Selected titles in the Continuum Education series:

George Antonouris and Jack Wilson: *Equal Opportunities in Schools: New Dimensions in Topic Work*
Patricia Broadfoot and Marilyn Osborn: *Perceptions of Teaching: Primary School Teachers in England and France*
Guy Claxton: *Being a Teacher: A Positive Approach to Change and Stress*
Guy Claxton: *Teaching to Learn: A Direction for Education*
Peter John: *Lesson Planning for Teachers*
Jennifer Nias, Geoff Southworth and Robin Yeomans: *Staff Relationships in the Primary School*
Andrew Pollard and Sarah Tann: *Reflective Teaching in the Primary School (2nd edition)*
Ron Ritchie (ed.): *Profiling in Primary Schools: A Handbook for Teachers*
Alan Rogers: *Adults Learning for Development*
Dennis Thyer: *Mathematical Enrichment Exercises: A Teacher's Guide*
Sheila Wolfendale *et al.* (eds): *The Profession and Practice of Educational Psychology: Future Directions*

Selected titles in the Continuum Education series:

Cedric Cullingford: *The Nature of Learning*
Mark Fox: *Psychological Perspectives in Education*
Andy Hargreaves and Michael Fullan (eds): *Understanding Teacher Development*
Michael Huberman (trans. Jonathan Neufeld): *The Lives of Teachers*
William Louden: *Understanding Teaching: Continuity and Change in Teachers' Knowledge*

This picture used on the cover is by Paul Cézanne (1839-1906) and is entitled 'Port de Maincy, près de Melun dit autrefois Pont de Mennecy'.

When Teaching Becomes Learning

A Theory and Practice of Teaching

Eric Sotto

continuum
LONDON • NEW YORK

Continuum
The Tower Building
11 York Road
London SE1 7NX

15 East 26th Street
New York
NY 10010

First published 1994, Reprinted 1995, 1997, 1999, 2001, 2002, 2003, 2004

British Library Cataloguing-in-Publication Data
A catalogue record for this book is available from the British Library.

ISBN 0-304-32792-1 (hardback)
       0-8264-5613-8(paperback)

Typeset by Colset Private Limited, Singapore
Printed and bound in Great Britain by CPI Bath

For Tamar and Leora

'There is nothing as practical as a good theory.'

Kurt Lewin

Contents

Preface

This book is intended to help anyone who does any kind of teaching. I begin by outlining a certain approach, and then I give descriptions of classroom practice which I have observed to illustrate it.

As I try to deal with fundamentals, I believe it is possible to spread the net this wide. For example, if we really understand the basics of soil cultivation, it won't usually take us long before we know how to grow cherries in California or melons in Tashkent.

Anyone especially interested in learning might also find something in this book, and I hope that anyone interested in the various branches of psychotherapy might find something useful here, too.

It gives me pleasure to mention that nearly everything I have written has come out of interacting with others, either in classrooms or in reading what others have written in their books. As for my more specific debts, one of the rewards of writing a book lies in the pleasure one gets from being able to mention them. I have indicated my debts in the notes at the end of the book. I have also added a reading list.

My biggest general debt is undoubtedly to the many taxpayers who have supported the various schools and colleges in which I have worked. That has enabled me to earn a living in a challenging but interesting way, and to these people my warm thanks.

Godshill Pottery
Fordingbridge
Hampshire, England

Acknowledgements

I should like to thank Rosemary Aikens, Herbie Goldberg and Dr Robert Ward for taking the trouble to read and comment on early drafts of chapters. I am obliged to Fanny Baldwin, David Griffith and Stephanie Pollard for reading and commenting on an early draft of the manuscript. I am very grateful to Professor Tony Becher for reading a late draft from cover to cover and making many detailed and encouraging comments. I am very pleased that my daughter, Leora, read and commented on some of what I wrote.

The anatomical drawings were done by my ex-student, colleague and friend John Holden, and I should like to thank him warmly for his help. I am also much indebted to my friend Gemma Hooper for help with the proof-reading.

I should like to thank the staff at Harrow College Library (University of Westminster) for their help. I thank in particular Janette Dollamore for getting me innumerable publications, and Juliette Dye and Alleyne Riley for much cheery aid in locating things. Writing a book like this one would be near impossible without such help.

Some of the best work on the book was done at Godshill. I have gained a great deal from Kate and Chris when there. I also had the pleasure of Susan's interest during one period.

The above said, I can claim all the infelicities which remain in the book as my own.

Like many people who have tried to write a book, I have had certain people particularly in mind while doing so. In the case of this book that has been very much my daughters. It is to them with much love that this book is dedicated.

Part I

Learning

Chapter 1

Introduction and Preliminaries

INTRODUCTION

When people write books, they seem to begin in one of two ways. They either begin with their topic, or they tell you how they got to their topic. I have always found the second way the more helpful, and readers may find it helpful if I begin in that way, too.

The first time I taught was in a private language school in Austria. I was a young man at the time and got the job almost by chance. I had two qualifications: I could speak English, and I vaguely knew the director of the school. The day before I was to take my first class she taught me the method of instruction they used.

She told me it was called the 'Direct Method'. She stood tall, thin and formidable in front of her desk, pointed to a book on it, and said slowly and emphatically in French, 'That is a book.' Then she pointed to the book and asked me in French, 'What is that?'

Although I did not know any French, I knew what she was getting at. But I felt rather silly as I could not remember what she had just said. She had to repeat the sentence a number of times before I could get the answer right.

Whenever I couldn't answer one of her questions, I sensed that she saw this as a slight on her teaching ability. That made me clumsy. Fortunately, she stopped after about twenty minutes. Her expression then suggested that she thought I was an idiot, but her next words, in English, were about administrative matters. So it looked as if I had the job.

At first I had two classes. Then I got some more classes. Sometimes I even came in during a morning to teach a single student. I liked meeting the students, but I did not care for being a teacher. I felt it put me too much out front.

Things improved when I got to know a few of the women students. There was one I particularly liked. She came in for private lessons so she must have had plenty of cash. She never mentioned her family, or a husband, or a lover or partner, but she seemed to have lots of time, and plenty of money because she was always beautifully dressed and had a swish sports car. She greatly intrigued me. She had a bright mind, a warm laugh and a delicious body, and we reached a stage when I spent quite a bit of each lesson kissing her hand and sometimes her cheek, and discussing in which language we were better at using the direct method. Unfortunately, I couldn't get any further than that.

But those were my favourite lessons. The director of the school also let me know that she warmly approved of the work I was doing with this very good customer, and those lessons helped to cheer me up when news came in about a new government regulation to the effect that everybody with a job like mine had to take an examination and acquire the official status of 'English Teacher'.

I had never sat a serious exam before, and it soon looked as if I would not have to sit this one either. A colleague discovered some small print which stated that you could keep your job, provided you registered for the final examination, paid the examination fee, and sat the examination within a year – and I had no intention of staying that long.

But I did.

Instead of sitting under the plane trees in the Beethovenplatz each morning, with the pigeons, the pensioners, and the young women and their prams, reading the one-day-old, *New York Herald Tribune* (Paris edition), I went and sat in the grandly housed Nationalbibliothek. There were lots of books in English on education there. I read about people like Pestalozzi and Montessori. Other times I practised translating from English into German, or from German into English. None of this had much to do with anything I ever did in my classes, but I did not notice this at that time. The important thing was to be able to pass the exam. After about ten months I sat the exam, and to my surprise and not surprise, I passed. A month after that I left, and thought I'd never teach again.

But I did. This time it was in Israel. I was farming at the time. I had got married, a second child had been born, we worked hard, crops grew and got sold, but we were never sure that there would be enough money for essentials. So when I heard that a few hours of English teaching were required at a local school, I applied for the job, and got it.

I taught children of twelve and thirteen. Very few children of that age see much point in learning a foreign language, and most of the ones I taught thought it an awful waste of time. They also showed this! So it wasn't enough to woo them, and to teach well. One also had to be coercive, and I hated that. But a small monthly cheque came in, and it helped to tide us over between the cauliflowers and the aubergines. Then, about ten months later, we moved, I began managing citrus groves, and again thought I'd never teach again.

But I did. After a few years that job came to an end, and some temporary teaching seemed the best next step. I saw an advert for a teaching job in a nearby town, and applied for it. At my interview it came out that the post had become vacant because the previous teacher had not been able to control her classes. It also came out that I had once been a sergeant in an infantry company. It was that which impressed the man who interviewed me; he offered me the job, and I took it.

It was a part-time job. I had another part-time job, in another school, in an immigrant town, miles away, and for a beginner like me, just controlling those classes required a very great deal of effort. I didn't know which job I hated more. But the teaching day in Israel starts at about eight and ends at about two, and my plan was to use the afternoons to look for another job.

But I didn't find one. However, as time passed, I found I could cope better, and I even began to see some advantages in teaching as a career. There were two things I particularly liked about teaching. One was that I did not *have* to be nice to anyone. The other was that the amount I earned was not directly related to how well I did my job. If I tried to do well, it was because I felt I should, and because of the inner satisfaction that this afforded me.

Controlling the classes was my main problem. However, at the same time, I was very slowly developing a teaching technique which seemed to work. I will describe that in a moment. First I should like to mention something I did not even notice at that time, something which comes to the heart of why this book came to be written.

Here I was, a part-time, temporary teacher, who had had a little experience, who possessed a kind of certificate, but who actually knew next to nothing about learning and teaching. Nevertheless, I had been given a responsible job, and let loose in a classroom.

At that time this seemed normal to me. The people who gave me the job must have thought it normal, too. They must have thought that teaching is a kind of art form which you either have, or do not have, and which, if you have it, you can develop through experience.

Such an attitude implies that we can all learn the fundamentals of sepsis from experience: that whether we wash, or do not wash, our hands before we perform an operation is our own business. That, after all, was precisely the attitude in medicine for hundreds of years when so-called 'doctors' maimed more people than they cured.

I shall be discussing the extent to which we can learn from experience later. Before that, I should perhaps note that slowly things began to improve for me. I found I was managing to keep order with less and less effort, and my pupils seemed to be learning some English, too. Perhaps I should now say a few words about the method I used.

In a previous lesson I would give out some homework. That would usually involve completing a few exercises, and reading a short story. In time, I learnt to give as little work as possible, but to ensure that that little was properly done. I began the next lesson by checking that the exercises had been done, and that the answers were correct. As time passed, and as my confidence grew, I found I could do that briskly. Then I'd start asking questions, in English of course, on the story I had set. I tried to involve as many pupils as possible, used their answers as part of an ongoing assessment, and tried to get a conversation going whenever I could.

That is what we would do for most of the lesson. And it seemed to work. By the end of a year, most of my pupils could speak some English; and, if I had them for two or three years, they were usually able to speak, and often also able to read and write, English quite well. In this approach there was a little explaining, a little correcting, and very little rote learning. Mostly there was a maximum of doing in a meaningful context. At that time I did not see the full implications of this, and I shall attempt to explain what I think was happening in the pages that follow.

Eventually there came a time when controlling a class ceased to be a problem. That wasn't because I was doing anything in particular; it was more that I was beginning to take it for granted that there would not be many problems. Also, we were usually so busy doing things, there wasn't much time for many problems.

I even began to feel that I was doing a useful job. I still didn't like what seemed to be an essential element in teaching: being up front, in charge of the show; and I often thought about finding something else to do. But nothing came of that. So the years passed, the better job became a permanent one, my pension rights accumulated, and I even made it to Head of Department. Then I left.

The details are not relevant here. I returned to Britain, and I discovered that the qualifications I had acquired after I had begun teaching would not entitle me to 'recognized teacher' status. However, without such status I could not get a decent teaching job. I seemed to have one of two options: either move into another occupation, or apply for a place at a teacher training college and obtain the qualification that was required. I did the latter. After all, I had had ten years of teaching and a degree behind me by then. I certainly did not want to go back to being trained. But I had to; and I found doing that very difficult.

One of my difficulties was that I felt I had to do extra well, and I wasn't at all sure I could. Another difficulty was money. I considered myself lucky to be in a country which gave me a grant, but there was a huge drop in income. Nevertheless, I began, and I very soon discovered that I knew very little about learning and teaching!

I could put it like this: I discovered that my previous ten years of teaching had mostly confirmed me in the kind of teaching that was all around me. But so all around me I had not really noticed it. I had been like that proverbial goldfish: the last creature on earth to discover water. That is one of the problems about trying to learn from experience: it doesn't take you out of your experience.

I came to none of this because the course at the college to which I went was so good. We had lectures on language in the classroom, comparative education, philosophy of education, a professional course (in my case the teaching of English), and the sociology of education. But fortunately I learnt as much from what we were not taught as from what we were taught.

For example, I was powerfully struck by the fact that our teachers were no better than any other teachers I had ever had. Some of them were worse. The fact that they had been trained to teach, and were training teachers, did not seem to make them one whit better than any other teachers I had ever had.

I hope I shall not be thought petty if I say this. I often saw teachers who clearly knew a great deal about teaching, but who did not teach well. (The one who taught psychology once gave us a lecture on the inefficiency of lecturing as a teaching method.) They did not seem able to use what they knew. Why not? How can somebody know something, yet not know it?

I also began to wonder how much learning results from being taught. This occurred to me because here I was on a course many of us thought poor, yet I felt I was learning a great deal. (Some of the students felt it was such a poor course they organized a protest about it.) This experience got me speculating about the relationship between learning and teaching, and it came to me that there did not seem to be much of one!

The nature of the material we were asked to study also raised questions for me. I had always enjoyed reading, but I thought many of the books we were asked to read downright poor: reading some of them felt like swimming in treacle. Worse, I was seldom able to relate what I was reading to the many years I had spent in class-roms.

This became especially noticeable when we had to write assignments. Many of the students went about this by lifting chunks out of a textbook and embellishing them with a few 'famous' names. Quite a few said that this was the best way to get by, and they did get by. They were a mixture of amused and cynical about it. Others did not set foot in the library the whole of the time they were on the course. It seemed to me that there was something amiss here. I was strengthened in that belief by the writers from whom I did learn. They tended to be either people who were not academics, or academics who were not in education.[1] That seems a curious situation to me, and I should like to return to it later in this book.

The most important thing which that course did for me was to raise questions. A few of those questions were framed by the teaching staff on that course, but others I stumbled on myself. And what I indirectly discovered thereby is that learning, real learning, seems to be more a matter of seeing a question than learning an answer.

After the course was over, I went back to teaching: first in a school, then in a technical college, and then in a teacher training department. The questions that had arisen for me while I had been at my training college, came back to plague me even more when I found myself trying to teach teachers, and this book could be described as an account of how I have tried to grapple with those questions ever since.

Of course, I have not managed to arrive at any final answers. However, I do hope that reading this book might help those engaged in teaching to make better sense of their experiences.

PRELIMINARIES

The Experience of Teaching

In my Introduction I noted that I encountered two main problems in my teaching. The first arose when I began to teach in a school, and it was how to maintain discipline. The second arose ten years later in my training college, when it dawned on me that many of the things I had taken for granted about teaching needed to be examined. I should like to discuss the problem of maintaining discipline for a few paragraphs first, and readers not concerned with schools might like to know that these comments are of a preliminary nature only.

I found it very difficult to maintain discipline when I began to teach. What seemed to be required was a man who could silence a class with one look. In those days I used to wish I were such a man. Today that strikes me as a little silly (if understandable), but either way, I am not that kind of a man. So I felt I had to act in a way which wasn't remotely like me, and I was very unsure of my ability to keep up that pretence for very long.

I would walk into a difficult class and try to be friendly. And it didn't work. It wasn't that the children in that school were particularly rowdy. Problems of discipline take different forms in different societies. Where I found myself, at that time, the youngsters didn't jump around much, or do anything remotely vicious. They simply talked loudly to each other and ignored me.

For them, going to school consisted mainly of sitting quietly behind desks. But they were bright and energetic. So, in the time it took one of their teachers to walk out, and the next one to walk in, they talked. At the top of their voices. And when a greenhorn like me walked in, they ignored him. And when I raised my voice, I continued to be ignored.

What does one do? I hated shouting. I hated imposing anything on anyone. But there didn't seem to be a choice. So I shouted. And there was quiet. But only for a short time. There were no detentions, so I gave out lines. It turned into a battle and I hated it.

Years later, when I became involved with training teachers, I realized it isn't possible to teach anyone how to maintain discipline. It isn't something 'out there', which can be learnt like a chemical formula. It is something which relates to who one is, mostly to how secure one feels. Qualities like that cannot be taught. They can only be developed in a supportive environment.

I propose to write about the training of teachers, and the question of 'discipline', in a separate book. In the mean time I am faced by a problem. On the one hand, I am aware that most people who intend to become schoolteachers are keen to gain information on how to maintain discipline; but on the other, I have come to realize that the problem of maintaining discipline (in a difficult class) hides an ever bigger problem.

That problem, as I noted, is that a great deal of what we tend to take for granted about teaching needs to be examined. Under these circumstances, it seems to me best to begin by discussing not the question of discipline, but how the experience of teaching has the odd effect of hiding the main problem all teachers have.

When I first began to teach, it often struck me that the teachers around me seldom talked much about how they taught. I regretted that because I was new to the job and often felt lost. Years later I discovered that most teachers are concerned about how they teach, but that they seldom express that concern. I believe that the reason for this is related to the fact that one's teaching also involves who one is as a person, and that is not so easy to talk about. So instead of talking about their teaching, teachers tend to follow roughly the same approach that was used on them. That is, they tend to walk into a classroom, perhaps ask a few questions, perhaps give out some material, but when it comes to their own input, they tend to do that by 'explaining'.

This 'explaining' is sometimes called the 'transmission method' of teaching.[2] In doing that, teachers sometimes use a handout, an overhead projector, or a model. Of course, they also do other things, like set an exercise, or have a discussion. But anyone who has observed teachers at work, including those who say that they use a 'student-centred' approach, will know that a great deal of teaching is done by explaining.

This method has certainly been going strong for a long time. It was extensively used in Europe during the Middle Ages. In those days, all books were hand-written and therefore very expensive, and far beyond what most learners could afford to buy. The main method of conveying knowledge to a group of people was by word of mouth. Also, as paper was very expensive, learners couldn't afford to take many notes, so they had to try and remember a good deal of what they were told. Now we have pens, paper and print, but 'teaching by explaining' is still very common.

In my Introduction I noted that I took this way of going about things so much for granted that I hardly noticed it. But it is also the case that I often felt an underlying sense of unease. Sometimes this took a concrete form, as when I felt uncomfortable about being out front. Other times I wondered what it was about me that had got me into teaching.

For a time I experimented with a cassette recorder. I asked my learners if they would mind if I brought one in, and when they said they did not, I recorded some lessons. Back home I listened, and tried to work out how I could improve. There would be my voice, sounding strange at first, and sometimes there would be the voices of some learners. Sometimes there would be a few things I wished I had said or done a little differently. But there was never anything solidly 'there' which gave me any clues about how I could improve.

Much later I realized that my trouble was that I didn't really know what would be 'better'. All I had was a vague feeling that my lessons *could* somehow be 'better'. To put it a little more precisely, I could say that I had no analytical tools with which to examine my teaching. I was like a quack doctor examining a patient. The patient says he has a headache, but the 'doctor' hasn't got any concepts like 'blood pressure' which might help to explain the ache.

Other times, I asked my learners what they thought of the lessons. I tried to convey that I was sincere; that I was not – as far as I could make out – on an ego trip; and to save them from embarrassment, I sometimes asked them for written comments and suggested that they leave their names off the page.

I have to report that I never got anything really useful by doing that. Whatever was said was always either friendly or peripheral; things like, 'We reckon your lessons are OK'; or, 'You could have told us so and so in an earlier lesson.' Of course, those learners had the same problem as me. They did not have any analytical tools with which to make any powerful suggestions.

Occasionally I have heard another teacher express the same kind of doubts. But then another teacher would usually say that ours was a 'tried and tested' method; that is, one which produces high examination pass rates. I found that unconvincing. Both personal experience and research had shown me that the single most important factor contributing to exam pass rates is what the learners themselves bring to their studies. Other factors could be the learners' previous teaching, the teaching of another teacher in another subject, or the general atmosphere in a school.[3]

During those discussions I also remembered that the way we teachers learn is often quite different from how we expect our students to learn. A good example is teachers who begin their career teaching one subject, then move into teaching another subject. Some go on courses, but many teach themselves; yet they use a quite different method when they come to teach others. I could not but ask myself: why use one method on oneself, and another method on others?

Years passed like this, and I did not resolve any of these questions. I think that this was partly because I was only half aware of them, and partly because I was gaining more confidence in what I was doing. It was only later that I realized that we teachers use whatever method we do, not because we have systematically studied it and found that it generates good pass rates, but because it was used on us.

Teachers are often accused of being rather conservative. I don't think that they are more so than the members of any other occupational group. But I have often noticed a strong resistance, among many teachers, when an alternative approach to teaching is mentioned. I am not sure why that is the case. It may have something to do with the fact that, in teaching, one does not have to put only a subject across, but also oneself.

Whatever the reason, it has been my experience that, whenever 'alternative methods' come up in a discussion among teachers, one of them will tend to say, 'We have to cover the syllabus.' That is no ordinary statement. It is a magic statement! When it is made, you sense that the person who has made it considers that the discussion has come to an end.

But there did come a time, in my own case, when I began to wonder: '*Who* covers the syllabus?' I mean, what is the point of a teacher covering a syllabus in class if the learners have to cover it at home? But I can't say that I began to see how to apply such thoughts to my own teaching. That came later, when I became involved with training teachers. But even then the change came piecemeal, as the rest of this section will show.

When we have something complicated to do, we often have to spend some time studying how to do it. We may decide to go on a course, or we may try to find out what has been discovered by others who have done some research on the matter. But after I had begun to think like this myself, I found that it is unusual to hear teachers talk about the value of research when it comes to teaching. The reaction of most teachers I have known has been sceptical. Here is a typical example:

> My attitude to educational research was antagonistic. I was irritated by the negative tone of many of the research reports, and suspicious of the methods used to collect data. The reports were often couched in jargon and statistics, and were published in journals that rarely reached staff-room shelves. . . . We seemed to live in separate worlds. A prestigious research industry seemed to be thriving at the expense of school practitioners rather than in support of them.[4]

Readers may recall the critical comments I made in my Introduction about the material we had to study in my training college. But there came a time when I began to have doubts. All around me I could see people doing a variety of jobs, and it was clear that some were happy to coast along on their personal experiences, while others went off and did some systematic study. What I could also usually see was that those who did some systematic study usually gained a better understanding of what they were about. What I could not understand was why teaching should be considered so different.

Many people believe that to become an effective teacher is firstly a matter of having a certain flair, and secondly a matter of gaining some experience. Experience is often considered especially important. That was certainly the way I had seen things for many years. But here, too, I was becoming doubtful.

Readers may remember that I had had to go to a training college ten years after I had begun to teach, and that the main effect of that had been to make me question the experiences of teaching I had had till then. Readers may also remember that I had felt considerable unease about the way I had been teaching – yet nothing much had come of that. The question I now found myself asking could therefore be put like this: if personal experience is so important, why hadn't I learnt more from my personal experience? After all, by then I had had about fifteen years of experience as a learner, and another ten years as a teacher!

By about this time I had also begun to do some reading, and it was becoming clear to me that one of the main effects of personal experience is to corroborate for us what we expect to experience. In other words, it looks as if, once we have got used to doing something in a certain kind of way, our experience often has the effect of reinforcing the way we are already doing it.

It was also becoming clear to me that what we can learn from personal experience is limited. Would personal experience ever teach us that water is a compound of two gases? Or that the earth is a ball? We could walk the earth for a thousand years and still think it flat! In fact, the more we walked, the more sure we would be that, aside from ranges of hills and valleys, it *is* flat. Those kinds of considerations suggested to me that we must often escape our immediate experiences if we are to make progress.[5]

I have often thought of the above when taking part in a 'teaching workshop'. At first I welcomed the opportunity which such meetings gave me to get together with other teachers. I enjoyed some of the contacts, and sometimes picked up an interesting idea. But I have seldom gained any powerful new insights that way. Indeed, if I am to be honest, my experience is that a great many platitudes tend to be expressed in such workshops.

I find I make substantial progress in one of two ways. One is when I begin to have fundamental doubts about what I am doing. The other is when I come across a new way of seeing things which puts my personal experiences into a new perspective.[6] In other words, before we can reflect on our experiences in a powerful new way, we usually have to view them from a new frame of reference. That seldom happens when we meet with others, discuss our personal experiences, or reflect on them on our own.[7]

I could put the matter a little more technically, like this. Although it is fashionable to say that theories grow best out of practice, and reflection on practice, my own practice has shown me that things are not that simple. We tend to see our practice in terms of our past experiences, that is, in terms of a theory we already have. In fact, I think it is safe to say that we tend to view everything we do in terms of an existing 'theory'. How could we do anything, even stretch out an arm, unless we had some kind of 'theory', no matter how tentative or unformulated, to guide us in the back of our minds?

In the case of teaching, our theory will be made up of all our past experiences of being a learner. We will then tend to view teaching from that frame of reference, and mostly without being clearly aware of it. In short, our theories tend to come before our practice. And not only do they help to determine our practice, they also shape how we see our practice.

None of the above is to deny the importance of experience. On the contrary. As readers will see, I shall often argue for the importance of experience. Here I am only suggesting that our personal experiences tend to be limited.

Another problem I have encountered, when teaching has been under discussion, is the variety of topics that can arise. Teaching touches on so many issues! Topics that often arise in most countries today include resources, race, gender, equal opportunities, minority interests, political influence, methods of assessment and, especially, administrative matters. These are important topics. But knowledge about them must surely be sought *in addition* to a knowledge of the learning process.

Unfortunately, because these topics are often of a pressing nature, they tend to shift the focus of attention away from actual classroom teaching. Learning and teaching then remain a matter of going into a classroom and learning from experience.

I could sum up this chapter like this. I believe that it is extremely important to have experiences, and to reflect on them. But I would argue that that is not enough. I would argue that, if we wish to make substantial progress, we must also do some systematic study.

Earlier I mentioned the disappointment I felt with the bulk of the material on learning and teaching I was asked to study at my training college. But that cannot mean that all research into learning and teaching is useless. The problem is to find material that is useful. Surely it makes no sense to believe that research can be useful in everything – except in teaching?

Attitudes to Training

For many years there has been a great deal of controversy about how one should teach. At present, there is considerable talk about 'student-centred learning' or 'resource-based workshops', and I happen to believe that these approaches have a great deal in their favour. However, if one observes teachers actually at work, one soon discovers that there are almost as many interpretations of these approaches as there are teachers.

Perhaps this is understandable. Many contemporary writers on teaching maintain that it is the kind of subject, or the kind of learners which one has, which should determine how one teaches. Others argue that, as teaching is such a complex activity, there is no one effective way of doing it. Others say that, as people are all so different, we must find a way to teach which suits our particular learners. Others point out that there is still a great deal of controversy among researchers about what constitutes good teaching. Others maintain that research can be helpful, but only if teachers themselves do it. Yet others argue that it is the learners who should determine how they are to be taught. Given this kind of conflicting advice, it is difficult to know where to begin if one would like to improve one's teaching.

Perhaps in reaction to this kind of controversy, many of those currently engaged in the training of teachers take a practical approach. They maintain that teaching is basically a skill, and can be compared with skiing. If you want to learn how to ski, the best thing to do is to get on to some snow and go. That is, you learn best by practice, with perhaps an expert alongside to give you some tips.

I believe that there are at least two things fundamentally the matter with this approach when it comes to teaching.

Consider surgeons. They also have to be skilled. They have to be able to use a knife and catgut with dexterity. But the 'skill' required to open, and mend, a damaged knee is obviously only a part of the expertise a good surgeon possesses. Such a skill is practised under the control of a much higher-order ability. In the case of a surgeon that must include, at the very least, a powerful understanding of physiology and anatomy. Is mastery of that kind of knowledge also a 'skill'?

We speak of a 'skilled' or an 'unskilled' craftsman, and the word 'skill' carries a distinct and very important meaning here. It refers to an ability to carry out a complex task efficiently, and often in an almost routine kind of way. Usually, too, the parameters are not too wide, and the subject matter does not require systematic study.

If so, what do we mean by the words 'an unskilled surgeon'? A person who is clumsy with knife and catgut? It is as if terms like 'knowledge', 'understanding', 'insight', 'scholarship', 'expertise' and 'skill' have all become interchangeable now.

The increasing use of that word 'skill' seems to be part of an attempt to make anything that requires systematic study easily digestible. Instead of trying to understand 'what is', you concentrate on 'how to'.[8] That may be good for computer maintenance, but it is surely an uneducational way of going about things.[9]

Commerce and the mass media seem to come into it, too. All over the world today there is an ideology of competitiveness, and from commerce it creeps ever more into all walks of life, including education. This ideology favours the 'fast solution', and hence action is preferred to reflection, and knowledge to understanding. In the mass media we have chat shows, quiz programmes, soundbites, and hence slick superficiality. As a result, we get an ever-increasing trivialization of everything.

How can anyone carry out a complex task unless he or she first studies the nature of that task? In the case of skiing, one does not have to understand much about the physics of acceleration or the chemistry of snow. But in the case of car mechanics, for example, it isn't enough to know how to wield a spanner. One must also spend a few years studying how cars function.

But if one believes that teaching is a 'skill' or a 'competence', it can hardly follow that it is necessary to systematically study how humans learn before one teaches them. 'Skill' in teaching usually includes things like being able to conduct a discussion, stand at a blackboard, show a video or draw up a lesson plan. Not surprisingly, all these 'competencies' are easy to demonstrate. But how can we be *sure* that these are important factors in teaching, if we have not first studied how people learn?[10] Or how can we be sure that these are the important factors which distinguish between a mediocre teacher and an excellent one?

I could put the matter another way. I believe most educators would agree that one of the most valuable abilities anyone can learn is the ability to question the validity of anything, including a 'competence'. But is such an ability a 'competence', and does this 'competence' head the list of 'competences' which we think a teacher should possess? Everyone agrees that the ability to pass a written exam need not indicate a competence to do an actual job. But is there not a danger, in going in the opposite direction, in emphasizing demonstrable competences, that we trivialize the educational process?[11]

When people begin to teach, they tend to like the 'skills' approach. It seems straightforward, and that seems a blessing when one is trying to master the highly complex activity of teaching. To teach, one must first master a subject, and then acquire the ability to convey that subject to others. And one has to work with the most complicated things on earth: other people. In such circumstances, it isn't surprising if one wants tools that will help, immediately.

This brings me to my second worry about taking a practical approach too quickly. Is there not a danger that, in stressing the practical, we may apply the practical in the service of a half-baked, perhaps even vicious, fad? Everyone who has worked in education for more than ten years will know that what most powerfully drives a new approach is seldom a carefully worked out conception, but often no more than a kind of flavour of the times, or a bunch of slogans.

I suggested earlier that the experience – the demanding experience – of being a teacher has the odd effect of hiding the real problem all teachers have. And that problem, it seems to me, is to understand how people learn. If that is broadly correct, it seems to follow that it might be best to ignore teaching altogether initially. In other words, it seems to me that deciding how to teach, without first having studied how people learn, is like deciding to use a screwdriver before one has understood the nature of the job.

There is another current attitude towards teaching which I should like to consider. It is the one which holds that a teacher's job is to 'meet the needs of students'. This belief is often coupled with the idea that students, especially adult students, 'know what they need'.

It sounds almost perverse to question such an attitude today, especially if we remember that it arose in reaction to the absurd belief, held for many years, that learners are empty vessels which teachers know best how to fill. But I find, when I act on such attitudes, in a real classroom, I often run into trouble.

For example, when I ask learners what they need, they nearly always voice immediate needs. But these are often in conflict with long-term needs. Here is just one example.

If I ask student-teachers what they need, they often say, 'Ways to motivate learners.' That was exactly the kind of thing I used to say when I began to teach! Many years later, it dawned on me that wanting to know how to motivate learners is a mistake because it takes one in completely the wrong direction – the wrong direction because it places an emphasis on teaching rather than on learning. More on that later.

I am of course aware that to suggest that learners often do not know what they really need may make them sound childish, and me condescending. But there is nothing unusual about teaching in this respect. In every profession one can hear thoughtful practitioners say that their clients often do not know what they really need.

One hears doctors and nurses say that they must sometimes work hard to convince their clients that they do not really need what they think they need. Solicitors will tell you that they often have a hard time convincing some of their clients that they should not do what they feel they need to do. And counsellors and psychotherapists soon learn that one thing is for sure: whatever a client may initially say he or she needs, it is seldom what he or she ultimately needs.

None of this is to suggest that 'experts' know best, or that one should not listen to a client. Such attitudes are so obviously absurd that they do not merit discussion. I am only suggesting that the question of 'needs' is a complex one.

Secondly, one of the best ways to describe learning is to say that it implies change, and we all know that change can be very difficult.[12] So if learning implies change, and if change is often difficult, then learning must sometimes be difficult, too. Also, the more powerful the learning, the greater the difficulty. A good teacher will try to minimize that difficulty, but there is no such thing as significant learning without considerable difficulty.

That is why, looking back, we often find that our best teachers were demanding or challenging, so challenging that they sometimes upset us, and sometimes even had to force us to consider things which we would rather not have considered. Such observations are not easy to square with the belief that it is a teacher's job to 'meet the needs of students'. Much current writing on teaching, especially the teaching of adults, makes the fate of Socrates and Jesus – the fact that teachers can be put to death for their teaching – inexplicable.

Thirdly, there is the problem of standards. For example, a learner may want to be an electrician. That is his or her 'need'. But how is a teacher to act if a learner 'needs' an electrician's certificate but is not prepared to put in the work required to become a competent electrician? What about the community which needs competent electricians?

It is possible to read current books on teaching and find a hundred references to 'the needs of the student', and not find a single reference to 'the needs of the community'. Yet in all the humanities (anthropology, sociology, politics, economics, history) a common theme is the frequent tension between the needs of the individual and the needs of the community.

Today there tends to be a strong emphasis on *self*. There is, it often seems to me, a kind of unexamined assumption that happiness or satisfaction is a matter of achieving 'one's potential'. It is a kind of 'cult of the self'.[13] One would have to look for a long time today to find some expression of the idea that our needs, and their satisfaction, are profoundly social in nature. It is even rare today to find an expression of the old-fashioned idea that there is a deep reward to be found in working towards something that transcends one's own needs.

I would not want to pretend that these are simple matters. I raise them here only to indicate why I sometimes take an approach which may not seem fashionable at present.

There is one more aspect of training I should like to consider. It is that, when we discuss the training of teachers, we also discuss the making of a 'professional'. But it seems to me that there must be some doubt about whether teachers really deserve such a status. In every profession one has to master a certain body of knowledge to become a member of it, but the profession of teaching is different. One does not have to study teaching in order to become a teacher. It is true that, to become a teacher, one has to study a subject such as chemistry, law, computing or English. But it isn't knowledge of one of these subjects that makes one a teacher. After all, one can be a chemist and not be a teacher.

It is true that to become a 'qualified' teacher one has to study for a Certificate of Education. But the course of study for this qualification does not usually include the systematic study of an agreed body of knowledge. And there are many educational establishments where no teaching qualification whatsoever is required before one can teach in them.

So teaching is quite different from all other 'professions'. Above, I mentioned car mechanics. Car mechanics are not always considered to be in a 'profession', but they have to study how cars function before they are considered competent to work on them. Not teachers: they are not required to study how people function before they attempt to teach them. One assumes that those who hold such a view must believe that people are a good deal less complicated than cars, and that teaching is an almost self-evident activity which you can learn to carry out effectively through 'experience'. In the previous section I tried to show how limited such a view is.

We consider a person 'a professional' because a professional has learnt both the 'practice' *and* the 'theory' of a subject. As a result, such people are usually able to tackle a practical task with a greater likelihood of success than a person who has had only experience. The best way I have heard that fact explained is by the observation that 'there is nothing as practical as a good theory'.[14]

I could sum up the above like this: I believe that teachers need to study *two* subjects. One is the subject that they teach; the other is how to teach it.

There are a great many books on teaching. On closer inspection, one will often discover that some of them are not so much about teaching as about education. The best of these help one to see that education is about much more than teaching, and such books are valuable.

Unfortunately, some books on teaching consist of no more than slogans. I find these irritating, and the ones which contain the slogans which express the ideas with which I am most in sympathy often irritate me the most. Examples of such slogans are 'empowering students' or 'student-centred teaching', and my irritation stems from the fact that the writers who use these slogans the most tend to give the fewest clues to how one can achieve such aims in a real classroom.

As for more factual material on teaching, there is no lack of it. There are many textbooks, a great many research papers, and lots of accounts of practical teaching experiences. I have found some of these helpful, but I don't think that they are enough. I believe that we need a general theory of learning and teaching which would embrace the most useful bits of information we already have, and serve as a guide for sound classroom practice.

As I do not know of a book which contains the kind of theory of learning and teaching I have in mind, I have decided – so help me – to try to put one together myself.[15] As if such an aim were not inflated enough, I am aware that there are people who do not believe in the viability of any general theory.[16] It is interesting to contrast such a view with what has been discovered about what differentiates teachers who find their work satisfying from those who do not.

For example, the Swiss investigator Huberman tells us:

> Put briefly: teachers who steered clear of reforms or other multiple-classroom innovations, but who invested consistently in classroom-level experiments . . . were more likely to be satisfied later on in their careers than most others, and far more likely to be satisfied than their peers who had been heavily involved in school-wide or district-wide projects . . . an early concern for instructional efficiency was one of the strongest predictors of ultimate satisfaction. Inversely, heavy involvement in school-wide innovation was a fairly strong predictor of 'disenchantment'.

And this writer sums up:

> there emerges an image of the harmonious teaching career that is perhaps surprising in its simplicity. It would seem that the . . . teachers in our sample thrive when they are able to tinker productively inside classrooms in order to obtain the instructional and relational effects that they are after. . . . To do this, they appear to need manageable working conditions, opportunities to experiment modestly without strong sanctions if things go awry, periodic shifts in role assignments, access to collegial expertise and external stimulation, and a good shot at significant learning outcomes for their pupils.[17]

The present book takes the more modest route. It seeks to find what is common in 'instructional efficiency' rather than to urge 'school-wide innovation'. That is not to argue that innovation is unimportant, but to suggest that it works best when it is first discussed in concrete detail, in the context of real classrooms, and in an attempt to build a testable theory.[18]

What I have noted in this section suggests a certain format for this book. It suggests that the first half should contain material on how people learn, followed by a second half on how that material could serve as a guide for classroom practice. I would hope that a reader who has examined both halves should be in a better position to make some informed choices.

Chapter 2

Motivation and Learning

A question teachers often ask themselves is how they can motivate their learners. That seems to be an understandable concern, for being able to motivate learners seems to be an essential ability. If so, it is troubling to think that one might not have this ability. In order to motivate, one has to be stimulating, and I think that most of us would be hard pressed to name more than one or two stimulating people. It seems rather daunting to think that one's learners won't learn unless one has the ability to motivate them.

How can one do this?

The questions we ask determine the answers we get, and to ask a question which takes one in the worst possible direction must surely be a bad way to begin. I say this because, in the next few sections, I shall try to show that no one can motivate anyone.

It took me a very long time to reach that position. For years I took it for granted that it was my job to motivate my learners. Many textbooks on teaching outline a hierarchy of human needs, followed by suggestions on how, once the learners have had a good sleep and a decent breakfast, one can motivate them. Since becoming involved in teacher training, I have become even more aware that many teachers are concerned with this, so it seems best to begin with that central issue.

The central issue, it seems to me, is this: everybody is already motivated.[1] To try to motivate somebody is like trying to breathe their air or to digest their food for them.

At this point, some readers may want to throw up their hands (or their latest meal) and say something like, 'Don't make me laugh. You should see my lot. About the last thing that they are is motivated! If I didn't try to motivate them, they'd all fall asleep.'

It isn't difficult to imagine the kind of learners such a speaker may have: rows of unresponsive faces, even if the teacher tries to do handstands. What does one do in such circumstances?

I have just suggested that everybody is already motivated, in the same way that everybody is already breathing and digesting. If so, when one of those functions does not work properly, we do not immediately set about carrying out that function for that person. We try to find out what is impeding it.

In other words, if being motivated is like breathing or digesting, then being motivated is intrinsic to being alive.[2] And if that is so, then it is the absence, not the presence, of motivation that needs investigating.

In comparing being motivated with breathing I have taken what might be called a biological orientation.[3] I invite readers to explore that way of looking at things in the next few sections to see where it may take us.

HOW TO BEGIN?

A lesson usually begins when a teacher greets the learners, announces the topic of the lesson, and begins to teach. But one could begin differently. To illustrate, perhaps I could describe what I sometimes do. Having greeted the learners, I give out the following case study.

Case study: Simon Simple

Please read the following account. Then, after discussion with your neighbour, jot down your answer to the question at the end.

For many years Simon Simple had an old-fashioned jewellery shop in Deansvale High Street.[4] He retired last year, and soon found that he did not always have enough to do. Being an active man, that upset him. Then, one day, his daughter Mavis, who teaches in one of the town's schools, put him in touch with the local adult education officer. Simon met her, and it was arranged that he teach a 'jewellery-making' class one evening each week, beginning the following September.

Simon had no qualifications, but he had always been interested in jewellery and had read widely. He was also a good craftsman. In fact, with the spread of chain stores, most of his trade in the ten years before he retired had been in repairing jewellery and clocks.

Simon put a lot of work into preparing for his class. He went to the Victoria and Albert Museum in London several times during the summer and bought a lot of slides. He did a good deal of careful reading, and he made many notes. The education officer was able to let him have £50, and with this he bought a few tools and a small stock of silver. He was told that at least twelve people would have to enrol for his class for it to run, so he was rather apprehensive when September finally arrived. On the day of his first class he was excited, then delighted to find twenty-three people there.

Simon greeted the students warmly, then launched into a history of jewellery-making. He was pleased he had the slides; they illuminated very well what he wanted to say. The slide-projector worked like a charm, and he felt he held his audience. He found that teaching came naturally to him. He had always known that teachers were born not made.

After a twenty-minute break he began on the second part of the lesson. For that first evening he had decided to talk about precious stones: their physical properties, and what this implied about working with them. He began confidently enough, but after a while he felt uneasy.

Some of the students did not seem to be listening. As there was so much to explain, Simon began to hurry. And what with the way time was passing, and the rather bored look on the faces of some of the students, Simon finished that second part of the lesson in rather a fluster.

For the next lesson Simon decided to show more slides. He felt that these had held the interest of the students well. And as he showed them, he would talk about the physical properties of stones. He had heard that it was important to use visual aids in teaching, and his first lesson had proved that.

At first the lesson went well. But after about half an hour he again sensed that not all the students were listening. That bothered him. He decided to change his plan for the second half of the class. Instead of talking about stones, he would take a practical tack and talk about the kind of tools that were used in his trade and the need for safe practices. Then he would show the class the tools he had bought and tell them that they would soon be using them.

And that is how he began. But after about five minutes, one of the women said, 'I came here because I wanted to learn how to clean and rethread some pearls I have. Forsters want £35 to do the job. I think that that's too much. I'm sure I could do it if I had a little help.'

The comment annoyed Simon. He said, 'It takes a lot of experience to clean pearls properly. Threading them isn't that easy either. But we'll come to that. I've got "Pearls" down as a topic for a fortnight today.'

Before he could continue, a man called out, 'I'm interested in old clocks. I've always found them fascinating. I'm retired now. I'd like to get my hands on a few old ones and mend 'em. I was told this class would be about that.'

Simon said, 'We can't do everything at once. I was an apprentice for five years. I worked at cleaning watches for two years before I ever mended one! But we're going to look at clocks and watches soon.'

Another man called out, 'Things go faster today. I really did hope we'd be making a few things by now. Do we really have to wait two years?' For the first time there were a few smiles.

Then a young man with an earring spoke. Simon was surprised he spoke so well. He said, 'I have a friend who makes modern jewellery. You may not call it jewellery.' He smiled. 'You know, it's made of wire and various beads. I must say I rather like it, and it sells quite well. I don't care much for the present office job I have. My friend sells in markets. I'd like to spend some time out of doors like that. I wonder if we could do something that would help me? Others may be interested?' He looked around. Several people nodded.

Simon said, 'Well, I must say . . . it hadn't even crossed my mind . . .' He was thinking of the boxes of slides he had prepared. He said, 'Let me think about it?' The young man nodded.

Simon brought out the tools. He was a little worried they might disappear. But they came back very quickly, much quicker than he had expected. The students didn't seem particularly interested in them.

He had a few precious stones in his pocket, 'just in case he needed to motivate the students'. He held up a diamond, and said something about carats. He thought he sensed some interest, but was relieved when the end of the lesson came.

On his way home Simon felt bad. The notes in his pocket seemed to mock him; the time and effort he had put into their preparation seemed childish; and he had always suspected that there were a lot of stupid people about.

But that young man with the earring obviously wasn't stupid.

Simon decided gloomily that teaching was not for him. The trouble was, he didn't know how to get out of his commitment to teach for two terms. Deansvale was a small place. He couldn't just chuck the teaching after twenty-three people had paid to do the class. As soon as he got home, he phoned Mavis. Perhaps she would have some advice.

If you were Mavis, what would you say to Simon?

This case study usually generates some discussion. The participants nearly always suggest that Simon should have consulted his learners much earlier. If the matter does not arise during the discussion, I ask whether Simon could have motivated his learners more. The participants usually shrug their shoulders; they clearly consider the question irrelevant. Several usually suggest that Simon should have enabled his learners to tackle practical tasks much sooner. It seems to me that this is an extremely important point, and I shall return to it.

In the above, the course is a non-vocational adult evening class. Can we extrapolate from that to a class of children learning maths, or to medical students in a teaching hospital? I believe we can. I believe it makes sense to begin by greeting the learners, then to say something like, 'We are here to study biology (bricklaying or business administration) and I wonder how you think we ought to begin?' Having asked that question, a teacher might end up doing a good deal of what he had intended to do. If Simon had consulted his learners in this way, they might well have asked to see some of his slides.

Matters are more complicated on an examinable course. What learners may individually want to do may not be what it is necessary to do. Nevertheless, it is surely helpful if a teacher makes space for these things to be discussed and to take account of what is said.

It is surely also helpful if a teacher consults the learners about how they wish to learn.[5] One could say: 'I could give you a lecture, or I could give you a case study, or there is some reading you could do. Or we could begin with a practical task. Which would you prefer?' More likely than not, a teacher will end up doing a mixture of these. But the learners' attitude will tend to be different if they are sincerely consulted.[6]

On some courses, learners are encouraged to do the bulk of their studying on their own, or in small groups. Sometimes learners negotiate what they will study and how they will be assessed. Such courses have strengths as well as weakness,[7] but they will not be discussed here: this book is about learning and teaching in a classroom.

I would not want to suggest that beginning a lesson in the way I have just indicated is some kind of magic formula. It has been my experience that, no matter how much I have consulted learners, many problems remain. I would only suggest that by beginning in this collaborative kind of way, teachers are less likely to inhibit their students' motivation to learn.

MOTIVATION AND THE PROCESS OF LEARNING

When we find ourselves in a room with other people, we usually talk to some of them. We may not begin to talk immediately, and we may not want to talk to everybody there. But most of us will feel like talking to some of the people in the room to some extent or other. This inclination to communicate seems to be true of most mammals. Sheep, goats, cows, horses, monkeys, seals – all these tend to seek the company of their own kind; and each kind communicates with others of its kind in some way or other. We consider this 'normal'.

Compare this with what happens in many classrooms. In most classrooms the learners don't talk much because it is usually the teacher who does most of the talking. But how appropriate is this?

Consider the work of Vygotsky, one of the most respected researchers who has investigated the relationship between thought and language in this century. In one of his experiments, he placed a desirable object in a cupboard so that a child would have some difficulty getting at it. He then found that a child not only *acts* in its attempt to get at the object, but that it also *speaks*, and that this speaking arises quite spontaneously. He also discovered that, when a child is prevented from speaking, its *actions* tend to be inhibited.

None of this will surprise parents: most will have heard their children doing exactly what Vygotsky has described. However, because a child talking, as it is trying to do something, seems so artless, we may not grasp its significance.

After repeating such experiments many times, Vygotsky concluded: 'A child's speech is as important as the role of action in attaining a goal. Children not only speak about what they are doing; their speech and action are part of *one and the same complex psychological function*, directed toward the solution of the problem at hand' (Vygotsky's emphasis throughout). He therefore goes on to say that children '*solve practical tasks with the help of their speech, as well as their eyes and hands*'. And he adds that when such speech is allowed normal scope in childhood, it eventually becomes internalized and evolves into an ability to think.[8]

A moment's reflection shows that this process does not stop when we become adults. I have often found myself talking to somebody and, while doing so, realized that the matter we are discussing has suddenly become clearer to me. I have then sometimes pretended that the matter has always been clear to me. Other times I have found myself saying, 'As we were talking, I realized . . .'

Teachers probably have this experience more than anyone else. If so, it is surely odd that we often adopt an approach to teaching which prevents learners from doing something that would help them to learn. Unfortunately, many classrooms contain fifty or more learners. One might agree that learning is helped when we are able to talk about it, but it is difficult to know how to facilitate such talk in a large class. Detailed descriptions of how this may be done can be found in Part II of this book. In the mean time, it might be helpful to continue by considering what happens in a typical place of work when something new has to be dealt with.

Here, too, we see that people often talk to each other when they are trying to understand something. Solving problems in a place of work without talking would be impossible. Yet it is still uncommon to see such an approach in many classrooms. Perhaps that is one of the reasons people often say that they learnt most after they had left school. I think it was G. B. Shaw who said that the only time his education had been interrupted was when he had gone to school.

What else is there about classrooms that demotivates?

Consider what pupils and students mostly do in them.

Everybody agrees that we learn best when we are actively engaged. If you want to learn how to ride a bicycle, you have to ride a bicycle. If you want to learn how to bake a cake, kiss a girl, understand thermodynamics, or kiss a boy, you have to do those things. Explanations from somebody who already knows can help. But no matter how good the explanation, the best way to learn is when we are actively engaged.

It follows that, if we can discover what people mostly do in a given situation, we will also discover what they are mostly learning.[9]

What do learners mostly do in a classroom? In many classrooms they mostly sit and listen. It follow that they learn

- to sit and listen;
- to believe that learning is a matter of sitting and listening; and
- that answers come out of a textbook or a teacher's head.

How do we get out of such an absurd situation?

In Part II of this book there will be some practical suggestions; here we are still examining why learners often seem demotivated. Another reason may be that most people do not like to sit and listen for hours at a time when they are trying to learn something.

Imagine you have just bought a new kitchen gadget. Imagine further that somebody tells you to sit down, and begins to read the instruction booklet to you – for the next hour. How would you feel?

I have just noted that in some lessons learners mostly sit and listen. I also implied that most of them would prefer to be actively engaged.[10] Is that true? This is surely an important question. For if learners would rather be actively engaged than passively listening, that is almost the same as saying that they are inherently motivated to learn.

Some interesting experiments have been done on this question. One of the most striking was carried out at McGill University in Montreal a number of years ago.[11]

Three researchers offered undergraduates $20 a day (big money in those days) to lie on their backs on a couch, with their ears and eyes muffled, in a soundproof room, but with access to plenty of food and water. If they wanted some diversion they were able to get old stockmarket reports piped in via earphones.

The experimenters reported that, after about six hours, the students began to feel very uncomfortable. Soon some of them started to hallucinate, and all gave up taking part in the experiment after two days. One is reported to have left and got a job on a building site at $8 a day instead!

But the above cannot mean that teachers should be more lively in order to motivate their learners. On the contrary: if it is true that we learn best when we are actively engaged, it follows that, the more a teacher is actively engaged, the more the teacher will learn. It further follows that, instead of trying to motivate learners, teachers would help their learners if they could devise a teaching approach which enabled their *learners* to be actively engaged.

In this chapter, I have drawn attention to two constraints on motivation: one is that teachers often do most of the talking in a classroom; and the second is that in many classrooms, learners tend to be rather passive. I am suggesting that both not only inhibit motivation, but also prevent optimal learning.

RESEARCH ON MOTIVATION

This section contains some findings which have come from research with animals. As animals are not humans, perhaps one should begin by asking whether one ought to be interested in such research when trying to understand humans. A comparison with medicine may be helpful.

When we become ill, we are sometimes prescribed medicines, and we know that these are tested on animals before they are given to us. Some people may not like this idea, and I happen to be troubled by that practice myself. However, what is clear is that animals have the same basic biological processes as we do.

In the same way, we know that animals have the same *basic* psychological processes as humans. If so, it seems fair to say that, provided that psychological experiments on animals are humane, and provided that there is a possible link between an animal's likely reaction and that of a human, experiments with animals *may* be helpful.[12] With these provisos in mind, here are a few accounts of experiments with animals which may help to shed light on the nature of motivation.[13]

In a laboratory, a small, white, tame rat is placed in an enclosure. It has two paths leading to food. One path leads directly to the food. The other path is longer, variable, indirect, and involves searching for the food. Which path does the rat take?

The researcher reports that, very often, the rat will choose the longer and more difficult path. Why? One guesses that rats, like many humans, are inclined to explore their environment when they have a chance to do so.

Another experiment. A well-fed chimpanzee is put in a cage. The walls are covered with cardboard, but in one place there is a covered window which the chimp can lift, and in this way it can look into the laboratory. But because of the way the window is built, each time that the chimp lifts the cover, it soon falls shut again. What does the chimp do?

The researcher reports that it raises the cover again and again to try to look out.

Why? Why not just lie back and snooze?

Here is another experiment. Again a cage with some chimpanzees inside. They have all had plenty to eat and drink, and into their cage the experimenter places a contraption consisting of a padlock, bolt and chain, all put together so that it can be taken apart again. What do the chimps do?

They spend hours fiddling with the thing. Why? It must be immediately obvious to them that fiddling with it will provide nothing to eat or drink, nothing to copulate with, nothing they could use, not even something to scratch with. Why fiddle with it, and for hours?

These simple experiments suggest that animals are often active, not in order to reduce some drive like hunger, or to gain some reward like food or status, but because being active is intrinsic to being alive.

Does the above also hold true for humans? A great deal of research has been done on that question, and here is a typical finding from the work of Hanus Papousek on infant development.[14]

This researcher was trying to find out how infants vary in their response to different kinds of conditioning, and in doing that, he was struck by the following.

He had arranged things so that when the infant he was observing did something relatively simple, like turn its head to the right, he rewarded it with milk. Papousek then found that infants as young as two months old were soon able to learn that turning their heads to the right got them some milk. However, he also discovered that infants would go on turning their heads in the correct direction, refuse the milk, and smile their pleasure when milk was offered to them! This showed that, having got all the milk they wanted, they gained no further reward from obtaining milk. Their reward now lay in being *offered* milk; that is, in gaining control of something.

In later experiments Papousek found that an infant as young as four months old could learn to turn its head first to the right, then to the left, then back again to the right, to get a light to go on. But the really remarkable thing was that it was clear from the infant's evident pleasure, and the direction of its gaze, that it did not gain a reward from looking at the lights. The reward lay in the fact that the infant had itself managed to get the lights to go on. That is, the main reward derived from mastery of the task.

Papousek proposes that, in acting like this, an infant is matching the information coming to it, with its actions; and in doing that, a model of the world is built up in the infant's brain. The infant gains its main reward when it senses that its actions bring about results which square with this model. That enables it to gain mastery over its environment; and such mastery must have enormous survival value.

The implications of the above could be summarized like this: when not resting or asleep, animals and humans are often active. Not in order to reduce some drive or to gain some reward, but partly because, through our activity, models of the world become established in our brains. These models will include things like objects, attitudes, colours, movements, people and words. Having such a model in our brains enables us to respond appropriately to the world about us. We could add that, the more accurate our mental model, the more appropriate are our reactions likely to be. And having an accurate model of the world around us must surely have enormous survival value.[15]

Take finally a few everyday examples. Consider a child who has just been put to bed, having had all the food and drink it wants. As most parents know, that is precisely when it will often be most active. A child of three will often lie in bed and repeat a word it has just heard over and over again. It is actively practising till it has achieved mastery. But notice that there is no one around doing any motivating.

Parents also know that young children are forever 'into things'. Fragile objects have to be kept out of their inquisitive reach, cupboards have to be kept latched, and dangerous objects hidden away. At this early age, a child's curiosity manifests itself mainly physically. But soon a child will begin to ask questions. Endlessly! Where does this propensity to ask questions come from?

From 'reinforcement'? Clearly not. Children often continue to ask questions even when their parents hardly answer them. Who then is doing the motivating? Probably thousands of years of evolution.

Barbara Tizard and Martin Hughes found that, when young childr‹ their parents (as compared with their teachers), the children ask ‹ questions an hour. Tizard and Hughes suggest that one of the main ‹ questions is to enable a child to fill out its understanding of the world.'‹

This tendency clearly does not stop when we become adults. The more we know abᴏᴜ the world, the better we will be able to cope with it. And to know about it we have to go out and experience it. We can see how strong this inclination is when we consider the experiment with McGill University students reported earlier.

To sum up: the findings to which I have drawn attention in this section suggest that living creatures are naturally active and motivated to learn when they find themselves in an environment which enables activity and learning to take place. If that is roughly correct, it again suggests that teachers need not be concerned with motivating their learners. The problem appears to be to find a way of teaching which does not inhibit motivation; and to find a way of teaching which is in line with the motivation already present in the learners.

I expect that some readers may be thinking that the above is easier said than done.

MOTIVATION AND THE PROCESS OF SCHOOLING

It seems fair to say that we like what we are good at.[17] If we are very interested in something, but cannot master it easily, our failure may spur us on to try again. But if we keep failing, we tend to give up. We then often justify that by reminding ourselves that we cannot be good at everything.[18]

We also know that a complex task requires time and effort: the more complex the task, the greater the effort. Hence, if we succeed, we tend to feel good; but if we fail, we tend to feel bad. So before we tackle a complex task we usually ask ourselves how likely we are to succeed.

In the next section I should like to comment on the experience of being a pupil, in a school, in England, and in the light of the above observations. Some readers may not be concerned with pupils in schools, but the experience of being a pupil in a school must surely be relevant to all learners; for even when they have left school, the experience of school will probably colour their attitudes to learning for years to come. In the same way, some readers may not be concerned with the experience of being a pupil in a school in England, but here, too, I think that my comments are likely to hold broadly true for most countries.

Until recently, to have done reasonably well at school in England is to have obtained five O-level examination passes (O = ordinary). How many pupils have left school in England having obtained five O-level examination passes? The relevant government statistics show that not more than 25 per cent do so. This means that 75 per cent failed to do reasonably well until very recently.[19]

It must follow, from the above, that the thing which the majority of pupils most powerfully learnt while at school in England (and probably in many other countries) is that they are failures. For, no matter how hard they tried, they failed. The Examining Boards saw to that. That is because an O-level examination does not assess what a candidate knows, but how a candidate stands in comparison with all the other candidates who sat that examination in the same year. That is, only a certain percentage, fixed beforehand, are allowed to pass.

In addition, those to be examined do not get examined when they are ready (like, for example, adults when they go for a driving test). They are examined at a set time, without regard to whether they are ready or not ready.

Imagine you have to go for a driving test, not when you feel you are ready, but by a set time.[20] Also, that you pass (or fail) not because you are competent (or incompetent) to drive, but because you are considered a better (or worse) driver than the other people who have taken the test that same year. In other words, it is as if it had been decided that there is room for only a certain number of additional drivers on the roads each year.

There must come a time, in such a system, when the 75 per cent majority realize that they are not going to make it, no matter how hard they try. Such a realization must surely demotivate many of them.

As if the above were not enough, much research (and what I have heard and seen over many years) strongly suggests that many pupils feel that a good deal of what they are taught at school is of little consequence.[21] As for employers, they usually do not know what the material really consists of. In England, the yardstick 'five O-levels' is used as a catch-all measurement signifying that the holder has a 'basic education'. This 'basic education' is then supposed to give learners the ability to do useful work.[22]

But a moment's reflection shows that a good deal of what is taught in school seems to be taught, not because it might help us to do useful work, but because it is likely to appear in an examination. Every reader of these lines must have had the repeated experience at school of being told that certain material had to be learnt, not because it is particularly useful, but because 'it might appear in the exam'. But an exam pass seldom helps one to *do* a job. It mostly helps one to *get* a job. It's as if quite a bit of schooling is about learning how to run a course – so that you can then go swimming.

I suggested above that, for many children, all over the world, the experience of going to school is painful, for it teaches them that they are stupid. It seems to me that nothing could be more demotivating than that, and, if that is roughly so, it must make sense for teachers to keep such a consideration in the forefront of their minds.

It may not always be possible to teach in a way which will enable all one's learners to pass whatever exam may lie ahead. But good teachers usually know how to structure the material to be learnt so that the majority of their learners are able to master it. They are usually also able to convey to their learners that the material to be learnt is within their compass – if they are prepared to put in the work necessary to master it.

Nor do good teachers have a need to make their learners feel small so that they can feel big. These kinds of teachers seem to know intuitively that an atmosphere of fear and stress is bad for learning. They know this because they are not afraid to look inside themselves and remember what it is like to be a learner.[23]

As for the question of 'relevance', I don't think that that can be simply a matter of teaching material which is 'useful' in the real world, for it is hard to determine exactly what is going to be 'useful'. Nor can 'being relevant' be a matter of trying to make unreal things seem real. I am sure I am not the only pupil who squirmed when a teacher began,

'Your team has decided to re-mark the borders of its football field. Now, if the vertical measures. . . .'

In contrast, there are teachers who can make the wars of the Romans seem very real, and they manage to do this because they have a realistic outlook. They are able to show that all wars have certain things in common; that intelligent study is a matter of seeking patterns; and that looking at the past can give us clues about the future. Nor do these kinds of teachers teach something because 'it is likely to come up in an exam'. Being realistic, they know how to make most of what they teach relevant to the real world, and in that way they also help their learners to pass exams.

In this section I have tried to draw attention to four factors which tend to inhibit the motivation to learn. One is the experience of having been a pupil in a school, because for many people this was painful. Two is to be set a task at a level which is likely to cause failure. Three is to be made to feel foolish. And four is to be asked to study something that seems unreal.

TEACHERS AND MOTIVATION

By now some readers may have become impatient. They may have thought the research findings I have reported quite interesting, yet feel that it is a plain fact that many learners do not seem to want to learn very much.

I agree. So what does one do? Try to motivate learners? The trouble is, when one tries to do that, the learners tend to sit back and expect a performance. If the performance is good, the learners are pleased. If it is poor, they are bored. Unfortunately, that happens quite often, for, after all, teachers are not entertainers.

In this way teachers become the victims of an impossible situation. Teachers expect to have to motivate, and learners expect to be motivated. No wonder teachers are sometimes heard to say, 'They don't seem to have any motivation at all. I don't know what they come here for.' Notice that, when teachers say this kind of thing, it is clear, on reflection, that their learners *are* motivated – they are motivated not to learn.[24]

That might sound perverse, but I don't think it is. For when teachers say that their learners are not motivated, what they often mean is that their learners are not doing what they want them to do, namely to sit and listen, and for hours at a time, and to be pleased about it.

It seems to me that the only way out of this vicious circle comes when one realizes that what goes on in many classrooms is based on a false perception of learning and teaching. Because we can teach someone, we risk slipping into the belief that we can also 'learn' someone. But we know that we cannot do that! All one can do is to try to arrange conditions which will enable people to learn.

That may sound a rather passive function. Many teachers feel that they must teach. Isn't that what they are paid to do? But when we focus on teaching, we tend to produce a performance. Can a performance generate learning? Surely teaching has to stop before learning can begin?

I have tried to show that nobody lacks motivation. Motivation is like breathing: if we are alive, we will be motivated – to learn, or not to learn. And if that is roughly correct, two things seem to follow. First, that teachers must be alert to factors which may inhibit their learners' motivation to learn. And second, that teachers must work with whatever motivation is already present in their learners.

Very broadly speaking, I believe that the latter is a matter of creating situations which enable learners to become actively engaged, but I know from many failures that that is much easier said than done. But what is for sure, is that such an approach causes a shift in focus away from teaching and on to learning.

Some readers may wish to object here. They may wish to say that there is no real difference between setting out to motivate, and setting out to create interesting learning situations. Such an objection misses an important point. When a teacher sets out to motivate, the focus is on the teacher. But when a teacher sets out to create carefully structured and inherently interesting learning situations, the focus is on the learners. The effect of such a shift is to lift a burden from the teacher, and it gives learners a chance to do some learning.

For thousands of years people learnt 'on the job'. If they were not motivated to do that, they went hungry. This soon made them motivated! Then learning moved into institutions called 'schools', and in these a method of instruction evolved (the transmission method) which inhibits motivation. The idea then arose that learners need to be motivated. That is surely like first putting cotton wool down people's throats and then pumping air into them because they are not breathing.

Perhaps I could illustrate this point for the last time by once again comparing the motivation to learn with the motivation to eat. Can we motivate anyone to eat? Surely not. What we can do is to provide a decent meal and some convivial company; when we do that, the other person usually falls to it. And if they don't, there is not much we can do about it.

If all that is roughly correct, the idea that learners have to be motivated must be a misconception. What clearly does require careful study is the conditions under which people best learn. That is the topic of the next few chapters.

Chapter 3

The Learning Process

THE BEHAVIOURISTS

Earlier I noted my belief that it makes no sense to decide how one is going to teach, before one has made some study of how people learn. (I consider that the single most important sentence in this book.) In line with that belief, I should like to present some research findings on learning. To make the presentation as orderly as possible, I report this research according to various psychological approaches. Of course, life is not ordered along the lines of psychological approaches! However, in later chapters I hope to show that, when one takes what I consider most valuable from these approaches, one gets the beginnings of a reasonably clear account of learning.

Let us begin with a group of researchers who call themselves behaviourists. Their work attracts much less attention today than it once did, but I believe that they have some important things to tell us about the process of learning.

First I think it is important to recall that behaviourists believe that, if you want to find out how people learn, asking them how they do it is unhelpful. They take this view because, as is well known, the reasons people give for their behaviour are often mistaken. Behaviourists therefore maintain that the only kind of evidence on which we can rely is observable evidence; that is, when researchers can see the way a person actually *behaves*. Such evidence, they say, is objective. A person's actual behaviour can be recorded and measured. This will allow other researchers to check those findings, refute them or extend them; and in that way we can make some progress.[1]

One might have all sorts of doubts about this approach. But, rather than discuss possible difficulties now, I think it is better to go straight into the kind of work which these people do by examining one of their experiments.

Imagine a laboratory. In the middle there is a table, and on the table there is a small cage. The cage has a door at one end, and a bar at the other. When the bar is pressed, a pellet of food drops into a food-trough below it.

A small, white, tame rat is put inside the cage. The researcher now has a reasonably simple situation to investigate. He or she wants to find out how the rat will learn that pressing the bar can get it food. Notice that, in this arrangement, the researcher is able to observe the *behaviour* of the rat.

Although this rat has never been put into such a cage before, it has been reared in a laboratory, so it will not be afraid of the cage or the researcher. Probably it will first sniff the air. Then, as it won't have been fed for quite a while, it will begin to move around to look for food. The researcher and the rat don't talk to each other. Even if they could, the researcher would not be interested. As noted, this is because the researcher would consider such oral evidence highly unreliable. So the rat runs around, and the researcher sits there with pad, pencil and stop-watch in hand, and observes the behaviour of the rat.

A word about what is intended by the term 'learn' may be helpful here. By 'learn' is meant the ability to do something which one could not previously do. It follows that, 'to learn', there will be 'a change'. For example, a dog is acquired by a certain family. Every time they put food out for it, they shout. Very soon the dog learns to associate the shout with its dinner, and comes running. Previously a shout hadn't meant much to it. So it has 'changed'. Or a person might move from Honduras to Hungary and learn to speak Hungarian. That is, he or she will have changed from not being able to speak Hungarian, to being able to speak that language. Here again we see that 'learning' implies some sort of 'change'.

So the rat runs around, and the researcher watches. As can be imagined, there will come a time when, half by accident, the rat will touch the bar. A pellet of food will then drop into the trough. The rat will notice it, and eat it. At this stage it will probably not have registered any connection between the bar and the pellet of food. However, pretty soon, it will again touch the bar, half by accident, and again a pellet of food will drop into the trough. This process will occur several times and, sooner rather than later, the rat will be pressing the bar and obtaining all the food it wants. It has 'learnt' that bar-pressing produces food.

Behaviourists explain the above like this:

- The rat *acted on the environment*: that is, first it ran round the cage looking for food, then it touched the bar, and then it pressed the bar.
- Its actions were *reinforced by being rewarded* each time it did something that got it what it needed.

Some researchers add that a connection was set up in the brain of the rat which links bar-pressing with obtaining food. When that connection is solidly established, and the rat presses the bar every time it wants food, 'learning' will be said to have taken place.

Behaviourists maintain that the above account also holds good for humans. They say that we are all driven by internal biological drives like hunger, thirst or the need for sleep. These drives make us act on our environment, and when we reduce those drives by acting appropriately, our acts are reinforced by being rewarded.[2]

Behaviourists also suggest that this account of learning can be applied to classrooms. They say that teachers can themselves take over the position of the environment. That is, teachers can reinforce each of their learners' actions which they consider desirable by rewarding them. In that way the learners will repeat those actions, and thereby learn what they need to learn.

On the face of it, this shift – from acting on the environment and being rewarded by *it*, to acting on the environment and being rewarded by a *teacher* – does not look very big. In the next section I shall try to show that this shift raises important questions about the process of learning.

LEARNING AND ACTIVE ENGAGEMENT

The behaviourist approach to learning was once extremely influential in the training of teachers. To some extent it still is (as when one speaks of 'reinforcing', although that term is often misused). However, one of the most prominent behaviourist researchers, B. F. Skinner, has stated categorically that the findings of the behaviourists cannot be used in a conventional classroom to aid learning. His reasons are as follows.[3]

Consider again the illustration of the rat. The rat was said to have learnt because

- it was *active*; and
- each time it did something which brought it a mite closer to learning that pressing a bar produces food, its action had to be *reinforced by being rewarded* immediately.

So, according to the behaviourists, learning is generated by two absolutely fundamental factors:

- the need for the learner to be *actively* engaged; and
- the need for the learner's appropriate activity to be *reinforced by being rewarded* immediately.

Consider what would happen if the rat sat in a corner of the cage and just watched the researcher. As the rat wouldn't be doing anything, none of its actions could be reinforced. That must be an important consideration for, in a conventional classroom, the learners will probably be sitting on their backsides and listening; or perhaps taking notes. If so, there isn't much in their behaviour that can be reinforced.

The strange thing is that, although the behaviourist theory of learning was once widely discussed, it seldom affected the way anyone actually taught. I say this remembering an occasion in my training college when I heard a man give a lecture on the behaviourist theory of learning – that is, he taught in a way which was completely at odds with the theory of learning he was explaining. I mention this episode here to add a rider to my previous suggestion: that it makes no sense to set about teaching without first studying how people learn. The rider is that, having studied how people learn, we then have to find ways of teaching which take on board what our study of learning has shown us.

The behaviourists' method of teaching in a way which is in line with their theory of learning is to introduce programmed manuals (or teaching machines).[4] Readers who have never seen one of these may like a brief description.

Programmed manuals have a paragraph of text, followed by a question on that text, then a blank for the learner to write her answer. Then comes the correct answer. If the learner's answer is correct, she is given praise. If it is incorrect, she is instructed to begin again. Then comes the next paragraph of text, then a question, followed by a space for the learner's answer. Then the correct answer. Then praise if the learner's answer is correct. Then comes the next piece of text, and so on, till the manual has been completed. In this way one gets

- the learner's activity; and
- an immediate reinforcement each time the learner makes a correct response.

Teaching machines work on the same principle. They consist of a box, with a roll of paper inside, which a learner can turn. As she turns the roll, a text appears in a window. She reads the text, responds to a question, turns the roll of paper, an answer appears, and the rest is exactly as previously described. Such machines have now been superseded by computer programs, but the principle remains the same.

At one time this teaching/learning method was much in fashion, and many thousands of 'programmed' manuals and teaching machines were sold and bought. However, from what I have seen, except where routine skills are to be learnt, they have now all been discarded.

I believe that their fate is not surprising. I believe that the behaviourist approach to learning is simplistic, and I believe that behaviourists' views on the nature of being human are bizarre.[5] Yet behaviourists must be right to insist that, in order to learn, an animal or a human has to be actively engaged.[6]

At this point some readers may wish to protest that this emphasis on the need to be actively engaged is based on work done on animals; that is, on creatures who do not possess the gift of language. Humans, however, do possess the gift of language, and, with its aid, it is possible to tell learners what they need to know. Surely, such a reader might continue, it is precisely our possession of language which has enabled us to accumulate so much knowledge from one generation to the next, and in this way to outstrip all other living creatures?

Such an objection must be partly correct. We certainly do not need to learn everything from scratch. But does our ability to understand a language release us from the need to be actively engaged if we wish to learn?

Consider the following illustration.

On a drive home, I sense that there is something the matter with my car. That evening, I go to a neighbour who is more knowledgeable than me, and describe the symptoms to him. He nods, and begins to explain how the fault can be repaired. He is using language to teach me. How well does this work?

I have noticed that one of two things always happens in such circumstances. If I have a working model of that which is being talked about already inside my head, I am able to follow what is being said. But if I do not have such a working model, I find I may understand the individual *words* said to me, but I do not really understand their full *meaning*. The result is that I begin to lose track of what is being said to me. I may then ask the speaker to repeat what he or she is saying, but pretty soon I find I am lost again.

The same happens if I consult the car manual. I can pore over it for an hour at a time, but, if I have never manipulated the actual parts before, I do not really understand what I am reading. In short, until I actually have the car in front of me, have the faulty section in front of my eyes, push it this way and that with my greasy fingers, look back at the manual (or my neighbour) – that is, until I am in this way actively engaged – I do not really learn.

This example is of a practical task, but do we need to be 'actively engaged' when it comes to more abstract things? For example, how can we be actively engaged in the study of history?

The discussion here turns on the meaning of the words 'actively engaged'. Of course, it is not as easy to be *practically* engaged in the study of history as in the study of car mechanics. But there is an important difference between simply listening to a teacher talking about history, and doing research on a historical topic.

Consider a history lesson which begins with a teacher saying, 'Now, most of you live around here, and most of you live in a house which was built some years ago. But how did that house get there?' Lots of answers will probably be forthcoming. A good teacher won't leave it at that. A good teacher will initiate a disciplined 'activity'. Pupils will be asked to make a search in local archives, investigate local authority plans, consider the structure of local commerce and industry, and study the development of the local community. Compare that with a teacher who talks for the next fifty minutes. In short real learning is not a matter of being 'practically' engaged, but of being 'actively' engaged.

Consider lastly a very common illustration of the above. When somebody drives us to a new locality, we are seldom able to remember much about the route afterwards. But when we ourselves do the driving, we usually can.

So we can say that we do not have to work out everything we want to learn from scratch. That would be absurd. We can consult a manual, or question someone who already knows; and these can save us a great deal of time and trouble. However, unless we already have a working model inside our heads of that which we wish to learn, it isn't usually enough to read or listen. If we wish to *really* learn, we must expose ourselves to situations which will build a model inside our heads; and that happens best when we are actively engaged.

Readers may notice how these comments relate to the research on child development noted earlier. There, too, we saw that models of the world are built up in the mind of an infant as it engages actively with its environment.

But being 'actively engaged' cannot be enough. The next section will be about other important factors in learning.

SOME LIMITATIONS OF BEHAVIOURISM

In the previous section I noted that programmed texts and teaching machines were once bought in their thousands, but that they are rarely used today. That may suggest that the behaviourists made some serious mistakes, and are best forgotten. However, I believe that, despite their failings, the behaviourists have some important things to tell us about learning. I have also realised over the years that one can sometimes learn quite a bit from trying to understand why someone may be wrong.

Consider first the way B. F. Skinner puts his position:

> The practice of looking inside the organism for an explanation of behaviour has tended to obscure the variables which are immediately available for scientific analysis. These variables lie outside the organism, in its immediate environment and in its environmental history. . . . The objection to inner states is not that they do not exist, but that they are not relevant in a functional analysis.[7]

The rat, as we saw earlier, learnt that pressing a bar got it food, and it was said to learn this because, each time it pressed a bar, its action was reinforced by being rewarded.

All these factors refer to the rat's environment, and how it responds to it. There is nothing about its 'inner state'.

Readers may recall that, according to the behaviourists, learning is said to take place when a link becomes established between a certain action and a desired end. In other words, learning is said to take place as a result of the automatic forming of associations. (In the case of that rat, it is said to have learnt because an association became established in its brain between bar-pressing and obtaining a pellet of food.)

Consider now the following experiments.

A researcher named Hunter placed a rat in a maze and eventually it found its way to the exit. As we would expect, on subsequent trials the rat found its way to the exit more quickly. A behaviourist would say that, each time it took a correct turning, the movement of turning was reinforced with the reward of getting out of the maze. Or we could say that the rat learnt the physical layout of the maze through a process of associations.

Next Hunter flooded the maze. When the rat was put back inside, it still found its way to the exit quickly by swimming. So what had the rat learnt during its previous visits to the maze? Clearly more than the details of the route. If that were all it had learnt, then changing the details of the route by flooding the maze should have prevented the rat from reaching the exit quickly.

In another experiment a researcher named Lashley trained a rat to reach food by carrying out certain movements. That is, when it performed certain movements, they were reinforced because it thereby reached some food. Lashley then removed certain parts of the rat's brain, and this operation prevented the rat from carrying out those movements. Nevertheless, the rat reached the food by going head over heels![8]

So what had that rat learnt? Clearly not that certain movements would get it food. If that were all, then it would not have performed completely different movements to reach the food after the operation.

In the following experiment reported by Tolman,[9] rats were placed inside a maze so that they were able to run along a path to reach food. The path was then blocked, and a series of quite new paths were made available, which pointed in different directions. When the rats were placed back inside the maze, the great majority quickly chose one of the new paths which led most directly to the food. This suggests that, on their first visit to the maze, the rats had learnt, not only the details of the first path, but also the direction in which the food lay.

We can see from these experiments that to explain learning by talk of 'reinforcement' and 'associations' seems to leave too much out.[10]

But what?

One way to consider that question might be to ask what would happen if the rats had been offered a waterproof, resin-strapped, illuminated, digital quartz watch as a reward. A behaviourist would say that a watch would not act as a reinforcer for a rat so it isn't a reward. Our next question might then be: 'Why not?'

Behaviourists would reply that that question is unhelpful, and the reason for their objection is clear: it falls completely outside their terms of reference. But perhaps their terms of reference are too narrow? Most people would say that a watch would not *mean* anything to a rat. Behaviourists would, of course, reject such an explanation, for a 'meaning' is clearly related to having an 'inner state', and behaviourists don't like such explanations.

What is a 'meaning'?

Let us ask instead, 'What is a watch?'

We could say that a watch is a mechanism which turns two hands so that they sweep in a circle over a number of figures. (In the case of a digital watch, it will show numbers on a dial.) To a rat, all this is double Dutch, and we only understand because we already know what watches 'mean'. We could fill 10,000 pages with descriptions of watch mechanisms, their chemical and physical properties and a detailed analysis of our concept of time, and we would still not have got near its 'meaning'. Yet, by the age of seven or eight a child will know what is *meant* by 'time'. This is because we grasp the 'meaning' of something *intuitively*.

Notice that if we fed all the information in the world about watches and time into a computer, the computer would still not *understand* the 'meaning' of time. That is because, ultimately, a 'meaning' isn't the sum of a set of physical properties. I shall have a few suggestions to make about some of the characteristics of a 'meaning' later. In the mean time I will just suggest that a meaning seems to be a compact, living, abstract 'something' inside our minds, which has to be *experienced*; in other words, I am suggesting that it is a property of life. And if that sounds vague, well, I am only saying that, at least for the present, 'meanings' are no more amenable to a final description than life itself is.[11]

I could sum up like this. It is quite possible for a man born blind to obtain a PhD in Perception, but unfortunately this would still not give him any real idea of what it is like to see.

The following may further illustrate the limitations of the behaviourist approach.

Behaviourism has been used extensively in the health services to modify behaviour, both among adults who are mentally troubled and among infants who may trouble us. Here is a passage by a student who has had some training in this technique:

> I spend much time discussing with parents how to cope with problems like sleep refusal, potty training, temper tantrums, etc. in their children. For instance, in the case of a child who refused to eat the food put in front of him, most parents are so terrified that he will starve, they will try and persuade him to eat, will try to feed him, threaten him, and probably end up getting very angry. The child sees his parents are very concerned about this and, although it is bad attention he is getting, at least it's some, which is better than none at all.
>
> My advice to these desperate parents is to sit the child at the table with his meal, and if he refuses to eat, to remove the food without comment and to let him see you couldn't care less. Give him nothing to eat or drink except water until the next meal and then repeat the whole procedure. The odds are that, after two or three meals, the child will think it is not worth the trouble and, anyway, he's hungry and so he'll eat. This is the time for the parents to show their praise, although not over-praise. It is important to be consistent, and for all the family to co-operate and not to give in at any step till the situation improves. The praise is gradually reduced.

The above is unsophisticated; a behaviourist could point to several inaccuracies. Yet this student has grasped the essentials of the matter. And the simplicity of her outline enables us to see the limitations of the behaviourist approach.

It is this. The person giving advice in the above ignores what the child's behaviour might *mean*. It might be that the child is unwell; or it might be that the child is not getting suitable attention; or something else might be the matter. What is most unlikely is that a healthy child would simply refuse food. But it would be impossible to find out why a child refuses food by simply observing its *behaviour*. One must investigate the *meaning* of its behaviour. To understand that child, one must consider its 'inner state'. The 'behaviour modification' approach sets out to modify behaviour. Occasionally, as with the severely mentally troubled, such an approach may be appropriate. But often it isn't. The view is too narrow; it tends to take things at face value; it is mechanical; it ignores meanings.[12]

Behaviourists tried to get away from a nebulous something we call a 'meaning' and went in search of something that was concrete, like behaviour. But being concrete has nothing to do with being scientific. What is concrete about the notion of gravity? Here is the originator of the idea of gravity, Newton himself, talking about it:

> that one body may act upon another at a distance through a vacuum without the mediation of anything else, by and through which their action and force may be conveyed from one to another, is to me so great an absurdity that, I believe, no man who has in philosophic matters a competent faculty of thinking could ever fall into it.[13]

One of the most striking things about the behaviourist account of human behaviour is the absence of any sense of mystery about it. They convey the belief that human behaviour is basically a straightforward affair. Certainly far simpler than the mechanics of moving planets.

Eminent scientists often speak about the mystery of things. They hold it constantly in mind. They try to understand the little things about the mystery first. But they do not, in doing that, ignore the main mystery.

A science should help us to understand things, and hence also to do things more effectively. A science of learning should put a person who has studied it in a position to help others to learn. But programmed manuals don't work. They bore people.

Consider a last and everyday example which suggests that much learning cannot be accounted for by the notion of reinforcement. Consider the widespread practice of prayer. People will pray for rain, a bicycle, the absence of rain, and many other things, even when they consistently get the opposite of what they have prayed for. Behaviourists have explanations for these things, but they sound contrived. They avoid the 'inner state' which all of us experience so vividly.[14]

We have already come across an approach which might help us to fill in what the behaviourists have left out in their account of learning. I refer to those studies of infants noted in a previous section. Those infants did not respond automatically to a stimulus and repeat their previous actions because they were 'reinforced'. Like that of all living creatures, an infant's behaviour has been shaped by millions of years of evolutionary pressure, but this does not mean that humans are simply machines.[15] Already at the age of a few days, human infants try to make *sense* of their world. They 'strive after meaning'.[16]

RESEARCH ON REWARDING

The last few sections have been about the behaviourists and their account of learning, and readers may recall that the notion of 'rewards' plays an important part in their approach. In this section I should like to invite readers to consider some of the implication of this position.

Let us begin with the work of Mark Lepper and his colleagues.[17] These researchers selected two comparable groups of nursery school children. First they visited one group, put out attractive new drawing materials for them to play with, and told the children that they would get a 'good player's award' if they played with the materials. (The award consisted of an impressive certificate with a blue ribbon and a gold seal.) Hence, when the children had finished their drawings, they were presented with their 'award'.

Next these researchers visited the second group of children, and put out the same kind of drawing materials for them to play with. However, they did not promise these children any kind of reward, and when the children had finished their drawings they were not given anything.

Two weeks later these researchers went back to the children they had visited; first one group, then the other. As before, they put out the same attractive drawing materials for them to play with, but this time nothing about rewards was said to either group. Instead, the researchers sat around and recorded the amount of time each group of children spent using the materials.

Lepper's results are clear-cut. The children who had not been rewarded spent twice as much time with the drawing materials as those who had. This suggests that, when an activity is associated with an extrinsic (external) reward, the activity ceases when the extrinsic rewarding stops. In short, it looks as if extrinsic rewards undermine intrinsic (internal) ones. What may be the reason for this?

There is a great deal of evidence which suggests that we enjoy a task most when we feel we ourselves have chosen to do it. In contrast, when we are extrinsically rewarded for doing the task we seem to feel manipulated.[18] And as most of us don't like that, we stop doing the task as soon as we can.[19]

Some readers may want to object here and suggest that the first group of children played less with the drawing materials on the second occasion because they were disappointed by the reward they received. This explanation may well be correct, and it highlights the importance of considering what a given reward might mean to its recipient. But consider the following finding.

When a chimpanzee is given the opportunity to use drawing materials, it will do so, and it will often show pleasure in doing so. Also, its productions are often indistinguishable from those of a young child. In an attempt to encourage a chimpanzee to draw more intensely, an experimenter bribed it with food; and when he did, he noted that, 'the animal took less and less interest in the lines it was drawing. Any old scribble would do, and then it would immediately hold out its hand for the reward. The careful attention the animal had previously paid to design, rhythm, balance and composition was gone.'[20]

Consider next the following finding.

Condry and Chambers introduced a problem-solving task to some learners. They let them work on it for a while to get practice, then they divided the learners into two groups. They asked those in the first group to work on a few similar tasks, and promised them payment for each problem correctly solved. They set the learners in the second group the same kind of task, but did not offer them any kind of reward.

These researchers then recorded the problem-solving strategies used in each group.[21] They found that the learners who were paid to solve the problems tended to be more 'answer-orientated' than those who were not. For example, they began to guess at the answers before they had managed to obtain sufficient information to do so intelligently. Furthermore, what information they did obtain, they used inefficiently. The result was that they tended to make guesses which contradicted what they already knew. In contrast, the learners in the second group, the ones who were not promised an extrinsic reward, tended to be more thoughtful and logical in their approach.

In other words, the extrinsically rewarded group, the group that was paid, focused on the answer. But the learners in the second group – the ones who gained an intrinsic reward – were more concerned with discovering the nature of the problem.

The above research was done with pupils in a school. Readers may now like to compare this with work done with students at a university.

As is to be expected, it was found that some students are happy with a superficial understanding, while others try for a deeper one. It was also found that one of the factors which makes for a superficial understanding is the anticipation of an extrinsic reward. The researchers whose work I am noting therefore tell us that, if we value deep understanding in learners, 'every effort must be made to avoid . . . conditions which rely mainly on extrinsic motivation'.[22]

The findings noted above suggest that extrinsic rewards not only undermine intrinsic ones, they also seem to cause poor learning. If so, these findings suggest that, instead of worrying about 'reinforcing' or 'rewarding', teachers would be better advised to try to devise learning tasks which enable their learners to gain intrinsic rewards.

Of course, none of the above implies that teachers should not express appreciation for work well done; only that the attempt to motivate learners extrinsically can have serious costs.

Is it possible to make learning intrinsically interesting so that external rewards are not required? Consider the work of a researcher named Rainey.[23]

Rainey selected a group of 124 pupils in the upper forms of a secondary school. All attended the same chemistry lessons once a week, and were then divided into two groups for laboratory work. In this, each pupil had to perform sixteen experiments. Those in the first group were given detailed directions, while the second group was asked to do the same experiments on the basis of their lesson notes only.

At the end of the year the pupils were tested. No difference was found in the examination results of the two groups. However, the following differences were found:

- The pupils in the second group took longer to get to work, and they expressed some resistance to being asked to work in a non-directed way; however, once they had got going, they expressed pride in their work.
- The pupils in the second group produced better write-ups of their experiments.
- The work of the second group tended to be unsystematic, even chaotic, at the beginning; however, by the end of the year it became necessary to hurry them along because they wanted to spend extra time checking work which was already good.

These findings suggest

- if a task is organized so that learners find it intrinsically rewarding, nobody needs to 'reward' (or 'motivate') anybody;
- one of the main characteristics of a learning task which offers an intrinsic reward is that the learners are actively engaged in it;
- the more responsibility the learners have for their learning, the greater is their intrinsic reward likely to be.

These findings seem to corroborate the comments made on motivation in earlier sections.

Above, I suggested that the more responsibility learners have for their learning, the greater their intrinsic reward is likely to be. Is there any further evidence for such a claim?

Consider the following finding.

Kavanau put some deer mice (very small mice) in a cage. In it there was a running-wheel which the mice used a great deal. He arranged things so that the wheel could be activated by a small electric motor, and placed a switch inside the cage so that either he or the mice could set the wheel in motion. He then found the following: when the mice had learnt how to control the motion of the wheel by using the switch, they would run on it only if they had initiated its movement themselves. If *he* set the wheel running, the mice would stop it, restart it, and only then begin running.[24]

That's at the level of deer mice!

For those still sceptical about the effect of allowing people as much responsibility as possible for their learning, here is another finding.

A researcher named Langer visited two large firms to sell one-dollar lottery tickets to their employees.[25] He sold the tickets in one of two ways. He either gave the purchasers a ticket in return for their cash, or he invited purchasers to choose a ticket in return for their cash. On the morning of the lottery he went back to the people who had bought tickets from him, and asked them if they would sell their tickets back to him.

He found that the people to whom he had *given* a ticket wanted $1.96 on average for it, while the people who had *chosen* a ticket wanted $8.67 on average!

So far in this section I have drawn attention to some of the effects of extrinsic rewards on the process of learning. But giving extrinsic rewards has other effects, for example social ones.

Consider first the work of Garbarino.[26] This researcher paired a number of children so that an older one taught a younger one. In some pairs the older child was paid to teach, while in other pairs the older one was not paid to teach. He soon found that the 'teacher' in each kind of pair tended to treat the 'learner' differently.

For example, where the older child was paid to teach, she tended to see the younger child either as someone who was helping her to gain payment, or as someone who was hindering her. Hence, when the younger child did not catch on quickly, the relationship between the teacher and the taught tended to become hostile. In the other kind of pair, where the older child was not paid to teach, the quality of the relationship tended to be better. The focus was more on the task at hand, and the learners in that kind of pair made fewer errors.

This is hardly surprising. We know that we learn best from a person who sees our attempts to grasp something with interest and good humour. We are not usually at our best when we have to learn from somebody who sees our endeavours as something which will, or will not, get them some cash.

As teachers' incomes in most countries are not directly related to their learners' progress, this piece of research might be thought of doubtful relevance. Unfortunately, there are some politicians who would like to make such a link, and one would hope that the above finding would make them think again. Also, I believe that there is another important implication of the above research.

Though most teachers' incomes are not directly linked to their learners' progress, their self-esteem often is. That is, some teachers tend to see their learners' failure to grasp something as a slight on them. Garbarino's finding suggests that, the more that teachers see their role as that of a 'reinforcer', the more they are in danger of seeing their learners' natural and necessary failures as their own.

Garbarino's experiment is interesting for another reason.

It is often claimed that, unless we reward somebody for doing something, nothing will get done. That must be true to some extent – but only to some extent. Consider the following scenario. I happen to work in a college. At its head there is a principal. Also working in the college are janitors, and these people earn a lot less money than the principal. The mythologies prevalent in Western and Eastern Europe hold that this difference in income is necessary for reasons having to do with the nature of the duties these two kind of people perform. That is, it is commonly believed that, if we do not pay principals more than janitors, the principals will take their talents elsewhere.

Is this true?

My friend Albert Einstein used to perform what he liked to call a 'thought-experiment'.[27] (He never carried out a practical experiment in his life.) Let us do the same.

Imagine a law is passed which lays down that, in a given college:

(a)   nobody can leave their employment for employment elsewhere;
(b)   everybody in the building must be paid the same; and
(c)   everybody can switch jobs inside the building.

In these circumstances, would a principal immediately elect to become a janitor?

Probably not. If they did, it would suggest either that they could not really cope with being a principal, or that they were doing their job only because of the money they were being paid. I would have thought that in neither case would they be doing a good job.

College principals not only get the satisfaction of being paid lots of cash, they also benefit from a host of other things like power, interest, and doing something useful. And it is surely because of these *intrinsic* rewards that no healthy and able principal would exchange jobs with a janitor, even if that meant that they would earn the same amount of money as a janitor.

Now, if we extend this thought-experiment over the whole world, it is easy to see that nobody would drop a job which affords intrinsic rewards for one that doesn't, if all jobs were paid the same.

The trouble is, many jobs do not afford any intrinsic rewards. So extrinsic rewards – mostly in the form of money – have to be given in their place. In other words, extrinsic rewards are often given to people when they are asked to do what they would rather not do. And if that is roughly correct, it follows that, when teachers offer their learners extrinsic rewards, their hidden message seems to be: 'What I am asking you to do is so boring, I know you would rather not do it, so I am offering you an extrinsic reward.'

Having conveyed that message each time we give a reward, how can we expect learners to want to learn anything except when we give them an extrinsic reward?

Learning establishments reflect the values of their society. If there is an emphasis on extrinsic rewards in our schools, that is not because of established facts about how people best learn. Behaviourism didn't arise in Borneo in 1928.[28] Neither the 'scientific' attitude nor the value system of Borneo in 1928 could have produced it. But the value system of the USA in 1928 did produce it. Just as it produced cheap and useful automobiles, a painfully rising crime rate, and a science that turns humans into machines. Everything, but everything, in any given society is a part of a seamless web.

The prevalence of extrinsic rewards in our society is probably not the only reason for the prevalence of extrinsic rewards in our schools. Another reason may be related to the fact that the teaching method most commonly used – the transmission method – destroys many of the intrinsic rewards that learning can itself provide.

Some readers may wish to object here. They may wish to say that, although some learners are motivated, there are a great many who are not. I agree! In my Introduction I said that I have had my share of difficult classes.

The extent to which learners are motivated to learn depends to a considerable degree on factors which lie outside the classroom, and teachers have no influence on these.[29] Nor can they motivate a person who has lost all motivation to learn. What a teacher can do is to try to create learning situations which are intrinsically rewarding, and a climate of learning which is friendly and supportive. When a teacher has managed to do these things, and learners still don't want to learn, why then there isn't much else a teacher can do. Teachers are not magicians. As for using extrinsic rewards, we have seen that they offer a short-term solution with many long-term costs – in as well as out of school.

THE GESTALTISTS

We now move to another approach, this one associated with a group of researchers called 'Gestaltists', from '*Gestalt*', a German word which can be roughly translated as 'pattern'. These researchers believe that a topic doesn't simply consist of facts, but of facts *and* the pattern in which those facts are set.[30] The example they most often use to explain what they are getting at is a melody.

Think of a tune, any tune, and whistle or hum each note separately. Pause the same amount of time between each note, and stress each note in the same way. Those are the separate notes of the tune, and they could be said to be its 'facts'. If you have whistled or hummed in the way I have just suggested, the sounds will not have produced a melody.

However, if you whistle or hum the melody in the way the composer intended, that is, with all the pauses, and the right beat, a *melody* becomes recognizable. That is because the notes are now arranged in a pattern, and because each note now has an effect on the other notes. In short, it isn't just the notes which make the melody, but also the way the notes are arranged. Gestalt psychologists like to explain this effect by saying: 'The whole is greater than the sum of the parts.'

The following may illustrate this point further.

About a hundred different elements make up everything on this planet. Those elements are separate entities. But what millions of very different wholes they produce! For example, water is a compound of two gases. But how unlike any combination of gases water feels!

Consider another effect of pattern.

I am writing these words with a word processor. One of its facilities can tell you how many words you have used in a given chapter. This facility can also tell you the number of *different* words you have used. Whenever I use this facility, I am always surprised to discover that, however long a chapter, there are seldom more than about 600 different words in it. For example, there are about 2,000 words in this section, but only about 560 different words.

How can a few hundred words (and just twenty-six letters) do so much? It is because we can produce millions of different patterns with that number of words (and letters). Again, 'The whole is greater than the sum of the parts.'

Incidentally, the above suggests that, in order to learn how to speak a foreign language, the important thing is not to know a lot of different words. As we have just seen, we can make ourselves perfectly well understood with not more than about six hundred different words. The important thing is to know how to put those words together in a meaningful pattern.

Next, consider these two strings:

'cable a clutch on a replacing Beetle is a job of a broken hell.'
'replacing a broken clutch cable on a Beetle is a hell of a job.'

The two strings contain exactly the same words. However, in the first string the words have been put down arbitrarily; in the second string the words have been put down in a meaningful pattern. This kind of pattern is called a sentence. A pattern makes sense. A non-pattern seldom makes sense.

Next compare these two sentences:

'The gnat bit the woman.'
'The woman bit the gnat.'

The two sentences contain exactly the same words (or separate 'facts') yet they have very different meanings. That difference is caused by the different arrangement (or patterning) of the same items. Notice again that, because of the pattern, each word has an effect on the others.

The importance of pattern can be seen everywhere in nature. Look at a leaf, a rock, a piece of bark, a patch of skin, a raindrop. Always one sees a pattern. In nature nothing is ever 'untidy'. Look at the outline of a tree against the sky. Notice how balanced it is. Pattern is everywhere.

The following illustration may again suggests the importance of pattern.

A brick can be used to build a wall, smash a window, warm a bed, or prevent a car from rolling. In each case it is a brick. But, in addition, it is also something else. And in each case the difference does not lie in itself, but in how it is used. In other words, we see that a fact (in this case a brick) gets its meaning from the way it fits into a pattern (or context).

In an earlier section, when I was discussing 'meanings', I said that I would attempt a definition of 'meaning' later. A moment's reflection now shows that everything gets its meaning from everything else around it. One could say that the world is an interdependent whole, and that the separate things in it get their meaning from how they fit into that whole. (It is also that effect which we have in mind when we speak about having 'a theory'. One of the attributes of a good theory is that it will show us how the various facts of a topic – especially seemingly disparate facts – hang together, and make 'sense'.)

I am not suggesting that the words of a language, or the facts of a topic, are unimportant. To say such a thing would be absurd. Rather, that the parts gain their meaning from the whole.[31]

Consider a last example.

Imagine you go into your garden one day and find a creature from outer space admiring your geraniums. It stands 20 cm high, looks like a dish of blackcurrant jelly floating on spun sugar, and has several antennae sticking out of it. Having been suitably radiated, it can speak a little English. So it says, 'Hello.' When you get over your surprise you begin to chat, and after a while you find that you rather like the creature. So you ask it into your house. The surprises then continue.

For example, just inside your door there is a picture. The creature floats up to it and asks, 'What is that?' You say, 'A picture.' The creature repeats the word till it has the pronunciation right. But you can see from the way that one of its antennae is twisting that it hasn't really understood what it is saying.

So you begin to explain that humans like to have pictures in their houses. 'Why?' asks the creature. Now you realize you really are in deep water! Why have a picture on a wall? You realize that you would have to explain about a thousand other things before you could get this creature to understand the *meaning* of the word 'picture'. That is because, to begin to understand what that word means, one has to have a few thousand connections inside one's head.[32] Or, as I was saying before, a fact gets its meaning from the way it fits into a whole.

Teachers should find the above helpful for a number of reasons. Take the following example.

Teachers are often told to give their learners one fact at a time, and perhaps that advice is based on the belief that knowledge is like a wall made up of separate bricks. Hence, if learners are given one brick at a time, they will be able to place them next to each other, and then perhaps on top of each other, and then, when they have the last brick, they will 'have' the topic.

But if the Gestalt approach is right, then a topic does not consist of only separate 'bricks', but also of the way in which they are held together. In other words, to understand a topic, one must understand the way its facts fit together to make a certain kind of pattern.

This means that, when a teacher begins to explain a new topic by stating a series of new facts, the learners will not really understand those facts till the teacher has finished. Put that way, it sounds as if one must begin at the end! But that's impossible. What one can do is to give a rough outline of the topic first. That might help the learners to see how the various bits, of which the topic consists, hang together.

It is interesting that learners who really want to understand a topic always feel that they don't really understand anything when they first begin to study. Unlike the kind of learner who is content to memorize facts, real learners tend to feel inadequate. They sense intuitively that knowing only facts is nothing, and that it is only when one sees the pattern that one begins to understand the facts.

These are the learners who ask the awkward questions. Or don't say much at all in class. These are the learners who find that the notes they take in class are mostly a waste of time because they are taken before one has grasped the pattern. These are the learners who read around their subject. And these are the learners who find, to their surprise and deep pleasure, that, when they persist in this way, there very slowly comes a time when the material which they are trying to understand begins to take on a shape, a pattern – that is, *a meaning*.

These are also the learners who can freewheel through questions at an exam, and note implications where others see nothing. Even an unintelligent examiner will see that they understand, not just remember.

Reading around a topic is particularly important. The best thing to do, when one wants to learn something theoretical, is to try to find a good 'gist' book. A good 'gist' book will provide an outline of a topic, and it will be written by a person who knows the facts inside out. Then one must get hold of a book which has all the necessary details – what might be called a 'list' book. Having read a good 'gist' book, one will be able to cope more easily with a 'list' book, as one will have a rough idea how the various facts of the topic fit together.

The above shows that learning is not the same as remembering. The distinction becomes clearer when we compare the kind of learner I have described above, with participants in a quiz show. These inanities are often given grand names like *Brain of Britain*. However, if one examines what is actually said in them, one soon sees that the participants are seldom required to do more than recall two or three words. The deeper implications of an answer are never discussed. For example, a participant may be asked the date of a battle, but never what justification there was for it. Snappy answers are preferred.

Compare the notion that intelligence is a matter of remembering 'facts' – as in quiz shows – with the following two comments made in a widely used textbook on economics:

'If all farmers work hard and nature cooperates in producing a bumper crop, total farm income may fall, and probably will.'
'Attempts by individuals to save more during a depression may lessen the total of the community's savings.'[33]

On the face of it, these two statements may sound absurd. But anyone who knows a little economics will know that they express a basic *understanding*. Such an understanding is not primarily a matter of knowing facts. Knowing facts is important, but only to the extent that they enable us to understand a total structure. In a quiz show all one does is reproduce facts. But in real learning the facts are merely the building blocks with which one constructs a meaning that helps one to understand the world.[34] To equate remembering facts with having understanding is like believing one can cook because one can put a potato in a microwave oven.

This section has been about one element in the Gestalt approach, namely, the importance of pattern. There is another element which is also important in this approach, and it is called 'Insight'. It, too, is related to the importance of pattern. But it is an important topic in its own light and deserves a new section.

INSIGHT

During the First World War a German psychologist named Wolfgang Köhler spent about four years at an animal research station on the island of Tenerife. We do not know how Köhler felt about being on that island for so long, but he produced a book called *The Mentality of Apes* while he was there which, I believe, has some very important things in it for a better understanding of learning, and hence teaching.[35]

As with the behaviourists, it may be best to examine the Gestalt approach to learning by immediately considering one of the many experiments Köhler conducted.

Imagine an empty room, and in it a chimpanzee named Sultan. To the ceiling is tied a bunch of bananas, and Sultan cannot get at them by climbing. Inside the room there are also two large boxes, and the researcher wants to find out whether the chimpanzee can learn how to place one box on top of the other, climb up them, and get at the fruit.

As Sultan has never made a ladder out of boxes before, we have a learning situation here: that is, a case of moving from not knowing how to stack boxes to make a ladder, to knowing how to do such a thing.

Some scholars have objected that Köhler's account does not constitute a clear change in behaviour.[36] They argue that Sultan is likely to have encountered box-like objects before. I believe that this argument misses an essential point, and I shall come back to it in a minute.

Here now is Köhler:

> Sultan drags the bigger of the two boxes towards the objective, puts it just underneath, gets up on it, and looking upwards, makes ready to jump, but does not jump; gets down, seizes the other box, and, pulling it behind him, gallops about the room, making his usual noise, kicking against the walls and showing his uneasiness in every other possible way. He certainly did not seize the second box to put it on the first; it merely gives vent to his temper. But all of a sudden his behaviour changes completely; he stops making a noise, pulls his box from quite a distance right up to the other one, and stands it upright on it. He mounts the somewhat shaky construction, several times gets ready to jump, but again does not jump; the objective is still too high for this bad jumper. But he has achieved the essential part of his task.[37]

I read this, and feel I know how Sultan must have felt. There is the aim, in this instance of getting at those bananas, and I just cannot do it. That makes me feel very frustrated.

So one kicks at a tyre, or one stares out of a window. Or, if one is a chimpanzee, one may tear around a room dragging a box behind one. And then, as if out of nowhere, the way to solve the problem becomes clear. A Gestalt psychologist would explain what has happened like this. He or she would say that the various facts of the situation have become organized in the animal's mind in the form of a pattern, and this makes the various facts meaningful.

In the example of a brick in the previous section, I noted that a brick could be used as a missile, a bed-warmer, or a wheel-chock, and that in each of those instances it is the context which helps to determine the 'meaning' of the brick. We could say that an object 'affords' a meaning depending on its context.[38]

In the present instance we could say that the room, the bananas and the boxes helped to form a meaningful pattern in Sultan's brain – and in terms of the circumstances in which he found himself. Translated clumsily into words, the pattern would convey something like: 'boxes-on-top-up-go-to-fruit-you-want-eat'.

Earlier I noted that some researchers would say that the mental process which an animal undergoes in such a situation is best explained in terms of associations. That is, that the objects before the animal trigger off appropriate action, based on associations established by past reinforcements.

Such an explanation may sound more concrete than the one suggested above. But is it really more concrete? What is an 'association'? Two nerves linked together? If so, such a link has yet to be found. And even if such links were found, precisely what is it that determines which links are activated and which not in a given situation? After all, each situation could activate many of the millions of links that are present in a brain.[39] What does the organizing?

The circumstances in which Sultan found himself provided literally thousands of possible clues as to what he could do next. What determines which clues are relevant and which not? In other words, how was Sultan able to decide what was relevant, and what not, before he knew what to do?

Notice also that the information which Sultan picked up could not have registered itself in his brain in the form of words. As Sultan is an ape, he does not have any words. This suggests that the information must have been registered in his brain in an abstract form, that is, in the form of 'a meaning'.[40]

I am aware that this may sound fanciful, but from the comment by Newton in a previous section we saw how inherently absurd he himself considered the notion of 'gravity' to be. Nevertheless, that notion enabled tremendous strides to be made in fields like mechanics and astronomy, till Einstein came along and improved on it. A notion like 'a meaning forming in a mind' may also sound absurd. But its value should not be judged by that, but by how useful it is in offering a tentative explanation, and guiding practical action.

I noted earlier that some researchers have objected that the description provided by Köhler does not suggest a clear case of learning. They maintain that Sultan must have encountered box-like objects before. But even if this objection is correct, it misses an essential point.

From the description Köhler gives us, it is clear that the facts before Sultan became organized in his brain 'spontaneously'. It is possible that Sultan had encountered box-like objects before. But it is also quite clear, from the description Köhler gives us, that the implications of the situation in which that ape found himself were new to him. And it is obvious that the meaning of the situation did not become clear to him for some time. However, when that meaning *did* become clear to Sultan, it did so in a flash. Köhler shows us that this flash was preceded by conscious thinking. But Köhler also shows that this conscious thinking was fruitless. It produced only frustration.

The above suggests that understanding is a spontaneous activity of the mind, in the same way that breathing or digesting are spontaneous activities of the body. That is, just as we do not consciously need to do anything in order to digest or breathe, we do not consciously need to do anything in order to understand. Indeed, seen in evolutionary terms, it seems to me inconceivable that nature should leave it to our fallible thinking to produce understanding.

If the above seems rather fanciful, perhaps the matter should be considered in a little more detail. After all, the ability to teach effectively must depend – at least to some extent – on having some understanding of the relationship between thinking and understanding.

INSIGHT IN HUMANS

In the previous section there was a description to illustrate the process of insight in a chimpanzee. Here now a description to illustrate the same process in a man. The person concerned is the mathematician Henri Poincaré, and he is describing how he reached one of his mathematical insights. Those whose knowledge of mathematics is as scanty as mine can ignore the mathematical jargon and still make good sense of the passage.

Here is Poincaré:

> Having reached Coutances, we entered an omnibus to go some place or other. At the moment when I put my foot on the step the idea came to me, without anything in my former thoughts seeming to have paved the way for it, that the transformations I had used to define the Fuchsian functions were identical with those of non-Euclidean geometry. . . . On my return to Caen, for conscience's sake I verified the results at my leisure. . . . Then I turned my attention to the study of some questions apparently without much success and without a suspicion of any connection with my preceding researches. Disgusted with my failure, I went to spend a few days at the sea-side, and thought of something else. One morning, walking on the bluff, the idea came to me, with just the same characteristics of brevity, suddenness and immediate certainty, that the arithmetic transformations of indeterminate ternary quadratic forms were identical with those of non-Euclidean geometry.[41]

This is how Poincaré writes about many of his mathematical insights, and it is also the way that many other creative scientists describe how they made their discoveries.[42] Readers may like to consider some salient points.

Poincaré tells us that there was nothing in his previous *thoughts* which paved the way towards his discovery. In fact, we see that he had to stop thinking before he could come upon his discovery. When first heard, that last statement may sound absurd.

It is certainly true that thinking often precedes or accompanies understanding. But it does not follow from this that thinking brings about understanding. Indeed, the opposite might be true: thinking could be what happens when we do not understand.[43] That is precisely what a careful reading of the descriptions of Sultan and Poincaré suggests. These descriptions show us that both had to *stop* thinking. But why? An answer might suggest itself if we consider the nature of thinking.

If we examine what happens when we think, it looks as if thinking is a matter of consciously considering what there is in our minds; and what there is in our minds is the sum total of what we have experienced. So thinking seems to be a matter of bringing our memories to bear upon the present.

If that is roughly correct, it follows that, when our present circumstances are similar to ones we have encountered in the past (and when we are able to consider these consciously), then thinking is helpful. For then we will usually be able to find a match between something we have experienced, and dealt with successfully in the past, and our present circumstances.

But if our present circumstances are quite different from any we have encountered in the past, then thinking might be a hindrance. For then we will not be able to make a match between what we have experienced in the past, and our present circumstances. When that is the case, we must stop thinking (i.e. bringing the past to bear upon the present), for the tools will be inappropriate.

Consider again the situation in which Sultan and Poincaré found themselves. They wished to understand something which was entirely new to them, so it made no sense to try to bring the past to bear upon it. When they did, they got nowhere. In fact, it produced only frustration. That is why they had to stop thinking. How else could the new come to them?

In such a situation, we must come to our problem with a fresh mind, unencumbered by memory. If we don't, and think about it instead, we go round and round in circles. But if we go off and do something else, or go to bed and have some sleep – that is, if we can stop thinking – then a solution may *come* to us. Of course, we must then check that solution against our present circumstances.

In solving something like a mathematical problem, the situation is more complex. In such a situation, it is obviously important both to know a great deal, and also to be able to come to the problem with a fresh mind. In other words, an agile and flexible mind is required, which can move from knowing, to not-knowing, constantly back and forth, till a solution slowly presents itself.

It sometimes happens that we don't really want to accept a solution which does manage to present itself to us. That is probably because the solution is in conflict with our present desires. So we go on thinking! At such times our thinking is caused by our wish to reconcile that which cannot be reconciled. But when we can allow a new situation to unfold itself to us, when we can allow it to come to us freshly, not through the screen of our past experiences, expectations or desires; and when we have immersed ourselves by degrees in it, so that all its facets are clear to us, we might then be able to understand it.

In the West, especially, we tend to find such an approach odd. We tend to believe that, unless we consciously *do* something, nothing will get done. Yet it is clear that we do not have to do anything (consciously or unconsciously) for our lungs to breathe or for our stomachs to digest. In the same way, we do not have to do anything in order to understand. All we have to do is come to that which is to be understood with an open mind; to immerse ourselves by degrees in it; to be patient; and to allow the situation to unfold itself. After that comes the need to check whether what we think we have understood corresponds to reality.

Does not such a description help to explain what happened to Sultan and Poincaré? To explain the process of discovery by reference to the 'unconscious' is unhelpful. What is required is a keen but passive alertness.[44]

Consider the following passage by another mathematician, Spencer Brown:

> To arrive at the simplest truth, as Newton knew and practised, requires *years of contemplation*. Not activity. Not reasoning, Not calculating. Not busy behaviour of any kind. Not

reading. Not talking. Not making an effort. Not thinking. Simply *bearing in mind* what it is one needs to know. And yet those with the courage to tread this path to real discovery are not only offered practically no guidance on how to do so, they are actively discouraged.[45]

Compare the above with the following passage by the poet John Keats:

I had not a dispute but a disquisition with Dilke, on various subjects; several things dovetailed in my mind, and at once it struck me, what quality went to form a Man of Achievement . . . I mean *Negative Capability*, that is, when a man is capable of being in uncertainties, mysteries, doubts, without any irritable reaching after fact and reason.[46]

Descriptions of how discoveries have been made often sound dramatic. They sound that way because Westerners are steeped in a mode of thought which tends to place them outside nature. Westerners tend to believe that they have to *make* things happen. But when a researcher 'makes a discovery', he or she isn't making anything happen; it is nature that is 'happening'! When a discovery is made, a human mind and nature get in touch. Nature unfolds its secrets to a mind which has immersed itself in it, and is keenly receptive to it. We could say that one of the properties of mind is that it can resonate to nature.[47] After all, mind must be an integral part of nature.[48]

Instead of being dramatic and invoking the unconscious, consider again the stages through which the chimpanzee passes in solving his problem:

(a)   He recognizes he has a problem.
(b)   He attempts to solve it.
(c)   He is unable to do so (because he is 'thinking', i.e. bringing his past experiences to bear upon it).
(d)   He becomes frustrated.
(e)   He becomes detached from the problem (i.e. he stops 'thinking').
(f)   There is a spontaneous reorganization in his brain of the facts before him till they assume a meaningful pattern.
(g)   This leads to appropriate action.

It seems to me that the mathematician goes through a similar process.

When we do eventually grasp a solution, it often seems self-evident. It is then often difficult to understand why it ever constituted a problem.[49] The above may suggest why this is so.

Let us now see how this account of thinking and understanding may throw some light on the process of learning.

THE LEARNING PROCESS 1

The psychological literature contains many descriptions of people trying to learn something in a laboratory, but I know of only one or two systematic reports of people trying to learn something in a real-life situation. One of these descriptions is by John Carroll and Robert Mack, and I believe that there is a great deal to be learnt from it.[50]

These researchers describe how ten office temporaries tried to learn how to use a word processor. They report that one of the difficulties their learners had was that they often had too much information to deal with at the same time. This is a problem most learners have! Carroll and Mack give an example of a learner who wants to delete a word. She presses what she thinks is the correct key, and sees a number of things come up on her screen. She looks at the manual, remembers a few things, and presses another key. But instead of the word being deleted, the screen assumes a completely different configuration!

What's gone wrong? She doesn't know. So she tries to get back to the previous screen. When she succeeds, she finds that she has forgotten what she did a moment ago. But Carroll and Mack report that, even when learners do not understand what they have just done, they usually try to press on. They often act on the flimsiest kind of hunch, and we know what the result of doing that is likely to be: even more confusion.

Observing such a situation, many teachers want to tell a learner what to do. But such intervention seldom helps in the long run, for, unless one understands how each 'fact' is related to the next one, simply knowing one fact will not help very much. In other words, unless a task is a very simple one, it isn't possible to master it by learning one fact after the other in rote fashion. One has to learn how the whole thing hangs together. In short, one has to see the pattern.

We now see why it is possible to follow a set of instructions exactly, obtain the required result – and learn nothing. The above explains why children can stay in school for ten years, and leave without having learnt very much. They learnt by drill and practice. They may remember, but remembering is not the same as understanding.

That is why people who really want to learn, strike out. They latch on to whatever they think they do understand, and act on that: they test their hunches. Of course, in doing that, they often get into a frightful muddle. But they also very slowly come to see how one thing relates to the next. In short, they begin to understand.

It seems to me that, at this point, we have come to the heart of the matter.

Learning, real learning, isn't what happens when we are fed information. Learning is what happens when we realize we don't know something which we consider worth knowing, form a hunch about it, and test that hunch actively.[51] In doing that, we may have to find some information first, but notice that finding that information is only a part of that process. And notice that the process begins when we realize we don't know something.

The above seems so self-evident, one hesitates to say it. But, if correct, it has very important implications. It suggests that the prime function of a teacher isn't to convey information. It is, first, to help learners to realize that they don't know something (worth knowing). Second, to provide conditions which will enable learners to pick up information to test their hunches. And third, to manage these things so that the learners can learn what they need to learn with as few redundancies as sensibly possible.

Notice that nearly everything we wish to learn exists in the form of a system, not an isolated 'fact'. It could be a word-processing system, a judicial system, a circulatory system or a play. At a more basic level, it could be how to build a fire, or how to catch a fish. In neither of these two 'simple' tasks is it enough to know isolated 'facts'.

It is also important for teachers to remind themselves that, to anyone who understands that 'whole', the system may be a model of clarity. But a learner will only see such clarity *after* he or she has come to understand how the various facts in it hang together. And the only way of finding out how something hangs together is first to take it apart and then to put it together again. In the case of learning how to use a word processor, it is often a case of looking at a manual and pressing a key. When you do that, the static array of information on the screen before you gets moved. You then get a chance to glimpse how one fact is related to the next. You may then consult your manual again, or the 'help' screen, or a teacher. But having done that, you must try out the information you have just obtained. And then the process begins once more. In learning another subject, it may be necessary to do other things, but the basic process remains the same.[52]

Readers may have noticed how this example illustrates a number of things to which I have already drawn attention. For example, the importance of active engagement; the need to immerse ourselves in a problem; how intrinsic rewards are the best motivators; how we strive after meaning; how parts get their meaning from the way they fit into a whole; how we are helped to see this when we test hunches; and how, in this way, slowly, models become established in our brains. I summarize now because I noted earlier that, although I had to present each section one after the other, I hoped that readers might soon see a coherent pattern emerging.

I noted above that we cannot learn how to use something as mechanical as even a word processor in rote fashion. A word processor consists of a set of procedures designed to produce a written text, and how it works is governed by a strict set of rules. What could be more mechanical? And yet, rote learning is useless even in such a task. Even when we try to learn the most mechanical of things, we never simply say, 'First this, then that, and then that, and then that . . .'

Learning is not the same as remembering. In real learning we always try to make inferences. We say to ourselves, '*If* I do this, *then* that seems to happen.'

Readers who are still not convinced that learning isn't the same as remembering might like to consider the following two sentences. Which is easier to learn?

When a boat faces directly into the wind, and its sails flap, it is said to be 'in stays'. Up so in so in up in we in so so than in than we so we.

The first sentence is longer than the second, and contains longer and more varied words. Yet most people would find the first sentence far easier to remember. If asked why, most people would say that the first sentence has a meaning. This is the same as saying that it is understandable.

A good deal of research has been done on this question. For example, Sacks found that people do not remember the exact words – or the sentence construction – used to convey a message. What they remember is its meaning.[53]

Or consider the following experiments reported by Jenkins.[54]

Two groups of people were asked to memorize a list of words. One group was also asked to rate whether the words were pleasant or unpleasant, while the second group was asked to note whether the words were spelled with an 'e'. The results showed that the first group – the group that was asked to consider the meaning – recalled twice as many words as the second group.

Another experiment went roughly like this. Two groups of people were read a series of sentences about animals. One group was also asked to arrange the animals in terms of size, while the second group was simply asked to memorize the sentences. Here, too, the first group, the group which was asked to consider the meaning of the sentences, remembered the sentences better than the second group.

In a searching review, Craik and Tulvig conclude: 'what determines the level of recall or recognition of a word . . . is not the intention to learn, the difficulty of the task, the amount of time spent . . . it is the qualitative nature of the task', that is, the amount of meaning it contains. They even found that their subjects remembered more when the task was meaningful than when the task was meaningless and they were paid to learn![55]

Rote learning is not about understanding. In rote learning we drill and practise until we remember. Interestingly enough, when we repeat a word frequently, it loses its meaning. But when we see the same word in a variety of contexts, its meaning for us increases, and we are then able to remember it more easily.[56]

A teacher (or the writer of a manual) expects learners to read instructions and then to practise a task until they have mastered it. I have tried to show that such an approach rests on a fundamentally mistaken view of learning. People seldom read through a set of instructions. They don't, because instructions

(a)   don't pose a problem; and
(b)   don't enable a learner to *find* an answer.

So normal people try to work things out. They probably do that because that is how the human brain has evolved over the 100,000 years that humans have been on this planet. (It may be interesting to recall that during this time they have had 'written instructions' for only about a hundred years.) When people are given a set of instructions, they usually first try to follow them passively. Then they put the instructions beside the thing they want to understand, read the first two lines, and begin to experiment.

Some teachers get exasperated when their learners ignore their instructions (or manuals) and begin to experiment. Such teachers become annoyed because their learners then make all sorts of mistakes. These exasperated teachers then say, 'Why don't they follow the instructions?!'

I hope I have managed to show that such exasperation is quite misplaced. To use instructions intelligently, one has to understand them. And to understand them, one *must* experiment. Carroll and Mack note that this process 'looks much more like slightly unsystematic scientific research than drill and practice'.

Unfortunately, the experience of going to school makes many people equate learning with remembering. So if their teacher gives them a string of instructions, and they don't learn anything from that, they blame their memories. They should blame a form of instruction based on ignorance.

This is not to say that there is no room at all for rote learning. There is no other way to learn the alphabet or the formula for sulphuric acid. But such remembering constitutes no more than a small fraction of what we need to learn, and it is useful only to the extent that it enables us to understand a 'whole'.

THE LEARNING PROCESS 2

The example of learning given in the previous section was of a relatively straightforward, practical task: learning how to use a word processor. But I believe that the description of learning given there holds broadly true for many kinds of learning, including the learning of an experienced practitioner.

I give next a description of what happens when a physician attempts to understand the nature of an illness when confronted by a sick patient. Research into how doctors go about such a task shows that they do not gather a great deal of data first. Instead, they leap directly to a small array of provisional hypotheses, based on their knowledge and past experiences. Then they test these. One researcher, Elstein, describes the process like this:

(a) attending to initially available cues;
(b) identifying problematic elements;
(c) switching between long-term memory and the present instance;
(d) generating hypotheses and suggestions for further inquiry; and
(e) informally rank-ordering hypotheses as to their likely correctness in the present instance.[57]

Although this list describes experienced physicians at work, much of it also holds true for novices trying to learn how to use a word processor.

Consider next what happens when we try to understand a page of text. Many readers will have had the experience of having read a page, thinking that they have understood it – only to discover that they have not really understood it when they are asked a question on it. One then often finds that one has to reread the page, try a tentative answer, compare this tentative answer with the text, and then reformulate the answer. If the page contains complex information, one must sometimes repeat this process several times.

Readers may have noticed that there was no mention of a teacher in the previous chapter. In a practical subject such as word processing, people are often able to learn by themselves. But in many subjects, for example medicine, there is a large theory component, and having a teacher for such a subject seems important. I mention medicine again because this chapter began with some findings from medicine, and the following quotation is also from medical education. It is by Michael Polanyi, who was once a medical student himself:

Think of a medical student attending a course in the X-ray diagnosis of pulmonary diseases. He watches in a darkened room shadowy traces on a fluorescent screen placed against a patient's chest, and hears the radiologist commenting to his assistants, in technical language, on the significant features of these shadows. At first the student is completely puzzled. For he can see in the X-ray picture of a chest only the shadows of the heart and the ribs, with a few spidery blotches between them. The experts seem to be romancing about figments of their imagination; he can see nothing that they are talking about. Then as he goes on listening for a few weeks, looking carefully at ever new pictures of different cases, a tentative understanding will dawn on him; he will gradually forget about the ribs and begin to see the lungs. And eventually, if he perseveres intelligently, a rich panorama of significant details will be revealed to him: of physiological variations and pathological changes, of scars, of chronic infections and signs of new disease. He has entered a new world. He still sees only a fraction of what the experts can see, but the pictures are definitely making sense now and so do most of the comments made on them. He is about to grasp what he is being taught; it has clicked.[58]

That last sentence may remind readers of the descriptions of Sultan and Poincaré solving their problems. In their cases there was first a puzzle, then frustration, then detachment, and then a sudden understanding of how the problem could be solved. That is, the leap from not-knowing to knowing was large. In the case of these medical students, the leaps in understanding are much smaller, but Polanyi's description shows us that they are present nevertheless.

Perhaps all understanding is like that. It seems to come in jumps as more and more connections are made.

And, like the office temporaries, the medical students must have become aware that they did not know something which they needed to know. They must have found that frustrating. They probably also made tentative guesses. It is true that they were not able to test their hunches practically to the same extent as the office temporaries. However, they must have been constantly engaged in the process of trying to find out whether they had grasped what they needed to know.

The medical students, the people learning how to use a word processor, the mathematician and the chimpanzee all had to immerse themselves in that which they wished to understand, and let the information *come* to them.

As Polanyi's description of learning is a rich one, it may be possible to use it to ask a central question: what essentially happens when we find ourselves trying to learn something in a classroom? Aside from the more general factors, like being in good health and awake, the following factors can be found in Polanyi's description:

- discovering that there is something we do not know which we need to know;
- immersion in the problem;
- puzzlement;
- active engagement, especially
  - obtaining information, and
  - testing hunches;
- repeated exposure to the learning situation;
- the presence of an expert who
  - sets up the situation,
  - acts as a model of competence, and
  - can answer questions;
- the inherent capacity of the human mind to understand;
- periodic insights;
- pleasure in gaining insights;
- doubt that one will ever really understand;
- faith that one will eventually understand.

These items hold true for both the medical students and the office temporaries. Two other things about that list seem important to me.

One is the absence of any mention of a teacher teaching. In part this is because my question was about the learning process. True, Polanyi refers to radiologists talking. But it seems to me that this talk is only one of the many things which those learners experienced while they were learning.

The other thing that seems important to me about that list is that a good many of the items in it refer to the way the students were *feeling*.

The next section will be about the relationship between teachers talking and learners learning. The section that follows will be on the relationship between learning and feeling.

LEARNING AND LANGUAGE

Most lessons have a teacher, and one of the things teachers often do in a lesson is to explain the topic of the lesson. That is a rather obvious statement, but it might be helpful to examine it for a moment. A practical way of doing so might be to consider another passage by Polanyi. This one is a little technical, but readers should still be able to make perfect sense of it:

> Unless a doctor can recognise certain symptoms, e.g. the accentuation of the second sound of the pulmonary artery, there is no use in his reading the description of syndromes of which this symptom forms a part. He must personally know that symptom, and he can learn this only by repeatedly being given cases for auscultation in which the symptom is authoritatively known to be present, side by side with other cases in which it is authoritatively known to be absent, until he has fully realised the difference between them and can demonstrate his knowledge practically to the satisfaction of an expert.[59]

I don't think anyone will find anything remarkable in this passage, except perhaps the clarity and elegance of the language. Polanyi is reminding us that a learner must often make repeated attempts at a task until he or she has 'got it'. A few sentences later, Polanyi sums up the point he is making, and I believe that what he now says really is remarkable. He states:

> The large amount of time spent by students of chemistry, biology and medicine in their practical courses shows how greatly these sciences rely on the transmission of skills . . . from master to apprentice. It offers an impressive demonstration of the extent to which the art of knowing has remained unspecifiable at the very heart of science.

What does Polanyi mean by the words: 'the art of knowing has remained unspecifiable'?

When we go to school or college, and study a subject like biology or electronics, we have some lessons in a classroom and some in a laboratory. But why have practical lessons in a laboratory? Why not have a teacher 'explain' that which needs to be learnt?

Laboratory lessons are expensive. They require space and equipment for each learner. It would be a great saving if they could be discontinued. But no serious teacher would be prepared to do away with practical lessons. And learners often say that they learn the most from a practical lesson. What is the exact reason for this?

When I ask students this question they tend to say, 'Because practical lessons strengthen what is learnt in theory lessons.' But Polanyi goes much further. He tells us that one cannot convey that which learners pick up in a practical lesson by 'telling' them, and that that is because a good deal of what is learnt in a practical lesson cannot be specified in words. He calls this 'tacit' knowledge.[60]

If Polanyi is right, the implications for teaching are surely very great. Polanyi is claiming that a great deal of knowledge cannot be stated in words. And he is not referring to emotional things, which most people agree are often difficult to state. He is referring to scientific knowledge, a problem I mentioned in a previous section in relation to my attempts to learn how to fix a fault on my car. I stated that, if we don't have a model of the thing with which we are concerned already in our brain, having somebody explain a matter to us will not usually help very much.

Consider now a more general example than fixing a car.

Many readers will remember having been told something important about life by their parents or friends when they were young. But they will probably also recall that, until they had had some actual *experience* of the matter, they often did not really understand what they had been told.

The trouble is, we often think we have conveyed the meaning of something when we have said something. But we only manage to convey a meaning when the person to whom we are speaking already has that meaning. We can give someone the words that stand for a meaning, but we cannot give someone a meaning by using words. Meanings can't be given. Meanings are a part of life, and, like life, they have to be experienced.

Many tests of learning hide this limitation of language. They assume that learning has taken place when a person can write or say something. This illusion is often exploded the minute that that person has to *do* something. With a practical task, that is often soon seen. But with a theoretical task, learners can often get by with words – until they have to apply those words.

This limitation of language has long been recognized, and I write this book at a time when the reaction to 'theoretical' knowledge has become so strong that there is now a growing attempt to test all knowledge via 'competences'. The trouble with this approach is that, just as the ability to pass a written exam does not show evidence of being able to do a task, so being able to do a task shows little evidence of being able to understand a task.

But even with the current emphasis on practical abilities, a good deal of teaching is still based on the belief that you can convey a new meaning by 'explaining' it. This belief is seldom examined. Sometimes it is glanced at, as when a teacher says, 'I went over that topic last week, and they still don't seem to have a clue.'

John Holt puts it well:

> We teachers – perhaps all human beings – are in the grip of an astonishing delusion. We think we can take a picture, a structure, a working model of something, constructed in our minds out of long experience and familiarity, and by turning that model into a string of words, transplant it whole into the mind of someone else. . . . Most of the time explaining does not increase understanding, and may even lessen it.[61]

When I was on my teacher training course, a great deal of attention was paid to the use of language in the classroom. This emphasis was probably related to the widespread use of the transmission method of teaching. When we see the limitations of language, we also see the limitations of that method.[62]

It is obviously important to use the right kind of language when we teach. There are teachers who talk in a way quite unsuitable for their learners, and some seem to be oblivious of the fact that half their learners do not understand what they are talking about. But the real problem here is surely not one of language, but of attitude. Teachers who have a sense of empathy take on the perspective of their learners, and speak so that their learners can understand. But even when teachers have a sense of empathy, and speak so that their learners can understand, they will still not be able to convey new meanings a good deal of the time, because that is beyond the scope of any language.

None of this is intended to suggest that language has no importance.[63] Language is obviously very important. It is often only with the help of language that we are able to gain a clearer understanding of something which we have experienced, like the little old lady who said, 'How do I know what I think till I've said it?'

So language is two-edged: it can help us to gain a deeper understanding, but it can also create illusions of understanding. The latter happens when a teacher believes that, if she gives us a word for something, she has also given us the thing for which the word stands. It is probably because of this that learners often find lessons either entertaining or boring, but seldom the source from which they really learn. And it is probably because of this that an unknown learner carved the following legend into a certain classroom desk:

> Here I sit bord as hell
> Waiting for the bloody bell
> > > T. S. Eliot

TELLING AND LEARNING

Most people would probably agree that there is an important difference between 'verbal' learning, and what might be called 'real' learning. We all know people who seem to carry around chunks of prefabricated thought, and when an appropriate slot appears, they slide the chunk in. Other people make quite a different impression. What they say seems theirs, and it seems alive. These kind of people can use their knowledge in varying circumstances. They can be creative.

How does such a difference come about?

I am beholden to several people for helping me to understand this matter a mite better than I might otherwise have done. One of them is Michael Polanyi, another is Carl Rogers. Rogers' thesis is 'simple'. It is that it is impossible to teach anyone anything of any real consequence, because teaching results in merely verbal learning.

This follows on logically from what was suggested in the previous section. Of course, it also sounds far-fetched. Rogers thinks so, too. He states: 'That sounds so ridiculous I can't help but question it at the same time as I present it.'[64]

When I first came across Rogers' work, I felt I had made an important discovery. I hope that people who have not yet read his work will be encouraged to read it if I quote a few more lines. For example, Rogers writes:

> self-discovered learning, truth that has been personally appropriated and assimilated in experience, cannot be directly communicated to another. As soon as an individual tries to communicate such experience directly, often with quite natural enthusiasm, it becomes teaching, and its results are inconsequential. . . .
>
> When I try to teach, as I do sometimes, I am appalled by the results, which seem little more than inconsequential, because sometimes the teaching appears to succeed. When this happens I find that the results are damaging. It seems to cause the individual to distrust his own experience, and to stifle significant learning.

I distribute photocopies of these statements in my classes, and ask the students what they think of them.

At first, most of the learners smile and nod their heads in thoughtful agreement. Then a few object. They say that they have learnt a great deal by listening to a teacher. Others echo this statement. Then objections come so thick and fast that Rogers is soon almost buried.

After the discussion has continued for some time, I ask how we could summarize the position we have reached. Somebody will say Rogers is right to some extent, but that he has overstated his case. Many learners will nod their heads. One or two will disagree, but they seem to find it difficult to justify their support for Rogers.

I never quite know what to do next. I happen to believe that Rogers is broadly right. But, if he is, if 'telling' is often a waste of time, even damaging, then it would be contradictory for me to 'tell' my students why I think he is right.

It may be helpful if I admit that I have sometimes tried to explain why I think Rogers is right. When I have done that, I have found that some learners repeat my comments in their assignments, and I have then had the strange experience of seeing Rogers vindicated. For the way students do this suggests that they have not 'really' understood what he is getting at. They convey that they have learnt merely verbally.

But it would be a great mistake to exaggerate. I have found that quite a few learners understand beautifully what Rogers is getting at, and it is then a great pleasure to see their thinking develop powerfully. But for some, a dilemma remains. Immediately after a lesson on Rogers, in which the main theme has been the danger of 'telling', they have complained that I do not explain enough.

How does one tell about the dangers of telling?

Rogers was a counsellor, and he came to his conclusions while working with clients who had come to him in distress. These were people who found that they kept falling out with their spouses; or that they were making a mess of their studies; or that their personal lives were unrewarding and painful.

In trying to help such clients, Rogers discovered three things. First, that even when he was able to discover the causes underlying their difficulties, telling his clients about these causes seldom helped them to change very much. Second, when he was able to establish the right kind of conditions, his clients were sometimes able to work out for themselves why they had difficulties. And third, when they made such discoveries for themselves, change for the better sometimes followed.[65]

Some readers may be thinking that, even if these findings are broadly correct, they cannot be applied to a classroom. It is true that clients in therapy and students in a classroom are both engaged in learning. But that is where the similarity ends. Clients in therapy are trying to learn how to conduct more rewarding lives. Students in a classroom are usually trying to learn new information.

In response to such an alleged difference, consider the work of Gertrude Hendrix on learning mathematics.[66]

Hendrix wanted to find out which kind of teaching helps learners to transfer their knowledge from one kind of mathematical task to a similar one. She discovered three things. The ability to transfer what one has learnt from doing one mathematical task, to doing a similar one, is more likely when

- a learner has been helped to discover the rule for doing the first task; and
- when the rule so learnt remains unverbalized until it is completely mastered.

Further:

- giving learners a rule before they have been helped to discover it, or asking them to verbalize a rule before they have mastered it, interferes with their ability to transfer their learning.

Readers will immediately see the similarity between the Rogers and the Hendrix findings. Some may find them odd. They certainly go clean against widespread belief and practice. But then, so do many discoveries. It is easy to imagine how people must have felt when they were first told that the sun does not move.

What is the explanation for the Rogers and the Hendrix findings? I believe the following may offer a start.

When we discover something ourselves, we have direct experience of it. This knowledge is encoded inside us in a compacted, abstract, living form. That enables us to grasp its meaning. We don't see the items bit by it, word after word. We dimly see the matter as an integrated living whole. We also sense how it interconnects with the thousands of other things we already know. This kind of learning permeates our being.

However, when someone tells us something, we do not need to strive to grasp its total *meaning*. We can simply memorize the words. That often gives us the illusion that we have understood. But we have seen that the words which describe something are not the same as the thing itself.

Consider an everyday example. A friend of yours visits Boston, comes back and tells you enthusiastically about his visit, and shows you some excellent photos. By chance, the following week you see a fine film about life in that city. All this whets your interest, and that summer you decide to visit the place. Anyone who has had this kind of experience will know that there is seldom much of a relationship between what one expects to see, and what one experiences when one actually sees a place. This is because, as I suggested, an experience cannot be communicated.

I have not found it easy to apply such a view of learning in my own classes. Rogers's learners differ in one very important respect from many learners in most classrooms. Clients don't come to a therapist in order to obtain a certificate; they come because they are distressed. But many learners come to a classroom precisely to obtain a certificate. After all, that is one way of getting a job.

I believe Rogers underestimated the importance of this difference. He maintained that people will learn if given the right conditions to do so. That must be basically true. The question is, learn what? Few people are happy to spend a lot of time and effort to master a certain body of knowledge. There is only so much time in any one day, and most people want to do other things besides study.

That can cause a conflict between what an individual learner may need, and what a community may need. An individual may need a particular certificate, but not be prepared to put in the work required to master the knowledge to merit getting that certificate. A community, however, needs competent practitioners. In short, although a client in therapy and a learner in a class are both engaged in learning, their aims may be very different.

There is a great deal in Rogers' work about the needs of the individual, but very little about the needs of a community, and the possible conflict between the two. He is very much the product of a certain Western outlook, with its emphasis on the individual, and it seems to me that though this has certain advantages, it also has some important limitations.[67] Nevertheless, I believe Rogers is broadly right in what he says about the effect of didactic teaching. This poses the problem I noted earlier: how does one teach without too much telling?

I shall attempt to answer this question in later chapters. Before that, I should like to draw attention to the fact that this is not a new problem. Many of the most thoughtful religious teachers have wrestled with it. They have known that preaching seldom results in significant learning.[68] We all know religious people who are scrupulous about keeping to the outward manifestations of their religion, but whose personal lives are far from moral. We also know that, for centuries, all over the world, people have been taught by religious teachers, yet the actions of both teacher and taught have often been in direct contradiction to that which has been taught. In short, it is not enough to know 'the truth'. To 'really' learn it, one has to act on it. That is not intended as a criticism of religion, only as another example to suggest that didactic teaching seldom results in significant learning.

'Real' learning is never a matter of listening to a teacher, religious or otherwise. Such listening merely runs us along grooves of pleasant reassurance. Real learning only comes about when we have had an appropriate experience. And the more we have to struggle during that experience, the more powerful is our learning likely to be. It is only when my knuckles are bruised, oil is dripping into one of my ears, sweat is beading on my forehead, the wrong spanner is in my hand, and I can't wriggle out from under my car, that I begin to learn how to fix a fault on it. In short, when computers can sweat, they will learn.

LEARNING AND PROBLEM-SOLVING

One of the topics most often discussed in the literature on learning is the way people solve problems. Unfortunately, I am unable to make much sense of most of the literature on this topic which I have seen.[69] Three things especially trouble me about it: the artificiality of the tasks set; the clumsy and illogical way the people described in it often act; and the absence of much comment about how the people involved feel.[70]

I have the same reactions to accounts of computer simulations of problem-solving. These also seem completely artificial to me (in that the computer is unable to recognize a cucumber although it is able to solve a problem in calculus); and because there is never any reference to the way anybody feels.

I should therefore like to try to describe my own experiences of problem-solving. Although such an account is likely to be subjective, it may at least be ecologically valid, and may enable readers to see whether my experiences tally with theirs.

The example of problem-solving I should like to consider here is the experience of writing this book, and I choose this example because I have often recalled times when I have been a student while engaged in this task. That is, I have found myself faced by the need to solve a series of problems, and I have not been at all sure I can. The office temporaries and medical students described earlier must have had the same kind of doubts.

Next come other feelings. For example, the wish to establish professional competence, to make a contribution, to argue a point, to make some money, to gain the esteem of friends, to get a new job, perhaps even to override death.[71] Most students must have at least some of these feelings. If so, how simulate them on a computer?

Another very powerful feeling I often have, while writing, is that I do not really understand. It is as if there is an air of mystery about everything; as if any topic under discussion is almost always somehow different from what seems immediately apparent to me. Then, occasionally, when I manage to pierce the fog of mystery, there is a feeling of pleasure. That is similar to how I have often felt as a student. How does one program a computer to have a sense of mystery?

The next thing which strikes me is that, whenever I write something which I later consider useful, it is seldom produced by my thinking. Rather, my thinking is what happened *after* I have had an insight. Whenever I have tried to force myself to gain an insight, my mind has gone blank. Useful insights have always *come* to me. And they have usually come in one of two ways.

One way is when I am engaged in an activity other than actually thinking. Typical activities include having a shower, or going for a cross-country ride on a mountain bike. That is, thinking has to stop before insights can begin. I made a similar comment when discussing the way Sultan and Poincaré solved their problems. How does one program this on a computer?

It has also been long established that progress in science is not made simply by accumulating facts, but when someone glimpses a discrepancy between what is commonly believed and what may actually be the case. Then come hunches as to how such an anomaly could be resolved, followed by tests of those hunches.[72] Readers will immediately see how such an account relates to what I have written about the process of learning in general.

The above may sound straightforward enough. But what is it that causes a productive hunch to come about? If that could be made clear, then we could all have a productive hunch fifty times a day. But if we cannot specify how a hunch comes about, we cannot program a computer to have one. It certainly hasn't been done to date.

The other way insights come to me is in the process of writing. Until I began to consider how this book got written, I had not realized to what extent the very process of writing has such a powerful effect. For example, I will want to draw attention to a piece of research. So I start writing about it. In the process of doing that, something else will suggest itself to me. So I'll write about that. Then, while I am doing that, more modifications will suggest themselves. None of this would have happened unless I had actually begun writing.

And what is most characteristic about the material that comes in this way is that it comes in the form of compacted hunches.

At first, those hunches seem clear enough. But only until I try to write them down. Then they sound clumsy. I have to have many, many attempts at writing, before a hunch becomes reasonably clear to me. Even then, the moment another hunch comes along, the previous hunch, which had seemed reasonably clear, either becomes more clear or less clear. All this is similar to how the office temporaries and medical students learnt.

I have also noticed that the thousands of strands which go to make up this book get put together in a decidedly piecemeal way. I'll write a few paragraphs on a topic, come to the end of a third or fifth paragraph, and then I find I have to rewrite the first paragraph in the light of the third. Several weeks later I have another idea, or come across another research finding, and another strand will suggest itself to me. When I try to add this to the network I already have, I find I have to rewrite many of the strands around it. Quite often, whole sections have to be rewritten or moved around. It is as if meanings come in compacted kernels which have to be clarified and expanded until they mesh with each other to make up a coherent whole. Readers will immediately see how these comments relate to the comments made in earlier sections on the way parts get their meaning from a whole.

None of this is like how a computer program works. All the information in a computer program is held in the form of discrete items. And when a program contains a great deal of information, that information has to be organized in segments or hierarchies to allow for processing. In writing this book, the opposite happens. I begin by using things like subheadings. But, as I continue, these organizational strategies blur. In fact, it is only when I can see all the details of a topic as one coherent whole that I begin to feel it makes sense.

The above suggests that one of the main characteristics of a powerful understanding of a topic is that the person concerned can see all its details as one integrated whole. How would one program a computer to see a thousand details as one aesthetically satisfying whole?[73]

I believe that the word 'aesthetic' is very important here. Whenever I have found myself struggling to get the various strands of this book to mesh together, I have often been struck by the way I have been prompted as much by aesthetic as by intellectual considerations.[74]

For example, I find I keep asking myself whether a section now 'sounds' or 'feels' right. This reminds me of a period when I was a boy and became interested in painting. A few strokes here, a few strokes there, until a picture was built up. It also reminds me of more recent times when I have tried to establish a garden. There is the same digging, planting, weeding, pruning, staking, replanting and thinning. And guiding such an enterprise there is always an indistinct but potent sense of aesthetics.

Another thing I have discovered is that I am often far from clear about the implications of what I am writing, when I write it. For example, after many revisions, I will complete a chapter and leave it at that. I feel I just cannot improve on it any further. Weeks, months, or even years later, something I had not considered before will suddenly strike me. Or I will come across another bit of evidence, or another person's insights, and these will throw what I have been trying to say into a new light. It is then as if I suddenly understood much better what I had been trying to say. Other times I realize I have been on the wrong track. It is as if I am heading towards a goal, which I am unable to specify clearly beforehand, but which I am able to recognize when I reach it.

How explain this? It seems to me that the only possible way is to say that what I am trying to do is related to life. I am alive, can therefore experience life, and in writing this book I am trying to make sense of those experiences (more specifically, my experiences of learning and teaching). And this process will never end, for always the goal is as complex and indistinct as the nature of life itself. So we can never determine the goal beforehand. We can only recognize it – often mistakenly – when we get close to it. If that is all roughly so, it follows that a computer could never simulate human problem-solving because computers are not alive.

At other times I become aware that what I have known tacitly has become conscious.

For example, I find myself saying, 'Ah, that's how it is . . .'. Yet again, how program this process on a computer?

And colouring all these processes there are often intense feelings. I began my account by noting some of the feelings with which one begins any complex task. But some kind of feelings are always present. These can be painful, pleasurable, and everything in between. For example, I sometimes doubt whether anything will ever come of all the work I am doing, and I then groan at the implications of this. Other times I feel hopeful, even elated. There must also be a strong inclination to persevere, for without this, the job would never get done.

Again, the same must be true of those office temporaries and those medical students. They must have experienced the same kinds of emotions in their learning. How does one program such absolutely fundamental factors into a computer?

There is one more factor which plays an essential part when one is trying to write a book. It also plays an important part in many learning tasks. This is trying to make what one wishes to say clear, both to oneself and to others.

There are plenty of tips on how to write. For example, we know that it is helpful to vary the length of sentences, and not to use the same words too often. But knowing these things will not save a person from using ten words where six would do. I find I have to rewrite things many times, sometimes hundreds of times, before I am half-way satisfied with them. In short, good writing cannot be reduced to a set of instructions. If so, how do we program a computer to write simply and clearly?

But the difficulty goes further than that. I would put it like this: the main difficulty in writing is to get the meaning one is trying to convey past the screen of language in which one must say it. How can one program such a factor into a computer when the basic element of a computer is language, not meaning?

What I have tried to say in this section can be summarized like this. First, I have suggested that the distinction often made between feeling and thinking is misleading. Second, I have tried to show that problem-solving is not a matter of using appropriate 'strategies' (as is usually maintained in the writing of those who base their findings on laboratory tasks, or computer simulations), but depends on the quality of one's exposure to the problem to be solved. I made the same point when discussing Sultan and Poincaré and how they solved their problems. In fact, I would argue that the fewer the strategies the better the exposure. And so it logically must be. For I am unable to specify the goal until I have reached it.[75] Nor could the office temporaries or medical students.

If I consider what I have written in this section I am also forced to conclude that, although the urge to write is somehow mine, it would be more correct to say that the book got written *through* me. I fear that this may sound mystical when I am trying to be accurate.[76]

I do not believe that we solve problems by magic or mystical forces (whatever that means). I believe that thought processes are as open to rational investigation as our respiratory processes; that is, in terms of an integration between organism and environment. In artificial intelligence there is no environment. Only a disembodied 'brain' working in a vacuum. And so it must be, because that 'brain' is dead.

In short, I can see no sensible similarity between the way this book has got written, and how a computer program works. The essential feelings are missing, and none of the most important intellectual factors can be simulated on a computer.

So far in this chapter I have drawn attention to the nature of motivation, the effect of intrinsic and extrinsic rewards, the importance of active engagement, the way a part gains its meaning from a whole, the phenomenon of insight, the nature of thinking, the process of understanding, the power and limitation of language, the need for experiencing, and the part played by a sense of aesthetics. These elements are not the ones most commonly discussed in current books on learning. The next section is a kind of interlude in which I speculate on why that might be the case. After that comes a new section on how we see.

PSYCHOLOGY AND EDUCATION

In previous sections readers were offered an outline of a behaviourist and a Gestaltist view of learning, then a description of some people learning how to use a word processor. Readers may now like to consider whether a behaviourist or a Gestaltist view better explains the learning that was described.

I raise this question because writers of textbooks often maintain that the behaviourist and the Gestaltist approaches to learning provide alternative, even opposing, views. I believe that the descriptions of learning given in the past few sections suggest that elements of both views were present. For example, the office temporaries would not have been able to learn much unless they had been actively engaged. It is also clear that their ability to see the consequences of their actions was very important. These factors are at the heart of the behaviourist position.

We can also see that the office temporaries learnt when they were able to see how the various parts of what they were trying to understand hung together. We have also seen that it is impossible to learn such things by simply listening to a teacher – one has to experience them. These factors are very much in the Gestalt tradition.

For about fifty years, the behaviourist position was the dominant one in psychology. In educational studies, the behaviourist position was certainly the strongest when learning was being considered. Only the work of Jean Piaget was studied to the same extent.[77] Today, the behaviourist position is much less strong; it has been superseded by the 'cognitive' approach.[78] Gestalt psychology gets as little attention as before.

Actually, little psychology is taught on teacher training courses in Britain today. In fact, it is almost dead. Occasionally the word 'psychology' is mentioned, as when fashionable peripherals like 'individual differences' are brought in, but even when psychological issues are discussed it is usually without any mention of 'psychology'.

There must be several reasons for such a state of affairs. The first which comes to my mind is the rise of the 'skills' or 'competences' approach, as this has the effect of making it seem that there is no need for theoretical knowledge to inform classroom practice.

But whatever other reasons there may be for the demise of psychology in teacher education in the UK, it seems to me that the main one must be the nature of the psychological material which teachers used to be asked to study. For my own part, I have found much of it unhelpful, so the demise of psychology in teacher education has dismayed but not surprised me.[79]

On the rare occasions when psychology is mentioned in teacher education in Britain today, it is in terms of the cognitive approach. It may therefore be helpful to consider it for a few minutes.

In cognitivism, the focus of attention is not on an outside stimulus and the resulting behaviour (as is the case in behaviourism), but on the mental processes that are thought to take place inside a person. As a result of this shift, fifty years of behaviourist research appears to have been scrapped. For example, there is no mention of 'reinforcement' in the research published today in the cognitive style.[80]

With the appearance of cognitivism, it is as if, in physics, we had come to see concepts like mass, velocity and acceleration not just differently; it is as if they had ceased to have any use. As if in medicine the notion of metabolism and respiration were now considered outmoded. There is surely something odd about a discipline that can change as dramatically as this.[81]

One of the main topics of interest to a behaviourist was learning. Today it is possible to read research in the cognitive style and find no mention of learning whatsoever. This is probably because many cognitivists like to compare humans with computers, and it is difficult to program a computer to learn. So the focus is on 'information processing'. In other words, one does not begin with a problem, but with an orientation, and it is that which determines what one looks at, and of course sees.

But what is perhaps most striking about the move from behaviourism to cognitivism is not the alleged differences between them. For example, just as in behaviourism, the focus of attention in cognitivism is on the individual. People are seen as isolated things, encapsulated in a bag of skin. Nor is there usually much suggestion that humans are social creatures, profoundly dependent on, and affected by, their social environment.

Also as in behaviourism, these 'individuals' are usually studied as if they were automatons. An examination of the cognitive literature shows that many cognitivists are even more inclined than behaviourists to compare humans with machines. To some extent, behaviourists considered humans biological creatures. They tended to compare humans with animals. Many cognitivists prefer to compare them with computers. Cognitivism is like the rebellious son who reminds one a great deal of the behaviourist father.

Critics of behaviourism used to say that, with the advent of behaviourism, psychology became the study of people who had lost their minds. Today it would be just as appropriate to say that, with the appearance of cognitivism, psychology has become the study of people who have lost their bodies.[82] In behaviourism, feelings were mostly ignored. In cognitivism, feelings have almost entirely disappeared. As a result, everything we most associate with being human and alive, things like joy, worry, hope, shame and fear, tend to have no place in the cognitive scheme of things. And the things which most often give rise to our feelings – other people; relationships – have little place in the electronic switchboard model of humans which is currently fashionable in much cognitive psychology.

This dehumanizing tendency appears to be common in the academic fraternity. Here is Oliver Sacks describing it in his field of neurology:

Folly enters when we try to 'reduce' metaphysical terms and matters to mechanical ones: worlds to systems, particulars to categories, impressions to analyses, and realities to abstractions. This is the madness of the last three centuries. . . . It is this Newtonian–Lockean–Cartesian view – variously paraphrased in medicine, biology, politics, industry, etc. – which reduces men to machines, automata, puppets, dolls, blank tablets, formulae, ciphers, systems, and reflexes. It is this, in particular, which has rendered so much of our recent and current medical literature unfruitful, unreadable, inhuman, and unreal. . . .

And a page later:

one mulls over whole libraries of papers, couched in the 'objective' styleless style *de rigueur* in neurology. One's head buzzes with 'facts', figures, lists, schedules, inventories, calculations, ratings, quotients, indices, statistics, formulae, graphs, and whatnot; everything 'calculated, cast-up, balanced, and proved' in a manner which would have delighted the heart of Thomas Gradgrind. And nowhere, *nowhere*, does one find any colour, reality, or warmth; nowhere any residue of the living experience; nowhere any impression or picture of what it *feels* like to have Parkinsonism . . . one looks in vain for life in these papers; they are the ugliest exemplars of assembly-line medicine: everything human, everything living, pounded, pulverized, atomized, quantized, and otherwise 'processed' out of existence.[83]

I believe that the above is an apt description of much cognitive psychology, especially cognitive science. When I read the work of many of those who work in this tradition, I often feel that the writer failed to get into a school of engineering. I read their work from the perspective of a journeyman teacher, as a man trying to understand how humans learn. And I find I can read a great deal of their work and not find one single thing in it that tallies with anything I ever see in my classes.[84] In their search for usable evidence, method often seems to replace insight.[85]

Fortunately, there are other approaches to learning from which, I believe, a teacher can gain a great deal. I have already drawn attention to some of these. Another approach is based on our understanding of the way people see. That is the topic of the next chapter.

Chapter 4

Perception and Learning

PERCEPTION

One way to gain a better understanding of learning may be to examine how we see. We catch a glimpse of this possibility when we notice that the word 'see' can refer to our ability to see, and also to our ability to understand.

How do we see? Consider the following illustration.

A little girl is out for a walk in the country with her parents. The child is two years old, and as they walk they see a cow, the first this girl has ever seen. Rays of light are reflected off the cow, reach the child's eyes, and cause chemical changes and electrical charges inside them. These charges travel along the child's optic nerve, reach her brain, and stimulate certain nerve cells inside it. The child then 'sees' a cow.

We could say that, as the child looks, 'pictures' of a thing called 'a cow' are traced upon the millions of nerve cells that make up the seeing part of that child's brain.

I have used the words 'picture' and 'traced' here, but an examination of a person's brain will never show such things. The people who study perception use other, more technical terms. But these are only words, too, and how these images are coded in the brain no one yet knows.[1] The technical term often used to correspond with a 'picture' in the brain is a 'schema'. The plural is 'schemas' or 'schemata'.[2]

So the child walks along, and thousands upon thousands of schemata of 'a cow' are coded in her brain. I write that 'thousands' of schemata are coded in that child's brain because, after all, next time that little girl is out for a walk she might catch a glimpse of a cow's backside in the shade of a big tree. As her eyes take this in, the thousands of images (or schemata) she already has inside her brain that remotely resemble anything that looks like the backside of a cow in deep shade are reeled off automatically. If the new images coming into her brain from the outside match any of the thousands of schemata already inside it, she will recognize what she is seeing.

It is as if, every time we look at something, it is matched against the models we already have inside our brain.

This description is similar to the description, given in a previous chapter, of infants moving their heads in order to control a flow of milk. I then noted that they were 'testing' the model of the world which they had inside their brain against the world around them. The same is true of the office temporaries learning how to use a word processor. In the process of learning, they were testing what was happening on the screens in front of them against the schemata inside their brains.

The above is not to say that there is a one-to-one correspondence between the things in the world around us and the schema inside our brains. As usual, things become more complicated when we begin to examine them closely.[3] But I believe that the above account provides a rough working model for us to get along with.

I could sum up like this: when we 'see', we test what we take in with our eyes against what we already have in our brains. If there is a match, we recognize what we see.

Here is some evidence.

If you look at Figure 4.1 you will see either a duck or a rabbit. But how is it possible for a drawing to be recognizable as two so very different things? Notice also that there is no in-between kind of image. One never sees a picture which looks a little like both animals.

How can a drawing remain the same, yet what one sees be so different?

Remember that 'seeing' is not just a matter of taking something in. In seeing, we match what is out in the world against what is already inside our brains. The act of looking is like the act of picking up clues. The clues we pick up make our brain reel off the millions of schemata stored inside it which resemble what we are looking at. So, at first, an image of a duck pops up in our brain; then an image of a rabbit. Of course, it could be the other way round. Which way depends on the general context, or in which animal we happen to be more interested.

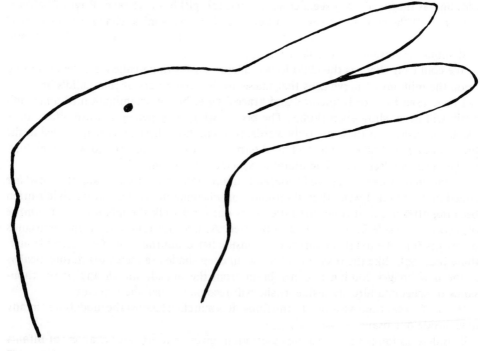

Figure 4.1

Figure 4.2

That last point illustrates the fact that seeing is an active process. We don't simply register the things around us passively. We nearly always have expectations, and these will influence what we see.

Note also that we see with our brains, not our eyes. The latter are merely receptors. I shall be discussing the implications of that fact in the next section.

Look next at Figure 4.2.

If you have never seen this picture before, you will probably not 'see' (better, 'recognize') anything. It probably looks like a mass of blobs and patches. Perhaps it reminds you of a badly drawn sea-coast. If you go on looking, you might 'see' all kinds of other things.

But notice what happens when we are given a few clues.

For example, towards the left there is the head of a cow. The cow is standing broad-side on, with its head turned at 90 degrees toward you. It is standing half in deep shade, and half in bright sunlight. Perhaps you have now 'seen' it?

If not, Figure 4.3 shows an outline of the animal.[4] If you now look back at the unclear picture, you will definitely 'see' it.

When we first see the cow, it comes in a rush. First there is nothing. Then, all of a sudden, one 'sees' a cow. How is this possible? The drawing on the page has not

Figure 4.3

changed. As pointed out earlier, whenever we look at something, thousands of schemata are reeled off in our brain, depending on the clues we pick up as we look. Then, as we pick up more clues, the possibilities are narrowed. Increasingly, what comes up in our brain begins to match what we are looking at. Finally there is an exact match, and at that point we *recognize* what we are looking at, and say, 'Ah!'

Of course, all this usually happens very quickly. So quickly there seems to be no gap whatsoever between our looking and our seeing. It is only in unclear instances, as in the case of the cow, that there is a slight gap. Whatever the length of the gap, like our circulatory system the process takes place completely beyond conscious awareness.

To sum up: 'seeing' is usually a matter of testing what we perceive of the world around us against the schemata already present in our brains. The next section will take this discussion a step further.

PERCEPTION AND LEARNING

It sometimes happens that a person is born with impaired vision. Such an impairment may be due to cataracts, or to an opacity of the cornea, and people with such a deficiency can grow up quite blind. However, many advances have been made in medicine and technology in the last fifty years, and it is now sometimes possible to correct such deficiencies by an operation. The cataracts are removed, or a corneal graft is made, and the person concerned obtains a corrected visual system. There are researchers who have investigated how people react to gaining sight after such an operation, and one of them, Richard Gregory, provides us with a striking account of a blind man who gained sight in middle age.[5]

Gregory reports that, immediately after the man's bandages were removed, he turned his face in the direction from which the voices of the nurses and surgeon around his bed were coming, but was unable to see anything except a blur. That will not surprise us when we remember that, to see, we must have appropriate schemata in our brain.

A few days later, things had much improved. The man was able to walk along the hospital corridors and tell the time from wall clocks. But his sight developed in selective ways. That is, if the man had had an experience of something via touch before the operation (e.g. telling the time by touch from a pocket watch), then his sense of sight in that respect developed reasonably well. But if he had not had such an experience, things were problematic.

For example, the man learnt how to read words written in capital letters by sight without too much difficulty. That was probably because he had learnt how to read those kinds of letters in braille when he had been blind. But he found it much more difficult to learn how to read words written in lower-case letters by sight, because these he had not learnt to read by touch. In fact, he never did manage to learn to read anything other than the simplest words written in that form by sight.

A more dramatic example came to light when the man began to draw. Gregory found that he was able to draw the back of a bus, but not its front, by sight. That was probably due to the fact that he had often touched the back of a bus in his blind years, but, of course, never the front of one. (Gregory is referring to buses in Britain, which used to be entered from the back.)

This example demonstrates that we have to learn how to see, in the same way as we have to learn how to walk or speak. That is, learning how to do these things is partly a matter of laying down appropriate schemata. The example also indicates that to lay down schemata late in life is not easy.

We are given some indication of how difficult this is by the following. Gregory reports that, although the man's sight continued to improve slowly, he unfortunately became so depressed that he appeared to give up the wish to live, and died three years later. Apparently depression is not uncommon in such cases, and Gregory suggests that some of these people feel a deep sense of pain at what they have missed in previous years.

This example furnishes yet more evidence for the common belief that it is difficult to learn how to do certain things in middle age which we can learn how to do almost without effort when we are children.[6] More exactly, if we have the necessary basic experiences when we are young, we can develop our abilities in those respects further all through our lives. But if we have not had a chance to have a basic experience when young – as was the case with this man's sense of sight – then there can be trouble in later years.

This and the previous section have been mostly about the process of seeing. But just as we must have the appropriate schemata in our brain before we can recognize what we are looking at, so we must also have the appropriate schemata in our brain to understand the words a person is saying to us.[7]

Consider what happens when somebody speaks to us in a language we do not understand. It sounds like noise. The reason is clear: we do not have the appropriate schemata in our brain which would allow us to 'recognize' what we are hearing.

This also helps to explain why it is that new ideas are often rejected out of hand, even if they are later shown to be sound. When we hear something which does not match what we already know, it does not usually make much sense. Or, in the language used here, if we do not already have a schema for something in our brain, we tend to find that something puzzling, even nonsensical. Many readers probably found the picture of the cow nonsensical when they first looked at it. The same is often true for new ideas in music, physics or cooking.

We have seen that a child has to learn how to 'see' cows by laying down thousands of schemata of cows. In the same way, a child will 'understand' the things she hears if she has had opportunities to lay down schemata of them. That helps to explain why children who have homes which offer rich experiences tend to be 'brighter' than children who come from impoverished homes. Among other things, we could say that they have more schemata in their brains.

We can see some of the wider implications of the concept of 'schemata' if we consider the extent to which our experiences – especially our earliest experiences – often have a powerful effect on the way we see things for the rest of our lives. These experiences are, of course, also laid down in the form of schemata, and we will often be no more aware of them than we are aware of having schemata for cows in our brains. I shall be discussing the implications of this last sentence later.

In the mean time, it may be helpful if I attempt to illustrate how the above material might relate to a lesson.

Imagine a classroom. The learners are nine-year-olds, all beginners, and this is their first lesson in biology. The teacher is up front, and he is giving a lesson on plant cells. He is using an overhead projector, and has thrown an image of a magnified picture of a plant cell (Figure 4.4) on the wall behind him. Now he is talking about it.

The children look at the picture, and of course they 'see' (i.e. recognize) very little. Some of them think that they see craters on the moon. We know that they don't really 'see' much, because there are no schemata inside their brains which could match what they are looking at. Hence, they are unable to make much sense out of what they are seeing.

But not only will they be unable to 'see' much, they will also be unable to 'understand' much. For when this teacher talks about 'cells', many of them will not really understand what he is talking about. That is because they are unlikely to have a schema for the word 'cell' in their brains.

Compare the above with a better teacher. She would first ask the children to bring some leaves to school. Then she would get them to look at those leaves under increasingly powerful magnifications. She might then ask them to draw what they were seeing. And only after that would she tell them that the shapes they were drawing are called 'cells'. Later still would come an explanation of how cells work. In that way, slowly, relevant schemata would become established in the children's brains. They would then be able to 'see' cells, and 'understand' how they work.

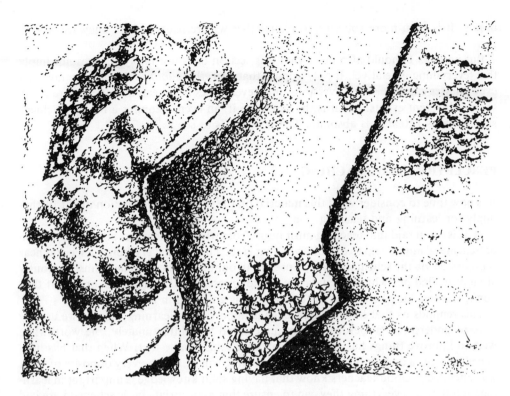

Figure 4.4

To sum up what this very brief account of perception might imply for learning and teaching:

- If a thing outside one's head is the same as the thing inside one's head, one will be able to make sense of it.
- If a thing outside one's head is completely different from the things inside one's head, one will usually not be able to make much sense of it.
- If a thing outside one's head is a little different from the things inside one's head, one will be unsure what one is perceiving – one might even see the things inside one's head.[8]

It follows that, if a teacher talks about something quite new, and the learners just listen, there is no way of knowing whether what the teacher is saying is what the learners are hearing.

We also see from the above that the human brain is not some sort of blank tape, able to take in any input provided that it is loud and clear. The brain is an organ which processes, and it processes information in terms of the schemata it already possesses.

That is why, after twenty-seven people have listened to one person talk for ten minutes, there may be twenty-seven versions of what the speaker has said. That is why eyewitnesses can be very poor witnesses.[9] That is why human memory is often so subjective, and why proof-reading requires a certain kind of attention.

It is sobering to realize that we think in terms of the schemata we already have in our brains. It is even more sobering to realize that we are usually quite unaware of that fact.

But perhaps I should also note what this section does not imply. It does not imply that 'everything is relative'. It only implies that everything *looks* relative. The fact that eyewitnesses can give several versions of an event does not mean that there were really several different events. (That is the case even if 'an event' requires a brain to achieve such a status.) Reality is absolute. The problem is to see it.[10]

PERCEPTION AND TEACHING

It is now time to consider what this material on the process of perception might further imply for learning and teaching.

1) It is often said that teaching must begin from where the learners are at. The notion of 'schemata' might help to explain why that is so. That is, if everything we see and hear is processed via the schemata already present in our brain, then teachers must obviously attempt to find out what schemata are already present in their learners' brains. If they don't, learners may be unable to follow what is going on in a lesson.

This reminds us that having knowledge is important in learning because we usually have to understand 'a' before we can understand 'b'. Unfortunately, the worthwhile wish to improve things has sometimes obscured this simple fact. When that has happened, there is a danger that a parody of learning will result, the very opposite of what was intended.[11] Good teachers know that having solid knowledge is important in learning, and they do everything they can to ensure that appropriate basic schemata are laid down before they introduce further material.

2) As each person has had different experiences, each person will have different schemata inside their brain. This means that each person will process information differently. It further follows that each person will make connections between any new set of facts, and the facts they already know, in their own way.

If so, good teaching cannot be a case of simply 'telling'. It must be a case of creating situations which will enable learners to tackle manageable chunks of new material directly. That will enable them to make links between what they already know, and the new material, in their own way.

3) We know that before we can learn something new, we must often unlearn something old. That is because new information is always processed via information already present in the brain. But getting rid of inaccurate schemata may be difficult. For example, many people will have had the experience of speaking to someone, but sensing from the other person's reply that they have been misunderstood. So you try again. But again it may become clear that you have been misunderstood. That can be frustrating, even painful.

We can explain such a state of affairs by saying that the person to whom we are speaking is using a set of schemata which does not match our own. It follows that mutual understanding will only come about when the schemata causing the misunderstanding are dealt with first.

In the same way, learners may continue to misunderstand something until they are able to see why they misunderstand. A good teacher is sensitive to such things. She will allow many opportunities for learners to say what they think they understand,

and she will 'really' listen. That will provide her with an entry into the learners' frame of reference (their schemata), which may then enable her to clarify things.

4) We have seen that the human brain does not simply take in new information, but always processes it. And as each person has had different experiences, each person will process information in a different way. It must therefore follow that the only way we can know for sure whether what we have taken in is what is actually out there is to test what we have taken in. This is most easily done when we are able to talk about what we have taken in, and hear someone agree or disagree.

That is what people frequently do, especially in places of real learning, like research laboratories. But not in all classrooms. But then, sadly, in some classrooms there is a great deal of teaching and not much learning.

5) Many people will have noticed that learning is not always a matter of picking up something new. Sometimes it is a matter of seeing what one already knows in a new way. When that happens, it is as if the schemata in our brain had been reshuffled into a new pattern. That new pattern will then give the old facts a new meaning.

6) In the previous sections on perception I repeatedly noted that learning is a matter of testing and interpreting, not simply recording. That observation complements the many comments made earlier on the way that 'real' learning is an active rather than a passive process.

7) When we look at something, we have the illusion that it is 'out there', not inside our brains. One of the effects of the transmission method of teaching is that it tends to reinforce the myth that answers are 'out there', either in a textbook or about to come out of a teacher's mouth. But just as seeing must take place inside our brains, so must understanding.

In the next section I shall try to show what that last fancy-sounding claim implies.

FACTS AND ANSWERS

At the end of the previous section I claimed that we must ultimately find answers inside our own brains. When I first came across that notion I whistled with pleasure. I felt it was packed with implications, and I also thought it new. Then someone drew my attention to the fact that Plato had made it in his *Meno* more than two thousand years ago.[12]

In this short work Plato describes how Socrates manages to get an uneducated boy to state the proof of several geometric theorems by asking him a series of questions. It could be argued that Socrates simply leads the boy by the nose. I doubt whether the boy fully understands his own answers; and I certainly do not think that Socrates demonstrates a good teaching technique here.

But that is beside the present point. Plato is attempting to demonstrate that, although the boy appears not to have the foggiest notion about how to solve geometrical problems, with Socrates there to guide him the boy is able to find all the answers inside his own head. It is partly that which I had in mind when I made the claim that we must find 'the answer inside our own heads'.

But the matter goes further than that. For to make the claim I did is the same as saying that the boy must have had the answers in his head all the time. All Socrates did was to help him find them there; and Plato is also saying that this is true of all of us. In other words, Plato is saying that understanding is not something entirely new, but a recognition of something already in our minds.[13]

One could summarize what Plato says like this: we never learn anything. We already know everything. What happens when we say we 'learn' is that we recognize something we have always known.

Many readers may find the above absurd. If so, I wonder what they will make of the following research on memory.

Consider first how we store things. If we want to store beans, we can put them in a jar. But if we want to store information, things are more complicated. We then have to write that information down. In the case of an image, we have to draw it, or take a photograph of it. And if we want to store sounds, we have to use electric gadgetry.

In other words, when it comes to storing *information* (in the form of words, pictures or sounds), some kind of physical change must be made in a medium. That may consist of marks on a piece of paper, chemical changes on a photographic plate, or physical changes in the magnetic particles on a cassette ribbon.

What happens in our brains when information is stored in it? What kind of change in the medium takes place?

One researcher in this field, Colin Blakemore, first notes that having a memory of something must involve some kind of physical change in the brain. How else is the memory to be stored? To illustrate, Blakemore reports the following experiment.[14]

A rat is placed in a maze, and allowed to run around inside it until it has learnt how to get to the exit quickly. It is then *immediately* cooled down to about 5°C. That stops all electrical activity in its brain. Shortly after, when it has thawed out again, it has been found that the rat will be none the worse for wear. But if the rat is then put back inside the same maze, it will run around in a way which shows that it has not learnt anything about the maze from its first visit to it. In other words, its behaviour shows that it does not have a memory of having been there.

Now consider what happens when the same rat is cooled down to about 5°C *several minutes* after it has run around inside a maze. It has then been found that it will retain the knowledge it has gained from having been there because, when the rat is put back inside the maze, it shows by the way that it gets to the exit that it learnt the topography of the maze from its previous visit. In other words, it now has a memory of having been there.

This experiment suggests that cooling a rat down to 5°C *immediately* after it has learnt to run a maze prevents a physical change from taking place inside its brain. That is, it prevents the establishment of a memory trace (or schema) in its brain.

The next thing that would interest a researcher like Blakemore is to identify the molecules in the brain which are changed when a memory is stored inside it.

Blakemore – University Lecturer in Physiology, and Fellow and Director of Studies in Medicine at Downing College, Cambridge, giving the Reith Lectures in 1976, some 2,500 years after Plato had given one of his lectures – concludes that no such molecules exist in the brain.

He goes on to note that such a conclusion leads to one of two possibilities: either memory does not have a physical basis in the brain; or, in his words: 'every memory is innately within us, in our genetic make-up'. And further, that this supposition is 'curiously reminiscent of Plato's nativist theory that all human knowledge is derived by the soul from a previous existence'.

Well, well, well!

So the answer might be in the learner's head after all!

Not quite in the case of that rat, perhaps.

Readers may be prepared to agree that *answers* must be found inside our own heads, but not specific facts. That is, we might be prepared to agree that an answer is obtained when schemata are rearranged so that they produced a meaningful Gestalt. But the topography of a given maze can surely only be learnt by having some actual experience of running around inside it.

So perhaps Blakemore is right to say that the problem he faces is 'curiously reminiscent of Plato's nativist theory'. That is, 'reminiscent' only. For the rat could not possibly know anything about the topography of a certain maze before it had actually run around inside it. Or could it . . .?

I do not know how to resolve the problem Blakemore poses. Perhaps consciousness is faster than light? If it is, it would also be beyond time . . . But this discussion is beginning to take us beyond the scope of the present book. However, readers unacquainted with Plato's views on learning might like to hear a little more about them.

Plato maintained that all human beings have a soul. Nobody quite knows what a 'soul' is. Whatever it is, it is commonly held that souls are immortal. It is also held, by those who believe in souls, that each time a person is born, a soul enters that person's body; and each time a person dies, that person's soul goes to a place called 'heaven'. It follows, Plato felt, that each time a soul enters a person's body it will carry with it the knowledge that it gained from its many previous visits to this planet when it inhabited another living body. So Plato argued that when we learn, we discover what our soul already knows from its previous visits to this planet.[15]

I noted earlier that many people must find such an account absurd. Yet it is clear that a living body and a dead body are very different. It is also clear that it is impossible to describe this difference in only physical terms. It is quite obvious that there is more to being alive than having a beating heart. So exactly what happens when a person 'dies'?

People have various answers to that question. Some believe in souls, others not. I find at least one widespread belief about souls (whatever they are) unsatisfactory. Rather than each one of us having a soul which continues living after we die, it seems to me far more likely that the thing we call a soul is a general 'something' which permeates the whole universe. Perhaps a comparison with water is possible here.

We know that our bodies contain a good deal of water, in the form of various fluids, and those fluids will be a little different in each person (depending on what they eat and drink). But when we die, those fluids reduce mainly to water, and go back to being a part of all the water on this planet. In the same way, while we are alive, we all have an individual soul, and that soul is likely to be a little different from person to person (depending on our individual experiences). But just as the water inside our bodies is a part of all the water in the universe, so may our souls be a part of a larger soul which permeates the whole universe. And when we die, our soul may go back to being a part of one large 'soul'.

I don't think it matters what we decide to call this general 'soul-something'. We could call it Soul, God, Tao or Nature. I quite like the word 'consciousness'. Whatever word we use, the advantage of the above account is that it suggests an intimate link between the world outside our bodies and what we call 'a soul' inside our bodies.

Or perhaps I could put the matter this way. Like many other people, I have a hunch that there must be something called 'life', or 'soul', or 'consciousness' in this universe of ours; and that this consciousness can only become manifest through a living creature. Now, if this 'thing' some people call 'soul' – and I prefer to call 'consciousness' – is ultimately not only the private affair we usually take it to be, and if it also permeates the whole universe as well as our brains, then that which we call 'understanding' may not be a case of processing the stimuli coming to us from the outside world. It may be more a matter of being open to the world, and becoming consciously aware of that to which we have opened ourselves.

All this may sound rather 'unscientific'. However, it is a line of thinking one frequently encounters among many eminent scholars. Consider the following comment by the biologist Sinnott: 'Mind itself, at least in essence, seems to be coextensive with all of life, and grows out of that self-regulation and goal-seeking which is life's distinctive quality. Mind and life are essentially one.'[16]

Or consider this comment by Schrödinger, one of the scientists most responsible for the revolution in modern physics:

> The same elements compose my mind and the world. This situation is the same for every mind and its world, in spite of the unfathomable abundance of 'cross-references' between them. The world is given to me only once, not one existing and one perceived. Subject and object are only one.[17]

Or consider this comment by the psychologist Gibson: 'Instead of postulating that the brain constructs information from the input of a sensory nerve, we can suppose that the centres of the nervous system including the brain, resonate to information.'[18]

These are speculations, but readers inclined to dismiss them might first like to consider some criticisms of contemporary accounts of learning,[19] and the way in which the thoughts of some very eminent Western scholars have begun to converge with those of an ancient Eastern tradition. For my own part, I have found this a liberating experience.

For now it is enough if I have managed to suggest two things: that learning is a matter of being open to the world; and that answers must be found inside our own heads.

Chapter 5

Real Learning

THE PERSONAL IN LEARNING

So far in this book I have drawn attention to the nature of motivation, the importance of active engagement, the effect of various kinds of rewards, and the abstract nature of meaning. I have also drawn attention to the phenomenon of insight, the influence of pattern, the scope of language, the importance of experience, and the establishment of schemata. In the previous section I drew attention to the need to look inside our own heads if we are to find answers.

There is one element in learning to which I have not yet drawn attention: the importance of personal feelings. Here is a true account to indicate what I mean.

For many years it has been a part of my job to visit student-teachers and observe them teach. After the lesson, the student-teacher and I will discuss how the lesson went, and there is always some concern in such discussions because, no matter what I say beforehand, student-teachers usually see such a visit as an assessment. Teaching is a very personal matter, and very difficult to do well. So anything but generalities, praise or the mildest suggestion for improvement will tend to be seen as criticism, at least initially. Hundreds of such visits have shown me that many people find them a threatening experience, and I have therefore come to see that it is wise to be as unobtrusive and gentle as possible. I am sure that no one who has done any teaching will be surprised by any of these comments.

That said, by way of an introduction, here is a description of how one of these visits has typically gone.

The day has come when I am to visit a student-teacher. This particular student-teacher is a tutor-librarian. As usual, this first visit is made towards the end of the first term, and by this time the student-teacher will have examined and discussed the materials presented in this book so far.

This particular student-teacher – let us call her Betty – has herself fixed a date for my visit. (My diary goes around the class, and people put in a time when they would find it convenient for me to visit.) Betty has chosen this afternoon. She has decided to have a lesson on the topic 'Using a Library'. She has placed eighteen chairs in a horseshoe, and when the learners come in she welcomes them and announces the topic of the lesson. She talks about the library organization, the various indexes, and the many things which library staff tend to feel users should know. Betty is a knowledge-able, pleasant, conscientious, middle-aged woman, and she speaks about these things in a systematic way.

Betty talks for about forty minutes. Her voice goes up and down, the learners sit and listen, glance at their notebooks, move in their chairs, look around, look at each other, sit and listen, and look at Betty. At the end of her talk Betty gives the learners a sheet of paper on which there are half a dozen questions. Very soon the learners jot down their answers with good cheer. Occasionally they get up to consult a catalogue. Sometimes they exchange a few words.

It takes them about ten minutes to do this work. Then they sit in the horseshoe again, and Betty asks for their answers. These are read out, and it is clear that they have caused few problems. Next Betty asks if there are any questions.

A girl asks what should be done if someone wants a book that isn't in the library. A boy says he can never find a book when he needs it. Another asks if there are any fines. Betty is conscientious and answers these questions in detail. Some of the learners look restless. Finally Betty asks if they have learnt anything that afternoon. As we stand up to leave, a girl smiles and says she has.

Betty takes me back to her office and offers me some tea. There is the usual touch of nervousness in her manner. She smiles and asks, 'Well, what do you think?'

I say I thought the lesson had gone well, and ask her how she felt about it.

Betty tells me that she wished she had had more time, that there was so much to get through, and that it is difficult to hold a lesson in a library.

I say I can appreciate all of that. Also that I had the distinct impression that she enjoyed her job.

And so we chat. And when I feel it is appropriate, I mention the course she is doing with me, and the material on learning and teaching we have considered so far. Then I ask her whether she has found any of it useful.

My question clearly makes Betty feel uncomfortable. From things she has said, and things she has written in her assignments, and from the way she has sometimes smiled in class, she has given the impression that she has usually found the material, and the approach to teaching we have discussed in my classes, useful.

It also becomes obvious, from the next few things she says, that she believes that she has used this material in her lesson that afternoon. She notes that she uses quite a few of the techniques I use: things like getting the learners to sit in a circle, and using a worksheet. But as we continue chatting it becomes increasingly obvious that her lesson that afternoon had remained largely untouched by anything of any real substance we had considered in my classes.

So I say with a smile, 'For ten weeks you have been examining material in my classes which strongly suggests that simply telling people does not help them to learn very much. You have certainly shown that this is broadly correct this afternoon.'

I wish I knew how to describe Betty's face. For it only took her about twenty seconds to work out that if little she had considered and discussed with others in my classes over the past ten weeks had had much practical effect on her, then it would be unlikely that anything she had said over the past fifty minutes in her class that afternoon would have much practical effect on her learners either.

So Betty took a sort of breath and said, 'Well, you seem to be talking yourself out of a job!'

I replied as mildly as I could, 'How about devising a question-sheet in which everything you said this afternoon, except for your welcoming comments, appears on it in the form of a question? That way you could get your learners doing practical things right from the start? Do you remember . . .'

But I was wasting my breath.

I could see that Betty knew exactly what I was getting at. I could see from her face that, for the first time, the materials she had been studying in my classes had *come alive for her.*

Betty had come to my classes. She had spoken about things she found problematic in her teaching. She had heard others do the same. She had heard me mention things which thoughtful people had suggested in response. She had examined materials on learning and teaching. She had discussed them in small groups. She had written assignments which invited her to reflect on her experiences, and to consider the relevance of the material she had studied. On the face of it, Betty had done my classes.

But had she really 'done' them?

I believe Betty had been a good deal more active in my classes than she might have been in some. And yet, it was still not enough to generate real learning. Till today, the material she had examined in my classes had been something 'out there', perhaps 'mine'. But when it comes to learning, 'out there' means that it has no real substance. It is just so many words.

Learning isn't a process that exists on its own. It is obviously a part of a much larger process. Breathing isn't a process that exists on its own either. Just as breathing cannot be found on this planet on its own, neither can learning. On this planet, breathing and learning can only be found in a living organism. Computer simulations of learning are like artificial lungs – very odd-looking things in the absence of a living person using them to stay alive.

If we take this kind of an approach, we can understand why Betty had 'really' learnt so little in my classes. Until she *felt* that the material she was studying could further her own needs, she didn't 'really' learn. For learning, like breathing, must have evolved on this planet to further felt needs. Until Betty deeply felt she had a need, she had learnt at a level that would get her by: verbally.

From what she was able to say, it appeared that Betty had learnt a good deal. But I noted earlier that language is two-edged: through it we can communicate, but through it we can also create an illusion of communication. A teacher may ask a question, a learner may answer, and there is a suggestion that some learning has taken place. But often nothing of any real substance has occurred.

And so, over the years, I have discovered a fact. It is that next to nothing my students discuss or study in my classes affects the way they actually teach (even when they say that the material is apt and interesting) until two things happen:

- they strongly feel its relevance to their personal needs; and
- they repeatedly act on those felt needs.

When I discovered that what we did in my classes had next to no practical effect, I was greatly upset. Here I was, encouraging them to exchange experiences, showing them all this rich material – and none of it had much practical effect! Even in those who were enthusiastic about it!

It took me several years to realize that my disappointment was quite misplaced. This dawned on me when I became aware that it had taken me years of struggle to work out an approach to teaching which half-way satisfied me. And the critical element had been my *felt* need.

I can now ask a question.

When we feed information into a computer, it can be said to 'know' that information if, when we ask it to perform some function on the basis of that information, it performs that function correctly. In that way it can be said to have simulated a human.

In my classes, I had introduced Betty to certain information. And whenever I had asked Betty a question about that information, she had usually been able to respond in a way which showed that she 'knew' it. Yet we have seen that she did not *really* know it, for she was unable to act on it. Nor would it have made any difference if Betty had been introduced to that information a hundred more times, each time in a some-how clearer way. Until she began to make that information hers, by feeling its relevance to her personal needs, and acting on it, she had really learnt nothing but words.

I had better add that it took Betty many practical endeavours until, to some extent, she was able to act appropriately on the information she had supposedly learnt. That was partly because this information was in conflict with her existing habits (and these habits exert a much stronger effect than anything we may intellectually believe); and partly because it takes time and effort before new habits become established. More on that later.

In the mean time, I can ask my question. It is this: How can we tell when computers know, as distinct from *really* know?

It may be helpful to consider the above question in another context.

While discussing her work as a translator, Barbara Reynolds describes a visit she and some Italian friends made to a British war cemetery in Italy. She writes that it was a beautiful place, and it is clear from her evocative description that she is touched. She notes that she was talking to her friends, in Italian, and she goes on to say that a moment later she read a notice, also in Italian, which told visitors what the place commemorated.

She continues:

> suddenly I walked a few places on and there was another notice, saying exactly what the Italian notice said, but in English. The shock was astonishing. I knew then that only my brain had taken in the meaning of the Italian words; my sympathies had been stirred, but only faintly. I realised this when I read the words in English: Here lie the bodies of British soldiers killed in action in the Asiago campaign during the War of 1914–1918. I knew then, with all my powers of knowing, as I had not known before, that British soldiers were buried there.[1]

Here again two forms of knowing: one verbal, the other felt. How does one model this difference on a computer?

I pose this question in an attempt to explain why I believe that so much psychology (especially cognitive psychology) is misconceived. As I said earlier, a great deal of academic psychology ignores the fact that humans are alive. (I believe that also helps to explain why psychology has almost disappeared from educational studies.)

In the next few sections I should like to discuss the implications for learning and teaching of that striking fact. Before that, I feel the time has come for me to admit to a personal dilemma.

Many times in this book I have noted the limitation of 'telling'. Yet this book is inevitably based on 'telling'! If so, there must be a serious doubt about the value of reading this book.

If I consider what I have written about the nature of learning, and if I consider my experiences with student-teachers, and if I am honest, I am forced to admit that I doubt whether anyone's teaching will *really* be affected by reading this book. In fact, I have had the experience of observing a colleague teach who had read the manuscript of this book, who had been generous enough to express enthusiasm for it; yet, when I observed her teach, it was obvious that it had not affected the way she actually taught.

I found this experience distressing and embarrassing, especially when she talked about her lesson afterwards. For it then became apparent that she was distressed and embarrassed, too! Being candid but human, she both criticized and defended herself; and the more she did so, the more contradictory she became. Looking back on the episode a while later, I felt that perhaps some good had come out of it after all. For it seemed to me that, though her actual practice had not changed, she was troubled, and she now seemed to view teaching from a new perspective.[2]

I mention this experience because it may illustrate a way out of my dilemma. That is, though I do not believe that reading any book is enough to change a person's practice, it is possible that such a reading may plant a seed in a person's mind which will grow, and eventually come to affect practice – provided always that it falls on hospitable soil and gains some support from a sustaining environment.

FEELING AND THINKING

Human beings are made of flesh and blood, bone and sinew. They feel. If they did not feel, they would do very little. They would certainly not want to show that humans are essentially machines. What would be the point? Who would *care*?

Imagine you felt nothing. Your arm would burn every time you touched a fire when you hadn't noticed it. Nor would there be anything to prompt you to eat, for you would never feel any hunger. It follows that you would be unlikely to go out and grow some food or earn some cash to ease that hunger. In short, if you did not feel, you would be as good as dead. You would be a machine.

Some centuries ago the philosopher Descartes stated, 'I think, therefore I am.' He wanted to begin with fundamentals, with things about which we could be *sure*. It seems to me that the way he began typifies a European tradition, but perhaps it also typifies an aberration.[3] I put the matter this way because it seems to me that seeing things like this confers on thinking a pre-eminence it does not have.

Consider again the fact that we are aware that we are alive. That is, if we *think* about it, we know that we are alive; but in some people the *feeling* that they are alive is missing. They say that they *know* that the things around them are real, but that nothing *feels* real to them.

Such feelings cause anguish, and the people who have them often seek a priest or a therapist because they are in such pain.[4]

One researcher, Weckowicz, describes such people like this: 'they think, but they do not exist'. He goes on: 'It is as if there were two kinds of knowledge; one supplied by . . . experience, and the other by rational judgement.'[5]

Notice the use of that word 'experience'. Experiences are felt, but these people do not feel. We also note that there is nothing the matter with the ability of these people to make a 'rational judgement' – that is, with their ability to think – yet they are in anguish. Why?

It must be because, if we *feel* that life is 'not real', then life does not *seem* to be real, no matter how much we are able to *think* it is. So saying that we know we exist because we can *think* must be misleading. It is the kind of thing typically said by a person who spends a great deal of time thinking.

So from where do we get our feeling that we exist? In the space available, I suggest that it derives from our sensing that we exist in another person's mind (and in particular that of a parent), and that this is why we invariably find trauma in the early and close relationships of troubled adults. It is also why most of us find the withdrawal of love intensely painful, both as children and as adults.

In other words, I suggest Descartes is wrong, first, to place such emphasis on cognition; and, second, to place such emphasis on the individual. I believe he would have been closer to the truth if he had said, 'They think I exist (and want me to exist), therefore I *feel* I am.'[6]

Another question which such considerations raise is: where do feelings end, and thoughts begin? When I try to establish this in myself, I find I cannot. Perhaps thinking is best seen as an extension of feeling?

But at least one thing is clear. It is that creatures existed perfectly adequately on this planet for millions of years before thinking – in the usual sense of that word – ever arrived on it. So I would suggest that whenever we do anything, the origins of what we do must lie in a feeling.[7]

This often becomes apparent when a topic like capital punishment is under discussion. Participants will usually put forward a variety of reasons for whatever position they hold. But if the discussion continues for long enough, we often come to suspect that these reasons are really justifications for the way the participants happen to *feel*.

Here are some pointers.

Place a Martian in front of a bicycle and he will smile and scratch his antennae. Never having seen a bicycle before, he has no idea what it is for. In other words, when we do something, it is often done on the basis of past experiences.

But in what form are our past experiences of riding a bicycle coded inside us? Clearly not in words. Imagine getting on a bike to go to the post office and having to verbalize every muscle contraction required![8] So only some of our past experiences will be coded inside us in the form of words. The rest will be coded in a 'felt form'.

This felt, pre-verbal form, is the state all infants are in before they begin to acquire a language. This stage must also be the stage out of which music arises. In short, there must be a felt, pre-verbal state 'behind' language.[9]

Take next a simpler example than riding a bicycle or learning a language. When a baby first stretches out an arm to reach for an object, it tends to be clumsy. However, after a few months of practice, it becomes proficient at such an action. This suggests that a kind of coding must become established in the brain and tissue of a baby before it can carry out such an action. In a previous chapter, the word 'schema' was used to describe such a coding. But in what form are such schemata laid down? Again, clearly not in words.

Sultan, the chimpanzee from an earlier chapter, eventually understood that he could reach some bananas by stacking boxes on top of each other. But in what form did his understanding take place? I argued that it could not be a matter of associations, and suggested that he grasped the 'meaning' of the situation he was in; I also suggested that this 'meaning' must have an abstract, living form. And as apes don't have the gift of language, Sultan must have *felt* that meaning.

Consider further the case of completely deaf people.[10] Many do not possess the gift of language (as we usually understand that word), yet they are usually able to take perfectly good care of themselves. They are not always able to perform as well on certain mental tests as people who possess natural language. But it is obvious that their brains must contain a wealth of complex schemata, and few of these will be in the form of words. If so, these, too, must be in the form of abstract, living, 'felt-experiences'.

Consider next what happens when we are faced by a problem. We tend to say to ourselves, 'Well, if I do "this", then "that" is likely to happen.' We do not say to ourselves exactly what the 'this' and the 'that' stand for. We know what they stand for. They are whole chunks of compacted 'felt-meanings' which we leave unsaid.[11]

When we try to verbalize some of these chunks of compacted felt-meanings, our listener might say: 'I'm sorry, I don't quite understand what you are getting at.' We will then tend to pause and reflect. Because, if we are to make ourselves clear, we must attend to those 'felt-meanings' deep inside us. Sometimes, try as we may, we cannot quite express what it is we want to say. This suggests that in order to say something rather complicated we must first get a clear, pre-verbal sensing of that something. It is only after we have managed to do that, that we can translate such feelings into words.

William James described something similar in 1893 when he considered what sometimes happens when we try to remember a name, and cannot:

> The state of our consciousness is peculiar. There is a gap therein; but no mere gap. It is a gap that is intensely active. A sort of wraith of the name is in it, beckoning us in a given direction, making us at moments tingle with the sense of our closeness and then letting us sink back without the longed-for term. If wrong names are proposed to us, this singular gap acts immediately, so as to negate them. . . . And the gap of one word does not feel like the gap of another, all empty of content.[12]

Notice the use of that word 'feel' in the last sentence. What other word could James have used?

It is as if inside us human creatures there are two processes. At bottom, a basic 'feeling' process, which we share with all other living creatures. Then, tacked on to the top of that basic feeling process, there is another process called 'thinking'.

But here I hesitate more than usual. Readers will be aware that I am trying to describe a kind of model of how the mind works. That is daunting, to say the least. But it is surely what teachers need.

A MODEL OF THE MIND

I have suggested that there are two mental processes: (a) a basic feeling process; and (b) a verbal/thinking process. It may be more helpful to speak of three mental processes. First, a basic feeling process when we have an experience. Second, a process which enables us to become consciously aware of what we are feeling – a process which we call 'thinking'. And third – allied to that conscious-making, thinking process – the language process which enables us to consider more clearly the things about which we are conscious (and also to communicate them).

Perhaps it is these latter processes which Bartlett had in mind when he wrote that an 'organism has somehow to acquire the capacity to turn around upon its own "schemata" and to construct them afresh. This is a crucial step in organic development. It is where and why consciousness comes in.'[13] (Readers may recall, from the section on perception, how schemata are laid down. Bartlett's comments throw further light on this process.)

Recent findings related to the phenomenon of 'blindsight' lend some support to Bartlett's position. Larry Weiskrantz draws attention to certain amnesic patients (whose ailment is caused by chronic alcoholism, a variety of poisons, or herpes simplex), and he notes that the most striking symptom these patients exhibit is an inability to remember anything from one minute to the next.[14] You might be talking to such a patient, leave the room and come back a minute later, and the patient not only does not recognize you, but will have no recollection whatsoever of ever having met you. Such amnesia is, of course, a very great disability.

At one time it was thought that such people could not learn anything. However, research has shown that they can, but that they have no recollection of having learnt. In other words, such people are able to learn; but, in Bartlett's words, 'they are unable to turn around upon their own schemata and construct them afresh'. Or, as we would say in more ordinary language, these people are unable to reflect upon what they have learnt.

Weiskrantz compares this kind of patient with others who have suffered an injury in their striate cortex (that part of their brain which receives input from the eyes). For a long time it was thought that such patients were completely blind when they received signals from their eyes in the damaged parts of their brain. However, it has been discovered that such people are able 'to detect visual events in this "blind" area, to locate them in space, to make judgements about the orientation of lines or gratings, to detect the onset and termination of movement, and even to do simple pattern discrimination'.

But these patients do not have any awareness that they have such abilities. When they are questioned, they say that they 'are just guessing and playing the experimenter's game'. And when they are told the results of their test, they express astonishment. Weiskrantz notes that such a patient will sometimes say that 'he does not "see", but has a "feeling" that something is there'.

Note that word: 'feeling'.

Weiskrantz goes on to suggest that in both kinds of patient there is a direct response to a stimulus, but without conscious awareness. In his words: 'What I think has become disconnected is a monitoring system, one that is not part of the serial information-processing chain itself.'

Again, it seems to me that what Weiskrantz calls 'monitoring' (taken from Lloyd Morgan) may be similar to Bartlett's 'capacity to turn around upon our schemata'; that is, to reflect consciously about what is unconsciously known.

Generalizing from the above, one might say that many of our actions are 'automatic': we are often not even aware that we are doing them. But we can be. We can stop and reflect on what we are doing, and in doing that, we make conscious some of what is unconscious.[15]

At this point we might recall a very important difference between our feeling process, and our thinking process.

First, we have seen that our *feeling* processes are often unconscious. (And when we can make them conscious, they will tend to be generalized, because it is impossible to make all the details conscious.)

In contrast, we have seen that our *thinking* processes are mostly conscious. That is, we can usually consciously reflect on our thoughts (and in some detail). This enables us to do such things as review a matter, modify it or plan ahead.

But our feeling (mostly unconscious) processes have advantages, too. They enable us to do several things at the same time. For example, we can drive a car, suck a gumdrop, chat with a passenger, scratch an ear, and take in a new route, all at the same time. By having many of our actions 'on automatic', we free our limited capacity for conscious thinking for those things which require our conscious attention. For the moment we begin to think consciously, we can deal with only one thing at a time. That is how language works: one word after the other, not holistically.

I have noted that we can sometimes make our feeling processes conscious, but we cannot *always* do this. It appears that what we feel – that is, what we have experienced – can sometimes be made conscious. Conversely, what we think cannot become encoded in our basic feeling process to a very great extent.

I attempted to illustrate the latter point when I noted that hearing a description of Boston does not have the same effect as going for a walk in that city. That is, a feeling, or an experience, does not become encoded in our brains when we are simply *told* something. Only the words do. Experiences have to be experienced; they have to be felt.

These are large claims; the following is some further evidence in their support.

Consider first the following finding which comes from work with so-called split-brain patients. These are people who have undergone an operation to ease epileptic seizures. In this operation, the two halves of the brain are surgically severed (Figures 5.1–5.4).

These figures show that, in most people, the language centre of the brain is located in the left half (or left 'hemisphere') of the brain. This language centre is extremely important, for it enables us not only to understand and use language, but also to reflect consciously about what we have experienced.

The right hemisphere of the brain is responsible for more global feelings; that is, it is in this half of the brain that most of our experiences are encoded.[16]

Normally, the two halves of the brain are so closely connected (via a bundle of nerve fibres called the corpus callosum) that most of what is processed in one half is

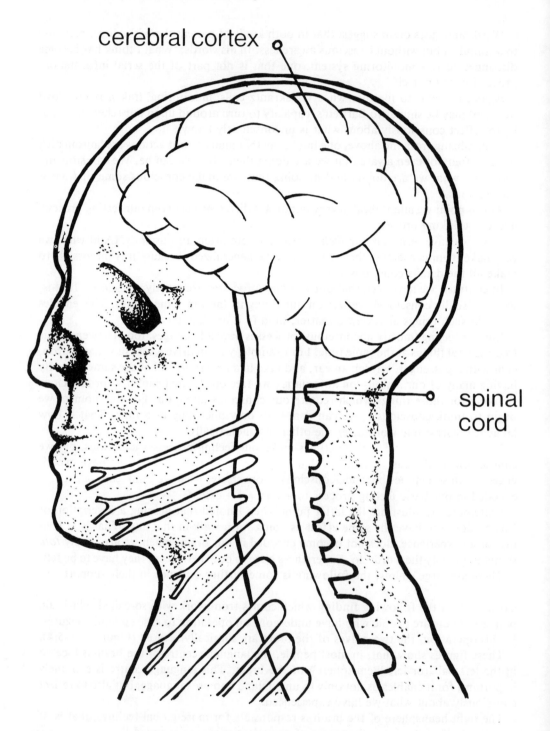

cerebral cortex

spinal cord

Figure 5.1

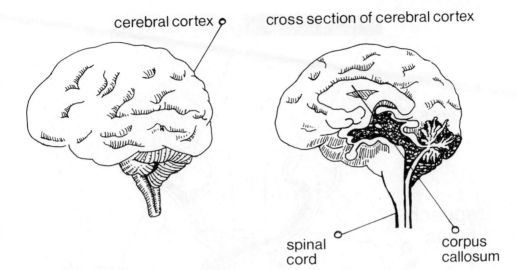

cerebral cortex ○——

cross section of cerebral cortex

spinal cord ○——

corpus callosum

Figure 5.2

view from top

corpus callosum

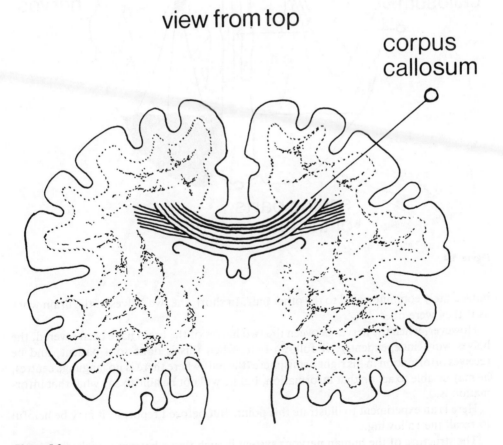

Figure 5.3

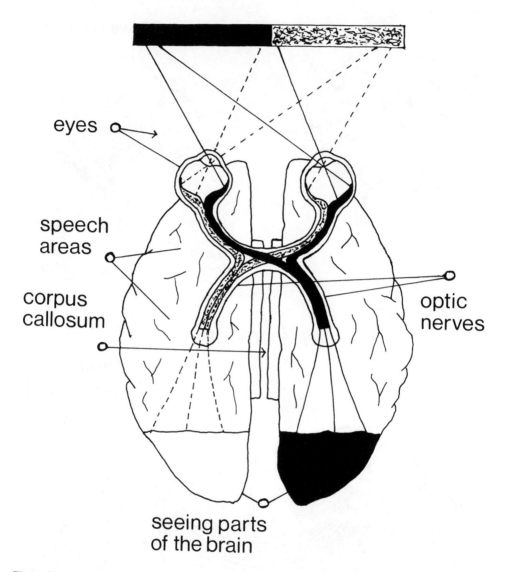

eyes

speech
areas

corpus
callosum

optic
nerves

seeing parts
of the brain

Figure 5.4

immediately communicated to the other half. In short, the two halves of the brain work as if they were one.

However, when the nerves between the two halves of the brain have been severed, the halves work independently. It follows that, when this is done to a patient, and he receives information in his right hemisphere (the half where there is no language centre), he may be able to act on that information, but he will not be able to say what that information is.

Here is an experiment to illustrate this point. But before I report it, it may be helpful to recall the following.

The structure of the human nervous system is such that whatever is picked up in the

visual pathway from eyes to seeing parts of the brain as seen from below

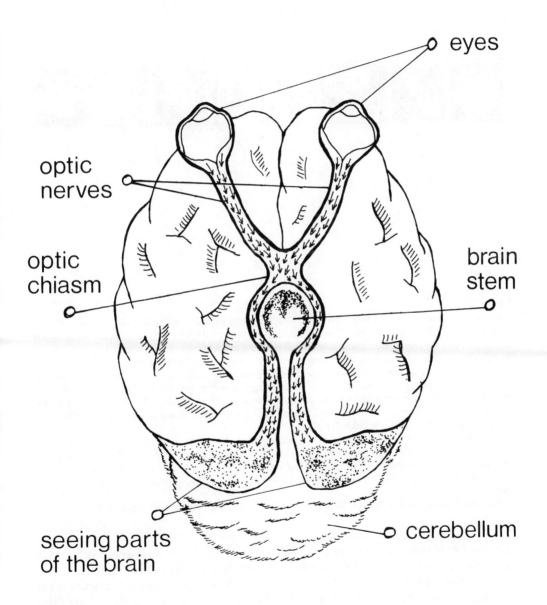

eyes

optic nerves

optic chiasm

brain stem

seeing parts of the brain

cerebellum

Figure 5.5

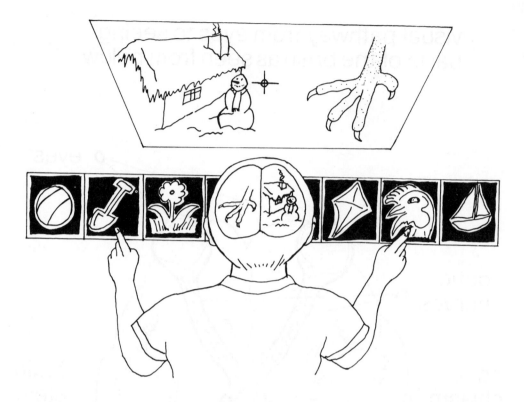

Figure 5.6

Figure 5.6 shows a man, the two halves of whose brain had been severed to ease his epilepsy, doing an experiment. A picture of a claw was presented to his right visual field, and was hence registered in his left hemisphere (i.e. the verbal and conscious one); and a picture of a snow scene was presented to his left visual field, and was hence registered in his right hemisphere (i.e. the non-verbal and unconscious one). In response to a request that he then select a picture to match what he had seen, he chose a picture of a chicken with his right hand, and a picture of a shovel with his left hand; and it is clear that these choices make good sense. However, when the man was asked why he had chosen these two pictures, he said that he had seen a claw, so he had chosen a picture of a chicken; and that, as you have to have a shovel to clean out a chicken shed, he had chosen a shovel with the other hand!

The man's reply shows: (a) that he was not consciously aware of the content of the non-verbal, non-conscious part of his brain – the part which had seen a snow scene; and (b) that the verbal and conscious part of his brain gave an explanation for his behaviour *on the basis of his outward circumstances*.

It is, I think, sobering to reflect that we all behave like this to a considerable extent throughout our lives.

Adapted from Gazzaniga, M. and LeDoux, J., *The Integrated Mind*. Plenum Press, 1978.

left visual field is registered in the right hemisphere of the brain. And whatever is picked up in the right visual field is registered in the left hemisphere of the brain.

In the experiment I am about to report, the patient had the ability to recognize single words with his right hemisphere, but, like most people, he was unable to state those words using that hemisphere because there is no developed language centre in it.

Now for the experiment.

A picture of the word 'Laugh' was shown to his left visual field. As is to be expected, this image reached the right hemisphere of his brain (i.e. the non-verbal, non-conscious half). The man acted on that request and laughed. The experimenter then asked him why he had laughed. His reply was that the experimenter was funny!

This experiment, and many like it, suggest that, when people act on the basis of promptings from the non-verbal, only partly conscious part of their brain, and are then asked why they have acted as they have, they tend to offer an explanation which is in line with their outward circumstances – that is, they do not offer an explanation which shows that they are in touch with the non-verbal part of their brain, the part which has actually prompted them to act as they have.

Consider next the following experiment.

The left half of a normal person's brain – the half which usually contains the speech centre, and hence the part which is conscious – is anaesthetized. That is done by injecting sodium amytal into the carotid artery, which feeds blood into the left half of the brain. The person is then asked to handle an unseen object (say a toothbrush), lying under a blanket, with his left hand. As we have seen, in such circumstances, the nature of the object handled will be registered in the right hemisphere: that is, in the non-verbal, non-conscious half.

When the anaesthetic has worn off – and the left half of the brain is again functioning normally – the person is asked to name the object he handled. It has been found that in such an experiment people are unable to do this. They say that they do not know. However, they are able to point to the correct object when shown a number of different ones.

Such a result again suggests that information coded, or processed, in the non-verbal part of the brain is often inaccessible to conscious introspection. These findings seem to relate to the findings of Weiskrantz. That is, the people reported in the experiment above also seem unable to 'turn around upon their own schemata', but in their case that is because the conscious-making mechanism had been incapacitated by an anaesthetic rather than a disease.

It may be helpful to pause for a moment to consider in what form information could be coded in the non-verbal parts of a brain. Clearly, it must be in a non-verbal form. But how? I have suggested that it must be coded in a 'felt' form, the form in which information is coded in the brains of many other living creatures.

Consider lastly the following finding reported in a medical journal.

Having undergone an operation, a certain woman patient developed a strong reluctance to see the surgeon who had operated on her. Her reluctance was surprising, for prior to her operation she had liked the man, yet now she was unable to furnish a reason for her dislike. However, under hypnosis the woman was able to quote her surgeon as having said, during her operation, 'Well, that will take care of this old bag.'

This, along with other such findings, shows that a level of anaesthetic which enables surgery to be performed without pain to a patient may not prevent certain patients from overhearing things said during their operation. However, they are not consciously aware of having overhead anything, so they are unable to reproduce it.[17]

This finding again suggests that information processed unconsciously often remains inaccessible to conscious reflection. Or, in the language of a previous chapter, schemata which were established in a non-conscious form cannot easily be made conscious.

The neurologist Kurt Goldstein discovered something similar over fifty years ago. In reporting on his work with brain-damaged soldiers, he noted that 'a phenomenon which is not experienced in conscious form can never subsequently become directly conscious; and, conversely, a conscious phenomenon can never work directly upon attitudes and feelings'.[18]

I have still not got over my astonishment at Goldstein's finding, for it explains one of Freud's clinical observations in a way very different from the way Freud did. After listening to his patients, sitting after sitting, Freud concluded that there were things in their minds which they were unable to confront. He called this phenomenon 'repression', and he came to the conclusion that these things were repressed because they constituted experiences which that person found too painful to allow into conscious awareness.

Goldstein's explanation is rather different. He maintained that 'things experienced in a non-conscious form can never subsequently become directly conscious'. Later investigations lend considerable support to such a claim, and I return to this point in a minute.

I turn now to LeDoux, a researcher who has reviewed a large amount of evidence of the kind reported above. Here is a typical comment from him:

> When input is registered by non-conscious systems, that input is not available to the conscious self. It is coded in a way that cannot be decoded by the verbally dominant conscious mechanisms. Yet, it is as much a part of the store of information that directs our moods and behaviour as input which is initially processed in consciousness.[19]

He concludes: 'It is through overt behaviour that the conscious self comes to know fully the passions and prejudices that rule below.'

If all we have to go by is our outward behaviour, it is unlikely that we will ever come to know 'fully' why we behave as we do. But such studies do suggest that much of our behaviour is determined by factors beyond conscious awareness. And further, that the causes of much of our behaviour cannot be easily accessed by the conscious, verbal parts of our brain.

I believe that this modern finding lends considerable support to Goldstein's much earlier one.

What also makes these findings interesting is the further finding that it is the right half of the brain which first develops when we are infants.[20] Then, as we develop further, and acquire language, the left half (the verbal, conscious half) takes over more control of our actions. In other words, if much of our early learning is registered in the right hemisphere it will be coded in a non-verbal, non-conscious form, and so will be difficult to access consciously at a later date. Even if some of our earliest experiences are coded in the left hemisphere, they will not be coded in a conscious form because an infant does not possess much language in either hemisphere before it is about eighteen months old.

In other words, if *some* of our earliest experiences are difficult to access consciously, it may not be due only to 'amnesia' or 'repression'; it may also be, as Goldstein maintained, because such experiences were coded in a non-conscious form, and hence very difficult to access directly.

Let me summarize the above like this. The findings I have reported suggest that many of our experiences are coded in a non-verbal and hence unconscious form, and are not easy to access consciously. If correct, these findings question the common assumption that we direct our actions by consciously thinking about them. It is rather that many of our actions are prompted by past experiences, that many of these will be coded in a form inaccessible to conscious awareness, and that all that conscious thinking does in such circumstances is to offer justifications for those actions.

We do not usually notice this process because the way we behave usually makes sense. It is only when our behaviour is not as sensible as it might be that we may have an inkling that things are not quite as is commonly assumed.[21]

Here is an illustration from everyday life.

I recall first that infants have experiences, that these will be coded in the form of schemata, and that, as young children do not have a language, these early experiences must be coded in a non-verbal form. We have also seen that such experiences are often unavailable to conscious awareness.

Now the illustration.

We often find that a girl who has got on well with her father will tend to feel comfortable in the company of most men later in life. Likewise, a boy who has had a tense relationship with his mother may tend to feel uncomfortable with many women later in life. (Of course, the illustrations could be the other way around.)

The interesting thing is that both will tend to find objective reasons to justify their feelings. They will also tend to associate with people, and to prefer situations, which corroborate their existing feelings. And, like the people in the experiments described above, they will tend to explain their feelings and reactions in terms of their outward circumstances. Again, it is as if one of the functions of thinking isn't to direct our actions, but to explain or justify them to us. In short, we not only tend to see and act in line with our past experiences (i.e. feelings), we also usually feel a sense of 'naturalness' when we do.[22]

The above could be restated like this. We commonly believe that first something happens to us, and that we then have a feeling in response to it. But it seems more accurate to say that, when something happens to us, it triggers off a feeling already present in us (the product of our past experiences). That is why the same event often elicits quite different reactions in different people. It is as if the world furnishes us with the same hooks on which we hang our different past experiences.

The model sketched above helps to explain otherwise paradoxical behaviour. For example, it helps to explain how it is possible to 'know' that smoking cigarettes can kill one, yet continue smoking; the finding that parents who abuse their children have a history of having been abused themselves;[23] that spending time in prison does not always deter the prisoner from committing further crimes; that people often behave like one of their parents whom they dislike; and that people are often their own worst enemies. We can understand such behaviour when we see that we *learn our experiences*, rather than learn *from* our experiences.

Although this model may sound far-fetched in some ways, it sounds quite ordinary when applied to practical things. For example, most people would agree that we use a tool or play a game in the way we do because we have *learnt through experience* to do it that way. What reason have we for thinking that the processes which determine the way in which we react to the angle of a ball are basically different from the processes which determine the way in which we react to the slant of an argument?

I am only claiming that we often know no more about our mental processes than we do about our physical processes. For example, the fact that we are able to reach out for an object accurately must be due to our having had numerous experiences of having done so. That is, those experiences have caused schemata to become established in our brain and tissues. But do we have access to such schemata?

Lastly, if correct, this model emphasizes the need for charity when we consider our fellow human beings, and some humility when we consider our place in the larger scheme of things.

This has been a long section, and perhaps over-ambitious. I have presented a variety of findings, and what I have tried to say can be summarized very briefly like this.

Learning can take place in both a verbal/conscious and a non-verbal/unconscious form. Both have advantages and limitations. The next section will further explore what that might imply for learning and teaching.

TACIT LEARNING AND CONSCIOUS LEARNING

I have suggested that we often learn a good deal without being consciously aware of it.[24] That kind of learning is sometimes called 'tacit'; and readers may remember that I drew attention to that word when I referred to the work of Michael Polanyi. He noted that learners must be given repeated opportunities to have practical experiences – as in a laboratory – because much of what we learn through experience cannot be conveyed in words.

Readers may also remember my mentioning the work of Carl Rogers in psycho-therapy, and that of Gertrude Hendrix on learning maths. Consider now an everyday example of tacit learning: most people's ability to speak and write their native language reasonably correctly, without being able to state any formal rules of grammar. For example, few English speakers know what is meant by the term 'subjunctive', and I believe that not many could explain why we use the word 'a' in English. Nevertheless, most speakers of English are able to use those forms perfectly correctly.

As this tends to be a contentious issue, perhaps I should give a concrete illustration. Consider first the following sentences:

I like to live near the sea.
A wave came in fast.

Most readers would have little trouble writing those sentences correctly. However, many might have a problem if I were to ask what is the function of the word 'the' in the first sentence, and the word 'a' in the second sentence.

Some may know that these words are called 'articles', that the first one is called 'the definite article', and the second 'the indefinite article'. But what is 'definite' about the use of the word 'the' in the first sentence? And what of my question about the function of these words? That is, what does the word 'a' do in the second sentence?

Anyone unable to answer those questions, yet able to write those sentences correctly, must agree that he or she is able to use the articles in English correctly without knowing the rules of English grammar.

I should perhaps add a very partial explanation of the use of articles in English and this is best done with another illustration. Consider the sentence:

Ship sails tomorrow.

Most readers would guess that this sentence is a shortened form telling someone that a certain ship will set off tomorrow. But there is another possibility: the sentence could be a request that we send someone some sails.

So one of the functions of the article in English is to signal whether the next word is a verb or a noun. I trust that even this incomplete explanation will illustrate that we are usually able to use our native language perfectly correctly without knowing the rules which govern its usage; and if we can, that must mean that we have learnt the rules 'tacitly'.

The above raises an important practical question, namely, should formal grammar be taught in school? (I had better note that 'formal grammar' does not include spelling or punctuation, but an understanding of things like the 'subjunctive', or the use of 'articles'.)

Many researchers have investigated that question, and their findings point consistently in one direction. They have found that pupils who are not taught grammar learn to write more accurately than pupils who are.[25] Some people may find this surprising. But then, evidence – in contrast to mere opinion – often is. Consider how surprising the evidence that the sun does not move. No wonder it was resisted for centuries! The evidence on the teaching of grammar noted here complements the evidence cited earlier on the teaching of mathematics.

This evidence strongly suggests that native speakers of English learn how to write grammatically correct English best when they are exposed to good models, are encouraged to do lots of suitable reading and writing, and when their work is responded to in a serious and sympathetic way. In short, when they have lots of appropriate *experiences*.

The case of grammar suggests that we often learn something of great importance, and considerable complexity, tacitly; that is, without being able to state explicitly what it is we have learnt. In fact, we have seen that the evidence goes further: it suggests that trying to apply rules (e.g. the rules of grammar) often interferes with effective action. A reader still inclined to dismiss this argument out of hand might like to consider the finding that attempting to attend to all aspects of a task consciously is characteristic of schizophrenia.[26]

What does this mean? It seems to mean that what we are aware of, when we carry out a task, is not the 'rules' (or thousands of details) which are necessary to carry it out, but the broader requirements of the task, and an opportunity to see the results of our actions. Trying to attend to everything consciously usually results in a mess. If you don't believe that, try to attend to everything you are doing while walking down a flight of stairs.

That is not to say that knowing rules is useless. For example, it may be helpful to know the rules of grammar if we wish to learn a foreign language. However, it looks as if that ability should come after the rules have been mastered tacitly in one's own language.[27]

Why is experiential (or tacit) learning so powerful? I would suggest the following.

When we have an experience of something, our basic feeling processes are engaged, and these:

- enable us to apprehend things directly (not through alleged 'rules');
- enable us to respond to many things at the same time;
- enable us to take a global view;
- do not require the medium of language;
- work in an abstract way.

Does that mean that being conscious of what we are learning is a waste of time? Of course not. I would suggest that our most powerful learning takes place when we have had a suitable experience, and when we are able to reflect consciously on that experience. Such an interplay allows us to view the experience from a variety of angles, rehearse it for a new action, store it in writing, or communicate it to others.

What about when we have learnt something wrongly, and have to relearn it? Here is an illustration.

We often learn how to play a game, say tennis, by going on to a court with a partner and playing. In learning like that, we learn through experience. We could put it a little more technically and say that, through the experience of playing, schemata become established in our brains, many of a quite unconscious kind, and these often enable us to play pretty well.

However, one day we may meet an expert who tells us that the way we hold a racket isn't 'right'. The expert may then show us a new way. Nine times out of ten, when we try that new way it *feels* uncomfortable.

We get used to holding a racket in a certain way. Trying a new grip may not only feel awkward, it may also make our game go haywire. We will then be very tempted to ignore the advice we have been given, and go back to holding the racket in the way to which we have grown accustomed. Schemata, once established, are difficult to override. We have also seen that doing things by consciously thinking about them seldom produces effective action.

But if the expert has managed to convince us that if we change our grip our game is likely to improve, we may persist. And if we do, no matter how uncomfortable it feels, and no matter how bad our game has now become, we may then sometimes have the very gratifying experience of slowly learning how to play a better game.

We could put it like this: if we wish to change our behaviour, we must first override the schemata which have become established in our brain as the result of previous experiences. At the same time, we must expose ourselves to new experiences which, we hope, may result in the establishment of new and more appropriate schemata. But these attempts will only succeed if we can do two things:

(a)   see the incorrectness of our previous learning; and
(b)   persist in a more appropriate way of behaving – in spite of the discomfort and failure which this may initially cause – until new schemata become established.[28]

The above is an example of relearning based on a game. Things are more complicated when the stakes are higher, as in personal relationships.

For example, a person may have had the frequent experience of having been made to feel unjustifiably guilty as a child. It would not be surprising if such a person then felt resentful when he or she is made to feel guilty later in life. But it is sometimes necessary to feel guilty.

For instance, in the course of interacting with friends, we may say something which hurts one of them. The friend will then usually indicate that he or she feels hurt. The effect of that should be to make us feel guilty or sorry. If we do, we will usually try to make amends, and the friendship may then continue. But if we are over-sensitive to feelings of guilt, we may feel angry rather than sorry. And if we do, we will be much less likely to want to make amends, and may then lose that friend. Such a person would obviously be well advised to try to relearn how to respond to feelings of guilt in a way which is less distressing to both himself and others.

In other words, we learn attitudes in the same way that we learn how to play a game. That is, the attitudes we hold are encoded in our brains in the form of schemata, and many of them may be encoded below conscious awareness. If our attitudes are reasonably realistic, we will tend to react realistically. If they are not, we will tend to react unrealistically. When that happens, we may become aware of it, and may then find ourselves saying, 'Why the hell am I behaving in the way I do?'

We may never discover the reason. Many of our most basic attitudes will have been formed in our earliest years, and these may not be accessible to conscious awareness. Nevertheless, we may be able to see, from the results of our actions, that certain of our feelings are leading us astray. We may then decide that we had better ignore them. And if we can persist in such behaviour, we may manage to override our inappropriate feelings until new and more realistic ones become established.

From the above we see that we should not always 'listen to our feelings', and that schemata for attitudes are far more difficult to override than schemata for holding a tennis racket. However, a change in attitudes appears to be possible, too, but only when the conditions noted above are met. That is:

* when we are able to see the nature of our mislearning;
* when we are able to ignore our inappropriate feelings;
* when we can act more appropriately;
* when we are able to cope with the stress that acting in a new way may initially cause; and
* when we continue in this new way until new and more appropriate schemata become established.

Perhaps the most important point is brought out if I note what I have *not* said. I have not said that being *told* will have the desired effect. Instead, I have suggested that we must first *discover* a mistake, and that we then have to have an appropriate *experience* from which we may learn to do whatever we wish to do more effectively.[29]

These comments echo what I noted in previous sections on the learning of maths and grammar. In short, I am suggesting that learning grammar, and learning a new way of being, have much in common.

To summarize: it is generally agreed that there are various levels of knowing. The strongest form of knowing comes about when we have had a suitable experience of something. That kind of knowing is coded inside us in a felt, compacted, living, tacit form, and is a part of our total mental structure. With some effort, we can sometimes make this kind of knowledge conscious and think about it verbally. That can help us to do things like rehearse it, modify it, extend it, plan ahead or communicate it. We can do these things because, through language, we are able to link events, or objects, which may be far apart in space and time. And it is this ability which has enabled us to outstrip all other living creatures. However, the extent of this ability always depends on the extent of our underlying experiential knowledge.

As an illustration, consider the behaviour of people who are good at something. They often convey a sense of effortlessness. Also, they often find it difficult to explain what it is they do, which enables them to carry out a task as well as they do.

This kind of knowledge can be compared with verbal knowledge. In verbal knowledge we have words. We can think about these, and that can give us an illusion of knowing. But it is unlikely that we will be able to use such knowledge in anywhere near as powerful and flexible a way as the knowledge we have gained through experience, and informed reflection on it.

HUMAN LEARNING AND COMPUTER LEARNING

In this section I should like to try to summarize what I have been attempting to convey in the past few chapters by comparing the way a human learns with the way a computer is said to learn.

When computers hove over the horizon some years ago, one writer typically claimed that 'duplicating the problem-solving and information-handling capacities of the brain is not far off; it would be surprising if it were not accomplished within the next decade'.[30] I am writing these words over thirty years after that claim was made, and 'duplicating the problem-solving capacities of the brain' still seems an awful long way away.

Those who have made such claims have often based them on their ability to write a program which can make a computer do something that humans can do. A favourite example is to play chess; another is to solve mathematical problems. And on the strength of such success, some of these people have then claimed – claimed, literally! – that humans are essentially machines.

I find such claims bizarre, in part because they are based on what I would consider trivial pursuits. However, there are people who take such claims seriously. They believe that computer programs can provide us with a model of human learning, so let us consider such claims a little further. But instead of games and maths, let us take something more characteristically human and mature. Let us take the problem of pain.

People sometimes suffer pain. They may have a broken leg, or a broken heart. Usually they want to get rid of their pain, and nature often does that for us. But sometimes a pain persists. When it does, it is a signal that action is required. That, after all, is the function of pain. But exactly what action?

Those who have examined these things suggest that four steps are required. The person must be aware of the pain; the person must be prepared to deal with the pain; the person must gain some understanding of the nature of the pain; and the person must be prepared to take appropriate action after the pain has been treated.[31]

Quite often, there is no problem in taking these four steps. Sometimes there is. For example, we know that some people will push awareness of a pain so far away that they are hardly aware of having it. (This is most common in the case of an emotional pain.) Or, with regard to the third step, the need to have some understanding of the pain, we may know that we have a pain inside our stomach, but, in the case of a persistent pain, such knowledge is not enough. We have to go to someone who has been trained to understand such a symptom. (Perhaps another function of pain is to make us go to someone with it. After all, that which causes a pain is often something with which we are unable to deal ourselves.)

If the pain is due to something obviously physical, we go to one kind of therapist. If it is due to something obviously emotional, we go to another kind of therapist. In each case, a trained therapist should have some understanding of the underlying factors causing the pain.

In the case of unremitting emotional pain, all therapists agree that such a pain is often due to mislearning. That is, the affected person has learnt to respond to certain situations in an inappropriate way. For example, a person may feel terrible each time he gets into a confined space like a lift. Lifts are not wonderful places to be in; but feeling so bad about them that one is unable to get into one is obviously unrealistic.

Another example may be a person who has had two divorces, with all the pain, loss of confidence, and mounting expenses which such experiences can cause. Such a person has also mislearnt. In this instance, how to find and remain with a partner who will make life better rather than worse is clearly a more complicated problem than feeling bad about lifts.[32]

Matters become even more complicated when the problem is a more general one. Life being what it is, all of us at times experience pain and stress. Some of this comes from the very nature of being alive. One example is bereavement. Other problems are generated by destructive social forces such as prejudice, war, loss of work, crime, persecution, or an attitude which can call people 'redundant'. These kind of problems can be intensely painful, but they are not under discussion here.

Feeling bad about lifts is a simpler problem. One could deal with it by never going inside one. However, if one lives on the seventh floor of a building, that might be difficult. It might then be a good idea to try to deal with the problem.

If the account of learning given so far is roughly correct, the problem must be due to some kind of mislearning caused by inappropriate past experiences. These will have been generated first through contact with one's parents. Two thousand years ago it was already known that if the parents ate sour grapes the children's teeth would be set on edge. Then there are relatives, friends, and society at large.[33] And of course there are also the general experiences of life from which we learn and mislearn. The question now is: how have these past experiences brought about a situation which causes a grown man to panic when he gets into a lift?

The obvious answer is: investigate the matter. Then, having discovered the causes, explain them to the man in a sympathetic way. Common sense suggests that if a man is helped to understand why he feels bad inside a lift he should be able to overcome such feelings.

But we know that things are not that simple. Common sense is as wrong here as when it shows us that the sun moves. We know that 'explaining' things will not usually help a man who is afraid of lifts to get into one. And we have seen why that is so. Explaining is verbal, and will therefore result in merely verbal learning.

The above can now be summarized with a question: how can we help a person to acquire new and more appropriate learning – so that he can, for example, enter a lift without feeling bad – when we know that explaining things will probably result in merely verbal learning, and have no practical effect?

That is a real problem. How simulate it on a computer?

When therapists discuss the progress a client is making, it is common to hear them say that their client is 'merely intellectualizing'. They mean that the client is just thinking and talking. That is the same as saying that a client finds it difficult to sense what he or she is really feeling.

Most therapists know that it is only when their clients are deeply engaged with what they are *feeling*, that they learn.[34] It is only then that they begin to gain some insight into the nature of the experiences (often coded in a non-verbal, unconscious form) which are responsible for the distress in which they find themselves. In short, at the heart of all good psychotherapeutic practice lies an attempt to help clients discover what they are really feeling.

On the face of it, it sounds almost perverse to say that a person may not know what he or she is feeling. Surely we all know what we are feeling! But we have all met people who seem to be much more 'in touch with themselves' than others. The trouble is, we tend to see this much more easily in others than in ourselves.

All this was known many years ago. Readers may recall the words 'Know Thyself', engraved over the entrance to that famous cave at Delphi to which people came many centuries ago to consult the oracle about their future. The oracle turned them back upon themselves.

It can be very difficult to know what one is really feeling. Early experiences may be difficult to make conscious. They may also be deeply painful.[35] And making them conscious may require us to see ourselves in an unflattering light.[36]

The dilemma is acute. For the more troubled we are, the less likely are we to find it easy to see ourselves objectively. But unless we can muster the confidence to take ownership of our inmost feelings, we will continue to lead troubled lives.[37]

So change towards a more appropriate response to life has little to do with thinking. It has much more to do with becoming confident enough to become aware of what one is really feeling. When one does, one may begin to understand why one's life has taken the course it has. Given support, such understanding may generate more appropriate attitudes, which may then result in that person having new experiences. And that, in turn, may bring about new learning.

Accounts of people supposedly learning in therapy, written by those who work in artificial intelligence, sound like schizoid people talking.[38] In these people, primary feelings have gone dead and everything is intellectualized. They talk like computers.

The neurologist Oliver Sacks gives a wonderful example of this. He presented one of his patients with a flower and asked him what it was. The man answered, 'About six inches in length. A convoluted red form with linear green attachments.'[39] His response to people was the same. Sacks writes: 'no face was familiar to him, seen as a "thou" . . . there was formal, but no trace of personal, gnosis'.

When most of us look at a face, we don't just see a *shape*. We see a *person* looking out. And this must be because we recognize something of our own humanity in that person. However, this man 'construed the world as a computer construes it, by means of key features and schematic relationships. The scheme might be identified, without the reality being grasped at all.'

That is the impression conveyed by many of those who compare humans with machines.

Some therapists are so sure that talking about the possible causes of a pain would not help a client that they ignore all talking about causes. They go straight into new experiencing.

Take again the case of a man who gets into a panic when in a lift. With such a person, this kind of therapist will first chat about lifts in a supportive way. Next, therapist and client will look at a lift from a safe distance. Next, they will approach a lift together. Next, they will stand near a lift. Each time they do this, the therapist will reassure the client. Eventually, when enough progress has been made, they will get into a lift together.

When such an approach works, it is obvious that this is not because the client has simply been 'reinforced'. It must be because, in doing what he is doing, the client is *feeling*. If the therapist is sensitive and intelligent, the client is probably feeling encouraged. And it must be because the client has had the *experience* of feeling better about lifts that he is able to get into one eventually.

Notice again that this client is learning because he is experiencing, not because somebody is telling him something. The talk between client and therapist is merely one of the surface features of the learning process.

The mode of therapy described above is called 'behaviour modification'. It affects behaviour only. The meaning of not being able to get into a lift is ignored. Earlier I tried to show how limited such an approach is. It is much less likely to succeed when a problem is less specific, as, for example, when a person keeps falling out with a spouse.

In such a case, therapy usually begins with talking. And after a few meetings, a client might say, 'Yes. Now that you have drawn my attention to it again, I can see how I let everyone dominate me. And instead of doing something about it, I tend to go away and sulk. But from now on, I'm going to tell people when I've had enough. I really am going to have it out with them!'

This client now seems to see that he is, himself, unwittingly helping to create the situations which cause him distress.

But we have seen that being able to talk about something is seldom enough to show that someone has 'really' learnt something. When people have really learnt something in therapy, they talk quite differently. They find themselves engaged in consciously *re-experiencing* their previous unconscious experiences, not simply talking about them.[40]

Rather than helping a client to change, talking may well prevent a client from changing. To change, to really learn, one has to experience. But once you can talk about something, you no longer have the incentive to grapple with that something, hence feel it, and hence really learn it. You can talk about it instead!

In 'analysing' a client's problem, a therapist does exactly that which the client is doing all the time to prevent himself from feeling: he is thinking and talking! Many clients are adept at learning the language of therapy. They learn to talk eloquently about things like 'repression' and 'projection'. They are like those learners who do well at exams and nothing else.

That is not to say that a therapist should never explain or interpret. There are times when that may be very helpful. I am only suggesting that a therapeutic approach based on explaining is unlikely to result in much experiencing, that is, in real learning.

I could put it like this, and I must begin with a digression.

In discussing the difference between mediocre novels and great ones, E. M. Forster suggested that mediocre novels consist mainly of a plot, in which this and that happens. However, although a great novel also has a plot (because a novel requires one), the plot is merely the vehicle which carries the message of the novel along.[41] That is why, many years after we have read a great novel, we often have only the haziest recollection of its plot, but are left with a powerful impression of the attitudes conveyed in it.

In reflecting on my experiences of being with clients, it came to me one day that the details which a client relates, and the rephrasing or interpretations which many therapists offer, are merely the plot which carries the message of the therapeutic encounter. That is, the message is what the client and the therapist experience while they are sitting together, and in particular the quality of their relationship.

I believe that the above approach is given some support by the finding that, when clients do make progress in therapy, it is not primarily because of their therapist's knowledge. Research has shown that the single most important factor contributing to success in therapy is the quality of the relationship between client and therapist.[42] Here is the voice of a thoughtful person reflecting on her experience of psychotherapy:

> My analyst wasn't cold and remote. I felt his personality all the time and he was a passionate human being. Caring, angry, demanding, observant. He asked very analytic questions, but the tone of his voice, his reactions . . . I knew when I was entertaining him, I knew when I made him angry, I knew when he thought, 'stupid bitch, absolutely hopeless'. It was projection, but also it was real. Yes, he was a real person. And I remember at the last session he asked me, 'What do you think made the difference?' and I said 'You. You came across as a real human being. And you were real enough to make me feel that it's worth while being real. That's all.'[43]

Such comments will not surprise us when we remember that a good relationship is much more likely to cause a positive experience than anything a therapist might say.[44]

People who have led troubled lives often say that they are 'going to begin a new life'. They usually mean that they are going to seek a new set of circumstances, or to adopt a 'new' attitude. But the only way of 'beginning a new life' – if that is what one needs to do – is to find out how one is unwittingly structuring the only life one has in a way which is making one unhappy. But that cannot be done on one's own. Trying to do that on one's own is like trying to measure a piece of cloth by using the same piece of cloth. The help of a trained and sympathetic person is often required. We can only learn about ourselves in a relationship.

To come back to the therapeutic encounter. It is difficult to identify the factors in a relationship which help to make it therapeutic. Carl Rogers and others have made a beginning on that task.[45] Part of the difficulty may lie in the fact that, when a client does make progress in therapy, much of the learning is probably tacit, that is, non-verbal, hence hard to specify. That is probably true of all effective learning.

Some readers may have asked themselves what computers and psychotherapy have to do with learning and teaching. It has certainly not been my intention to encourage teachers to take on the role of therapist. It is rather that a client in therapy is also a learner. And if we can see what helps this kind of learner to learn, we may discover something of value about all learning.

The main thing I have tried to indicate in this section is the limitation of explaining, and the importance of experiencing. And if what I have noted is broadly correct, we also see that it is impossible to simulate such a process on a computer because a computer cannot have a felt experience.

Furthermore, to claim that humans are essentially machines has implications far beyond an attempt to understand learning. For clearly, if humans are essentially machines, it is perfectly proper to call them 'redundant' when sacked, or to talk about 'body counts' when they are dead. In other words, the debate about whether humans are essentially machines is ultimately a debate about the nature of being human. Now, I get *worried* when I hear that word 'redundant' applied to a human. Do computers?

At the very best, the attempt to show that a computer can simulate human thinking reproduces a second-order phenomenon. It produces a model which obscures what is most vital about being human. That isn't thinking. It is experiencing. That is why birds, hedgehogs and worms can learn, but not clouds, silicon rock or electronic computers.

LEARNING AND EXPERIENCING

I have called this chapter 'Real Learning', and it has been mainly about personal things like feelings and experiences. I should now like to return to something I mentioned in Chapter 1, namely, my surprise that some of the teachers I had in my training college clearly knew a good deal about teaching, yet did not teach well. I noted then that it seemed to me that, if one could understand how it is possible to know, yet not know, one might be in a better position to understand the nature of all 'real' knowing.

I would now suggest that those teachers' knowledge had been merely verbal. To teach well, one must have repeated *experiences* of teaching well, in addition to thinking about it. Without the experience, the thinking is only a potential.

Is there any direct evidence, independent of anything I have already written, for such a claim? I believe there is, and report three findings.

The first is from a researcher named Oliver. He first notes that, for many years, there has been broad agreement among many teachers about what constitutes effective teaching. He then describes how he contacted 119 teachers, sent them a questionnaire about effective teaching, and asked them to express their agreement or disagreement with the statements in it. When he got the questionnaires back, he found that most of the teachers who had replied had tended to agree with the statements.[46]

He then arranged to visit these teachers. He observed them teach, but found that few of them taught in a way which tallied with their replies. Oliver concluded that his findings did not justify condemnation of those teachers, but condemnation of their training. They had not 'really' learnt.

Oliver conducted his research among primary school teachers. Combs and Soper conducted similar research among teachers at a university.[47]

They got their students to nominate 'the very best teacher' and 'the very worst teacher' they had ever had. They then wrote to the teachers so designated (without of course telling them how they had been designated!) and asked them if they would participate in some research. In contacting these 'very best' and 'very worst' teachers, they hoped that the replies they received might indicate how one could distinguish between good and poor teachers.

But not a bit of it. The people who had been nominated as the 'very worst teachers' sent in the same kind of replies as the people who had been nominated as the 'very best teachers'! Here again is an example of teachers who know, but do not 'really' know.

The third finding is from medical education. Gonnella and his associates report research in which 113 patients were screened by a physician. Responsibility for them was then taken by a patient care team consisting of experienced physicians and senior students. The initial screening had shown that 108 of the patients showed signs of urinary-tract infection. However, a review of those patients' clinic charts, during their stay in hospital, showed that the patient care team picked up such signs in only 68 of the patients; and in only 31 patients were further investigations undertaken.[48]

A test given to both the experienced physicians and the senior students in the patient care team showed negligible differences between them. This suggested that the test was not a good predictor of actual performance. These investigators therefore note that it is

> disturbing to learn that, in an examination, the students and physicians indicate that a history of catheterisation, nephrolithiasis, past treatment of urinary tract infection, hypertension, and diabetes mellitus are critical data, but in actual treatment situations they either fail to ask these questions or fail to follow through once the information has been obtained.

They conclude: 'There are many instructional methods for correcting a deficiency in knowledge, but it seems the same methods are less likely to be effective when the issue is that of translating knowledge into action.'

Poets knew all this many years ago. In Shakespeare's plays it is often the worst characters who have the best lines. For example, many people know Polonius's words: 'Give every man thine ear, but few thy voice.' But what Polonius actually does in the play contradicts the advice he gives his son; and Hamlet tells us that he was a 'foolish, prating knave'.

A few sentences later Polonius tells his son, 'This above all: to thine own self be true, and it must follow, as the night the day, thou canst not then be false to any man.'[49] But it is clear from the play that Polonius was about as 'true' as the night is the day.

In another play, Shakespeare has one of his characters say, 'It is a good divine that follows his own instructions: I can easier teach twenty what were good to be done, than be one of the twenty to follow mine own teaching.'[50]

Shakespeare has often been described as a keen observer of the human scene. He knew that the people who don't 'really' know are often the ones who are best at talking about it.

I can still remember how struck I was when I discovered, a few years after I had begun teaching, that the people who talked most eloquently about teaching were often the worst teachers. The second thing I noticed was that it was the talkers who tended to get promoted.

Years ago Vygotsky began his classic work on thought and language by noting that he intended to examine the relationship between feeling and thinking. He first deplored the fact that these two topics tend to be studied separately. Then he noted that separating them 'makes the thought process appear as an autonomous flow of "thoughts thinking themselves", segregated from the fullness of life, from the personal needs and interests, the inclinations and impulses, of the thinker'.[51]

He continued: 'Such segregated thought must be viewed either as a meaningless epiphenomenon incapable of changing anything in the life or conduct of a person, or else as some kind of primeval force exerting an influence on personal life in an inexplicable, mysterious way.'

I cannot think of a more apt description of much cognitive psychology.

Because I have the words 'think' and 'feel', I tend to have the illusion that there are two quite separate entities corresponding to those two words in the real world.[52] Readers may like to try to find in themselves where one of their feelings ends and a thought begins.

The interplay between feeling and thinking interested Vygotsky profoundly, but he only touched on this topic at the end of his book. He then noted that the last step in his analysis is this. That thought 'is engendered by motivation, by our desires and needs, our interests and emotions'. And finally: 'behind every thought there is an affective-volitional tendency, which holds the answer to the last "why" in the analysis of thinking'.

Bartlett came to much the same conclusion when he wrote:

> Here is the significance of the fact, often reported in the preceding pages, that when a subject is being asked to remember, very often the first thing that emerges is something of the nature of an attitude. The recall is then a construction, made largely on the basis of this attitude, and its general effect is that of a justification of the attitude.[53]

Here is another finding which seems to corroborate the above. Luria quotes the work of Slobin, who found that children are often unable to repeat a word which they have just spontaneously said. Slobin explains this inability as due to the fact that a child's spontaneous speech is organized by its motives. If these are absent, the child is unable say what it knows.[54] In Vygotsky's words, when a child is asked to repeat something it has just said, and cannot, its inability is probably due to the fact that the 'affective-volitional tendency' is missing.

At this point, readers may remember my description of an encounter with the tutor-librarian named Betty. There I attempted to illustrate that she began to 'really' learn only when she discovered that she had a personal need, and only after she had made repeated attempts to act on what she had supposedly learnt. Cognition no doubt comes into this. But if it does, I believe it is a secondary matter.[55] In Vygotsky's words, it is an 'epiphenomenon'.

LEARNING AND TEACHING

We have almost come to the end of the first part of this book, and it is time I tried to outline the idea of learning I have attempted to put forward.

Living creatures are alive. Because they are alive, they feel. And because they feel, they have experiences. When a living creature has an experience, some kind of coding is established in its nervous system. This coding has a felt, non-verbal, abstract, tacit form. This coding could be given the name 'schema'. As schemata become established, a creature 'learns'.

Human beings can go further. They can 'go back upon their schemata'. That is, we can consider some of our experiences consciously. This often enables us to clarify them. Through language, we can also recombine experiences, communicate them, store them in writing, read books, listen to others, and plan ahead. Given the right conditions, we can sometimes also modify our learning.

But being able to do these things does not mean that we are able to bypass the need to have experiences if we wish to really learn. The possession of language enables us to listen to somebody talk. But this experience will be of the talk, not necessarily of what the talk stands for.

We do not have to do anything in order to have an experience except to expose ourselves to it. In that sense, experiencing is the same as digesting. If an experience can be experienced, it will be experienced. We can interfere with this process, but we cannot make it happen.

However, the way we expose ourselves to an experience can make a difference. That is where teachers come in. They can can help to arrange things so that their learners have experiences which suit them. They can also help to foster a climate which facilitates learning. But that is not always easy. When some learners are presented with a problem, they seem to see it as a threat. They then focus on the seeming threat, rather than on the problem. Other learners seem much less worried. They tackle a problem with interest, even pleasure.[56] They open themselves to it. In short, for both teachers and learners, when the attitude is right, a good deal else often comes right.[57]

The personal seems to be very important in learning. Most people would agree that it is when we feel personally engaged that we learn the best. In fact, we could say that 'real' learning is usually personal learning.

But what a learner may want to learn may not be what a community may need, and learners are always a part of a community. Until recently it was often a community's needs which were imposed upon the learners. More recently there has been a shift toward the learners' needs. The danger here is the creation of a 'Kentucky-Half-Baked-Chicken-Consumer' kind of learning, hiding behind slogans like 'student-centred' and 'student-led'.

And although real learning is usually personal learning, it does not follow that we can learn only from our own experiences. One person's experiences are sure to be limited. They can also be highly misleading, for we tend to experience that which we expect to experience. If we want to make progress, we must consider the experiences of those who have spent a good deal of time investigating the thing in which we are interested. But if we are to really profit from the experience of others, we must try to experience at least some of what they have experienced.

Many teachers will probably agree with the above. But teachers are engaged in teaching, and that tends to make them concerned with how they teach. The trouble with this understandable concern is that it can have the effect of making teachers concerned with the wrong thing. For, if 'real' learning requires experiencing, then it looks as if teachers need to shift the focus of their concern away from teaching and on to learning. This follows because learners won't have an experience of something if they are simply told about it.

With didactic teaching, with the transmission style, with the teacher standing up front and 'teaching by telling', there will be a good deal of verbal learning. However, with repeated exposure to real-life situations, some learners may find how to use some of this material in practical ways. The method is wasteful, absurd really, but some real learning may eventually result from it.

In the mean time, too, the learners may feel that they are getting somewhere if they have a sheaf of notes after a lesson. That reassurance is illusory, for a good deal of the learning is likely to be verbal learning. But if those lesson notes are coupled with good examination pass rates, the illusion may maintain the confidence of some learners and most administrators.

But the cost will be heavy. The learners will be given a false experience of learning, and their own capacity to 'really' learn may be undermined, perhaps for ever. That is a heavy price to pay, both individually and collectively, for no society can ever have too many real learners.

It may appear that helping learners to learn, as distinct from teaching them, is easy. Anyone who has tried to do such a thing will know it is very difficult. They will know that it isn't enough to tell learners to go to a library and read, or to sit in a wood and listen. To teach in a way which takes account of the way people learn requires systematic study of how they learn, followed by a great many struggles to translate such study into effective teaching practice.

But that is surely necessary. The world is a complex place. Verbal learning – like computer programs – is effective only so long as the parameters are fixed, but life has few fixed parameters. Even so, we usually manage to respond to life pretty well. And if we do, that cannot be because of any 'problem-solving strategies' that we bring to it. It must be because we are a part of life, and therefore able to experience it.[58]

I am aware that the above may sound woolly. It is difficult to be precise about learning. Many people much brighter than me have considered the matter for centuries, and they have found it difficult, too. To talk precisely about learning, one must be able to talk precisely about the nature of life, and so far no one has managed to do that.[59]

Not only may the above sound woolly, the outline of learning put forward in the previous chapters is likely to be faulty, too. If the history of knowledge is anything to go by, it is sure to be faulty! I don't enjoy thinking about that, but such a state of affairs is both inevitable and useful. It may spur someone to come along, show us what is wrong, and in that way we can make some progress.

Near the beginning of this book I noted that I would attempt to suggest a theory of learning and teaching, and I said that I would do so because I thought that this would provide us with some tools to guide us in our classroom practice. It may be helpful if I now summarize the theory of learning suggested in the first half of this book a little more formally like this.

First, it may be helpful to recall the characteristics of a good theory. (I shall follow that with an illustration.) A good theory:

(a)   indicates connections between (often seemingly unrelated) data, suggesting a pattern;
(b)   suggests explanations for these data;
(c)   suggests an approach to sensible practice;
(d)   is likely to throw up anomalies, leading to the need to modify (or discard) the theory;
(e)   will suggest lines of further research to improve the theory and hence our practice.

The example I use for the purpose of illustration is the theory of gravity (which, roughly, holds that bodies exert an attraction on each other that is related to their mass and distance).

In line with points (a) to (e) above, the theory of gravity:

(a)   indicates that the fall of an apple and the movement of the tides (tugged as they both are by the sun, moon and earth) are connected;
(b)   explains why apples fall towards the earth rather than drop off it;
(c)   enables us to go about throwing apples, or shooting rockets, in a planned (if seldom completely certain) way;
(d)   enables us to modify our theory when our practice goes awry;
(e)   suggests lines of further research to improve our theory and practice of apple throwing or rocket shooting (if that's what interests us).

Shooting rockets and teaching students are not the same! But, as I believe that this world of ours is an integrated whole, I also believe that, just as there is a pattern in the way apples and the heavenly bodies move, so there is likely to be a basic pattern in the way we learn. Readers will be better able to decide for themselves if I now summarize the theory of learning put forward here something like this.

If people's natural capacity to learn has not been impaired, it looks as if they learn when

- they find that there is something they wish to learn;
- they are able to tackle this task reasonably directly;
- the task affords intrinsic rewards;
- the task is sensible and manageable;
- they can formulate hunches, test them, and see the results of their actions;
- they are able to see patterns (or gain them tacitly);
- they find themselves in a challenging but friendly and supportive environment.

I would summarize the virtues of this theory of learning like this (and readers will again be able to see for themselves whether the following points tally with what I have noted about the characteristics of a good theory).

The theory of learning put forward in the first part of this book:

(a)   is based on a wide range of interconnected data (including research findings and personal experiences) producing a pattern;
(b)   provides some explanation for the circumstances in which animals and humans best learn;
(c)   suggests an approach to the practice of learning and teaching;
(d)   is likely to throw up anomalies leading to the need to modify or discard the theory;
(e)   will suggest lines of further research to improve our theory and hence our practice.

To sum up: If the theory noted above is on roughly the right lines, then, like all theories worthy of that term, it suggests a tentative approach to practice. In this instance we are considering a theory of learning; so, in line with point (c), it suggests an approach to the practice of teaching.

The purpose of the second half of this book is to outline such an approach.

Part II

Teaching

Chapter 6

The Transmission Method and an Alternative Approach

THE TRANSMISSION METHOD

This section and the following one contain descriptions of two different teachers at work. The first description is of a teacher in a school, the second of a teacher in an industrial training establishment. Having read the descriptions, readers may like to consider which teacher's approach is most closely related to the material on learning presented in Part I.

Imagine a researcher named Wertheimer observing a class of pupils being taught how to calculate the area of a parallelogram.[1] The teacher is up front, and begins by asking if anyone can remember how to calculate the area of a rectangle. A pupil puts up her hand and says, 'Sir, the area of a rectangle is equal to the product of the two sides.' The teacher nods, draws a rectangle on the blackboard, notes its dimensions, and asks the pupils to work out its area. A few minutes later, when it is clear that they all know how to do this, the teacher says, 'Now we are going to learn how to calculate the area of a parallelogram. A parallelogram looks like this.' He turns to the blackboard and draws a parallelogram.

He labels the corners of the parallelogram 'a', 'b', 'c' and 'd', looks around to make sure that everyone is attending and says, 'I drop one perpendicular from the top left corner like this, and another perpendicular from the upper right corner like this' (Figure 6.1).

Then he says, 'I extend the base line to the right, and I label the two new points "e" and "f".' He turns round and gives the proof that 'the area of a parallelogram is equal to. . .'. He does some calculations neatly on the board, and explains each point as he goes along.

This is an experienced teacher. He speaks clearly. He looks around the class to make sure he is getting attention. He rubs the chalk dust off his hands and says, 'You will find what I have been explaining to you on page 62. Read what the writer says, and then do the problems on the next page. You will have enough time to do about half the problems now. I want you to finish the rest at home. Are there

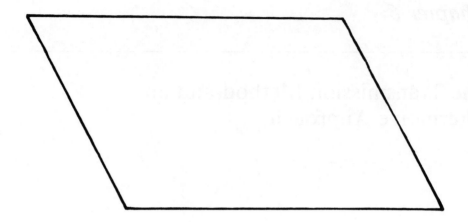

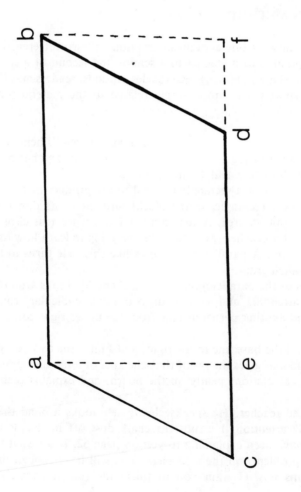

Figure 6.1

any questions?' As there are none, he smiles and tells the pupils to get to work.

They do, and it is soon clear that most of them know how to calculate the area of a parallelogram. Notice how many things this teacher does, which are generally considered to be the things a teacher should do. He:

- has a clear sense of aims;
- revises and checks on work previously done;
- begins from where the learners are at;
- speaks and illustrates clearly;
- states the appropriate rules correctly;
- elicits learner participation;
- checks on learning;
- refers the learners to a textbook;
- gets the learners to practise;
- knows his subject;
- is systematic;
- has a pleasant manner;
- manages the class well.

What more could anyone want?

But Wertheimer is troubled. Have those pupils 'really' learnt?

The next time this teacher meets that class, Wertheimer is there again. The teacher begins by asking if anyone can tell him how to calculate the area of a parallelogram. A hand shoots up and a pupil gives the correct answer. The teacher nods, smiles, turns to the blackboard, and sets the class a problem. The pupils get to work, and soon it is clear that most have the answer right.

But Wertheimer is still troubled. He asks the teacher whether he might ask the class a question, and the teacher readily agrees. Wertheimer goes to the front, and on the blackboard draws a parallelogram standing on its beam ends. Then he turns round and asks the class to calculate its area. Some of the pupils look puzzled. One of them says, 'Sir, we haven't had that yet.' But most are busy. They copy his drawing, drop the usual auxiliary lines – and then most are stuck.

These pupils have learnt like parrots. What they learnt was the rote application of a rule. Hence, when the conditions are changed, the pupils are lost. They have missed the central principle governing the way in which the area of a parallelogram can be calculated, hence they are unable to transfer what knowledge they have.

What went wrong? This teacher did everything teachers are commonly expected to do. Yet these pupils did not 'really' learn. What else could this teacher have done?

Perhaps the pupils should have been given some paper and scissors, encouraged to cut up a parallelogram, and to fit the bits together again to see how it is similar to a rectangle. Such a suggestion is along the right lines, but it may miss an essential point. I believe that the trouble with the above lesson is that the teacher 'taught', instead of 'helped his learners to learn'. This teacher based his approach on *telling*, and the central argument of this book is that, to 'really' learn, we must experience. Too much telling gets in the way of experiencing.

Readers may remember Gertrude Hendrix's finding that telling learners a mathematical rule before they have been helped to discover it for themselves gets in the way of their being able to transfer their knowledge. This teacher told his pupils the rule for doing something before he enabled them to experience it. He thereby took that experience away from them. Had he helped them *to find* the rule for calculating the area of a parallelogram, they would have grasped its *meaning*.

This does not mean that this teacher should simply have told his pupils to find the rule for themselves; or to go to a library; or to do a project. To do those things would have been an evasion of his duties. He should have devised a carefully structured learning situation that would have helped the pupils to grasp the rule for themselves, and so experience it. He could have done that by posing a series of judicious questions, or setting a series of simple problems which hint at a solution.[2] Or he could have posed a number of problems of steadily increasing complexity, set some investigational work, or perhaps devised a game. Best of all, a combination of all of these, followed by practice to consolidate the learning.

This teacher did ask questions, but notice that, when he did, he always led by the nose so that his pupils were really asked to guess what was in his head. He never encouraged them to look for an answer inside their own heads. This man's teaching was damaging. And the more successful it appeared to be, the more damaging it actually was.[3] Not only was there no transfer of learning, but the pupils had not been given the tools or confidence to find their own answers.

The kind of damage noted here may be conveyed like this. It has been found that beginner teachers like to be told about a class before they begin to teach it; however, experienced teachers do not.[4] They prefer to make up their own minds. Readers will immediately understand why that is so.

Notice also how these pupils were not encouraged to form and test hunches; or to discuss a problem and so clarify it for themselves. Nor were they able to derive much intrinsic reward from their work. And notice that the mode of teaching that this teacher employed is widespread, but that it is not related to anything known about the way humans really learn.

But there is nothing evil about this teacher! He has merely practised what was practised on him, and probably done a much better job of it. And when one is in the midst of trying to explain the nature of a problem, it seems 'natural' to try to show how that problem might be solved. Unfortunately, such a situation also provides an opportunity to shine, a temptation which good teachers intuitively resist.[5] A good teacher will have the ability to clarify the nature of a problem, and then the generosity to give the learners an opportunity to discover the solution for themselves.

Abercrombie has beautifully summarized what I have tried to convey in this section. She suggested that a teacher's task is to tell the learners what to look for, without telling them what to see.[6]

AN ALTERNATIVE APPROACH

The lesson to be described in this section is on computer engineering. As this book is about fundamentals, it could be on space-capsule horticulture.

The name of the teacher is Frank, and he works in the training establishment of a large computer company. Here they run courses to train field engineers in the maintenance of existing equipment, or to upgrade their knowledge when the firm introduces new equipment.

Lessons are divided into 'theory' and 'practice'. In the 'practice' lessons, the students work in 'labs'. These are rooms which contain examples of the various computers which this firm sells and maintains, and these 'practice' lessons usually go quite well.

The theory lessons are more problematic.

In these, the students (field engineers) sit behind rows of tables facing a teacher. The teacher stands in front, with several whiteboards behind him and an overhead projector next to him, and lectures according to a detailed course guide which includes a long list of objectives. The teacher will have literally hundreds of transparencies (or 'foils', as they are called here) at his disposal, and as he lectures, he projects these on to a screen above him, often at a rate of several a minute. These transparencies are all machine-made using the latest technology. Sometimes the teacher refers the students to the manuals stacked in front of them. Often he will draw diagrams on the various surfaces at his disposal.

When I first visited this establishment, I was repeatedly struck by the glazed look on the faces of many of the students attending these theory lessons. The teachers noticed this, too, of course, and they frequently reassured the students that the topic would become clearer to them as soon as they had got to their 'practical' lesson; and even more, when they were dealing with problems in the field. In the mean time, these teachers tended to say, they had to plough on as there was 'such a lot of material to cover'.

It will be seen that the mode of instruction employed at this establishment rests on the belief that, if you can tell somebody something, then that person can learn it. Everything is then geared to making that 'telling' as efficient as possible. This is a prestigious organization with huge resources, and a very great deal of money is spent on training. It sounds positively in bad taste to suggest that what is being done here rests on a myth.

In practice, what happens is that the students sit through these 'theory' lessons as best as they can, while most of what is said washes over them. When they come to their practical lessons, they pick up a few strands and weave them together into a shaky whole, but their real learning does not usually begin until they get into the field again.

When I first observed Frank, he taught in the manner just described. (It was often called 'foil and toil' by these instructors.) On my fifth visit this is what I saw.

The students, all field engineers, came into the class and Frank welcomed them. He gave his name, and asked the learners to introduce themselves briefly.

The tables were arranged so that they formed a square in the middle of the room. The students sat behind them, and Frank sat at one of the tables next to a student. Everyone could see everyone else. When the introductions were over, Frank asked whether anyone present had had any experience of the new computer system which they had come to study. A few people nodded. Frank asked what they thought of it and there were several replies.

Then Frank said that he would outline very briefly the way in which the new system differed from the previous one. He had a clear and simple way of talking, and conveyed the impression that they were doing a job of work together.

As he was speaking, Frank asked one of the students to describe the salient features of the earlier system. The student began, and when he stopped for a moment to get his bearings, Frank suggested he might find it easier to continue at the whiteboard. After a second of hesitation, the student, a man of about forty, went to the board, began to draw, and continued explaining. In this way, within a few minutes of the opening of the lesson, roles had been changed without any fuss.

As the student out front drew the system, Frank invited and got contributions from the other students. After a while he went to the front himself and sketched some features of the new system.

So far the lesson had lasted about fifty minutes. Frank stretched his lanky frame and suggested a break. The students got up and went to the vending machines present on all the floors of this very well-equipped building.

The break over, Frank gave out a sheet with about ten questions on it. He announced that, instead of lecturing to them, he was going to ask them to examine the new system directly. The questions on the sheet should help them to determine in which way it differed from the system they already knew. He urged them to work in pairs, and added that he hoped that the people who already knew something about the new system would help those who did not.

Frank led the students down a corridor, and ten minutes later they were busy at work on computer equipment. Frank sometimes moved around and exchanged a friendly word. Mostly he sat with me to one side. He had just read Jane Abercrombie's book, and was full of enthusiasm for it. Twice he said it felt odd not to be teaching.

Now and again one of the students came over to ask something. When Frank answered, he often rephrased the question, or asked another. When he explained something, it was always briefly. Then the student went back to lift covers off bits of machinery, turn switches, or watch what looked to me like garbled Hungarian on screens.

All the time there was a hum of conversation in the room. This period of work lasted for about forty minutes. When the students had finished, Frank got them to sit in a rough circle. He asked how they had got on, and it was soon clear that they had found what they had been doing useful. Frank said it might be an idea to compare their answers. A woman read out her first one, there was general agreement; a man read out his next one, and there were murmurs of assent. And so it went, with Frank seldom doing more than nod in reply.

It was now time for lunch.

In the afternoon we met in the room in which the course had begun. Frank exchanged a few comments with the students in his genial manner, then gave out another work-sheet. This contained a dozen questions relating to what they had been examining that morning. Frank said that a consideration of the questions would further develop what they had already discovered. He asked the students to reply to the questions in pairs, using the manuals on the tables in front of them when necessary.

Again Frank sat to one side while the students worked. All the time there was the sound of students talking, turning pages, and scratching heads. Occasionally one of them got up to consult someone on the other side of the room. They had clearly got to know each other a little by now. At one point Frank took me next door to show me some equipment. While doing so, he again said how odd it was not to be teaching all the time.

Half an hour later most had finished, and Frank called for a short break. When we reassembled, Frank suggested that one of the students might like to invite somebody in the room to answer the first question. If everyone agreed the answer was correct, the person who had answered should ask another person the next question. And so on, till all the questions had been answered. Frank said he intended to remain silent unless he was the only person to spot a mistake.

For a moment there was silence. The learners, twenty men and four women, ranging in age from twenty-five to fifty-five, were obviously surprised by this approach.

More silence. Then one of the men said something comical, pointed at a man opposite him, and read a question. The man addressed looked thoughtful, and began. And for the next half-hour I had the great pleasure of seeing humans learning.

Here is one incident out of a dozen.

A man began by saying that he was unsure if he and his partner had got that answer right. But he thought that 'so and so' might be the case. He paused and looked around. His partner and two other men nodded. One man shook his head. Prodded, the doubter said, if 'so and so', then things could not be quite like the first speaker had said. But he wasn't sure himself because . . .

The first speaker and his partner exchanged a few words, looked at a manual, looked up, but did not say anything. Another man began to speak, but was interrupted. A general hubbub ensued which continued for about a minute. This was followed by an uneasy silence.

Several students looked towards Frank. He remained silent.

The silence continued.

Then, quietly at first, the partner of the first man who had spoken began. He got to a certain point, then asked a question. A woman who had not said anything so far spoke. A man took up where she had left off. Then the man who had first answered the question said something in reply. He stopped, thought for a second, nodded hard, and went on. As he spoke, his eyes and face seemed to light up. He finished with a burst and ended on a mock-triumphant note. There were nods all round. The learners looked at Frank, who remained silent, half suppressing a delighted smile.

Readers may notice how different this is from what goes on in many classrooms. In these, the learners either sit listening passively; or, when they are asked a question, they compete to provide the correct answer. In this way learners seldom make a mistake, so nobody can learn from a mistake. In this class the opposite was happening. Notice how this replicates real life and how experiential it is.

And so this lesson continued. Four times Frank spoke. Once to give a clue when the students had thrashed around and got themselves into knots; twice to give a page reference; and once to suggest that the learners had gone too far in a certain direction.

At the end of that period we all got up for a fifteen-minute break. It was striking that many of the learners continued talking about the topic of the lesson as they walked out. None had that glazed look I had noticed when they had listened to an instructor teaching by telling.

After the break, Frank summarized some of the points that had been made. He then asked for a volunteer to go to the whiteboard to draw the outlines of the new system.

One man got up almost immediately. He began to draw against a background of humorous references to his cackhanded drawing abilities. For the next half-hour, never once moving from his seat, Frank made comments, asked questions, and invited people to go to the whiteboard to add other components to the system. Finally he asked the students to respond to a quiz in one of the manuals.

At the end of the afternoon Frank put his hands behind his head and said he reckoned they'd done enough for one day. No one got up. Someone sighed, another person made a wry comment. Slowly people got their papers together, stood up, and left the room.

I believe that the approach to teaching described in this lesson will foster better learning than the transmission method. But a belief is only a belief. It does not provide evidence. One way to obtain some evidence would be to carry out an investigation.

If this were done, it would not be enough to assess these learners' ability to write correct answers in an exam. The research would have to be designed so that it assessed whether they were able to apply their knowledge practically, in situations which were only marginally similar to those they had experienced in this classroom. The teacher would also have to be at least as well trained as Frank. The result of such teaching could then be compared with the result of teaching in the manner described in the previous section.[7]

In the absence of such research, it may be helpful if I report the following. When Frank asked these learners (in my presence) which approach they preferred, most expressed a strong preference for his approach. This response was corroborated by their written comments when they came to evaluate the course.

The above may sound like special pleading, so I will draw attention to three things.

1. The focus of this lesson was on the learners' learning, not on Frank's 'skills' or 'competences'. Frank does have skills and competences. They are important, and required lots of practice. However, they are best seen as the unobtrusive and surface features of his understanding of learning.
2. Frank's teaching is closely based on the material on learning presented in Part I of this book.
3. The learners in this lesson are adults, but the approach illustrated here could be used with any learners.

Finally, readers may like to ask themselves in which lesson they would prefer to learn: the one described in the previous section, or the one described here.

DOING CLASSROOM RESEARCH

In the previous section I claimed that the teaching described there rested closely on the material on learning presented in Part I of this book. A question which might now come to mind is this: is there any research on teaching which might support this claim?

Unfortunately, there is very little evidence which shows that one method of teaching is better than any other. This unsatisfactory state of affairs exists in spite of over fifty years of research into teaching.[8] However, there are a few pieces of research which do suggest that teaching in a certain way helps learners to learn, but before I report this I will briefly discuss some of the problems it can raise.[9]

If we wish to find out which kind of teaching helps people to learn, we could begin by observing as many lessons as possible. Most people feel that they can recognize good teaching when they see it. But there are at least two problems with such an approach. First, as we saw from the description of pupils learning how to calculate the area of a parallelogram, the conventional wisdom about what constitutes good teaching can be questionable.

Second, it is clear that relying on one's ideas about what constitutes good teaching would not produce any objective evidence. How could we be *sure* that what we believe is good teaching really is good teaching? That is, how could we be sure that it helps people to *learn*? After all, it isn't that easy to distinguish between a good teaching performance and teaching which results in 'real' learning.

One way to find objective evidence might be to look at exam results. If learners have passed an exam, it looks as if their teaching must have been good. But if we consider the matter for a moment, we realize that it is difficult to be sure that learners have passed an exam because of something their teacher did. After all, they may have passed their exam because they are bright, or because they studied hard at home. Did we all pass our exams because our teachers were so good?

But perhaps we could make a beginning with exam results? For example, we could look for a class which did consistently well at its exams, and carefully observe the behaviour of its teacher. After that, we could compare her behaviour with that of a teacher who had a similar class which did not do as well at exams. If that were done in several classes, a pattern might begin to emerge.

Another way to look for objective evidence might be to carry out an experiment. For example, one would have to find two comparable classes. To be sure that they really were comparable, one would first have to give both classes a test in, say, maths. If the results were about the same, one could assume that the learners in the two classes are about equal. Then a teacher would have to be found to teach both classes maths in exactly the same way, but with just one difference. That difference could be, for example, that in one class she did revisions, while in the other she did not.

At the end of the research period, say after a year, both classes would be given a second maths test. If it were then found that the class which had been given revisions did better than the other class, one could assume that doing revisions had helped them to learn more.

Of course, one such experiment would not be enough. Next year the experiment would have to be repeated, and with another teacher. The trouble is, when that has been done, inconclusive results have often been obtained. This is mainly because the variables involved are so complex. For example, even if one class initially scores (on average) the same as a comparable class in a maths test, that class might be very different in other respects; and it may be this difference which is responsible for the higher scores at the end of the year, rather than the revisions.

Another factor which might be important in learning is a teacher's personality. Many researchers have found that effective teachers tend to be firm, kindly and demanding. But do all learners respond to the same kind of teacher? A good deal of research has been done on this question, and here, too, the results are far from conclusive. In short, it is very difficult to isolate one factor and show clearly that it is that one factor which helps people to learn.

Another difficulty in doing classroom research is getting agreement between researchers on what they are seeing.

Imagine two researchers called Lavan and Black observing a lesson. They have decided to investigate whether a teacher's clarity affects how well the learners learn. In the course of a morning, they observe three different teachers. In particular, they try to observe how clear each teacher is. But what criteria are they to use to determine clarity? The two researchers might agree that one of the teachers is clearer than the others. But on exactly what grounds did they decide that?

Yet another problem lies in deciding what the aims of teaching are. Some people argue that the main aim is to help learners to pass exams. Others say it is more important to help them to become inquiring, independent, creative and responsible people. Are these two aims contradictory? A good deal must obviously be considered before one can answer that question sensibly.

The above outlines a few of the problems involved in doing classroom research. There are many others! But perhaps enough has been said to suggest that one must be cautious when considering the findings it produces.

The next few sections are shaped around the work of two researchers named Rosenshine and Furst.[10] These researchers did not do their research in classrooms; they examined the published work of others who did do their research in classrooms, so one gets a kind of composite picture from their work.

Rosenshine and Furst basically tried to do three things:

1. select only pieces of research which had been very carefully conducted;
2. use only those pieces of research in which a specific behaviour of a teacher could be shown to relate to the amount the learners had actually learnt – as measured by their exam results; and
3. see whether any pattern of effective teaching behaviour emerges when all these pieces of research are examined together.

By the end of their investigations, Rosenshine and Furst came to two tentative conclusions:

•   that they had found fifty pieces of research which were sound; and
•   that there are certain teaching behaviours which seem to help people to learn.

These researchers take pains to stress that they consider both the findings which they examined, and their own findings, tentative. With that in mind, let us examine their findings.

Chapter 7

The Teaching Process

CRITICISM

Rosenshine and Furst found that the following teaching behaviours help learners to learn:

- being clear;
- being enthusiastic;
- using a variety of approaches;
- good questioning;
- being task-orientated (not wasting time);
- being indirect (not giving straight information);
- giving learners an opportunity to learn;
- making structuring comments (periodically summing up what has been done and signposting the way ahead).

They found that one teaching behaviour inhibits learning, and it is:

- being critical.

Whenever I have drawn the attention of a class to the above list, I have found that it does not usually generate much interest. The items seem to strike most people as self-evident, and I have found that it takes some time to see that the list is loaded with powerful implications. However, there is one item which does tend to elicit an immediate response. It is the last one, and many people seem to want to distinguish between destructive and constructive criticism.[1]

Such a distinction seems to make sense. But I have found that the people who most want to make it are often the ones who become most upset when I attempt to be constructively critical of their work. I have nearly always found, when I have tried to be constructively critical with them, that they feel hurt. This has tended to make them defensive, and this very natural defensiveness has then hindered their learning.

It may be important to remember that this is a discussion about making mistakes in a classroom. It is not a discussion about, say, student nurses taking a mistake when they plunge a needle into a patient on a ward. Educational establishments are educational establishments. They are not 'the real thing'. They prepare students for 'the real thing'. Student nurses can learn how to do their thing with needles on oranges in a classroom. It is surely because classrooms are not the real thing that mistakes can be made in them.

It follows that there is no contradiction between allowing learners to make mistakes inside a classroom and ensuring safe practices outside them. Indeed, I have found that the more mistakes learners feel able to make in a disciplined way inside a classroom, the fewer they tend to make outside them.

So what can a teacher do when a learner makes a mistake?

Imagine that a learner has just said something, and, in doing so, makes a mistake. Instead of saying that he has made a mistake, a teacher could ask him how he has got to his answer. The learner will then very likely begin to think and say, 'Ah, yes . . . what I meant was . . .'

Another thing a teacher can do is to turn to the others in a class and ask them what they think. Seven times out of ten, someone will then give the correct answer. Doing this turns mistake-making into a part of the learning enterprise, and it also has the effect of combating the absurd belief that the answer is inside the teacher's head. And where the friendly atmosphere which I associate with good teaching exists, other learners will not wait for a teacher to correct mistakes, but will themselves object in a friendly way when an answer is incorrect.

In the illustration given above, there is an absence of either destructive or constructive criticism, yet incorrect responses have not been ignored. That is because the focus of attention has been on helping learners to learn, not on evaluating them; for, in good teaching, questions are not asked primarily in order to test understanding, but to generate it.

The above examples are of mistakes learners might make when they respond to a teacher's question. Mistakes are dealt with even better when lessons are so structured that the learners are able to discover and correct their mistakes themselves.

Learners can be asked to design and build an electronic circuit from an outline plan and a set of incomplete instructions. When the task has been completed, they can be asked to test their work against a list of specifications. The same approach could be used with a text, photograph, graph or model, and is often best done in small groups.

When I taught English in school, I sometimes asked my pupils to show their written work to a neighbour, and to ask him or her for comment. At first, some of the pupils didn't like that. Most had never been invited to do such a thing before. However, I found, if I persisted, and if a relaxed but purposive atmosphere developed in a class, that not only did the pupils get used to this approach, but most of them came to like it.[2]

We reached a stage when many of my lessons contained a period during which pupils showed each other their work. That way they didn't always have to wait for me to get a response. In any case, the response of a peer often carried more weight than anything I could say. By the end of the year, many said that they had learnt a good deal that way, and most came to feel that the practice was perfectly natural. After all, when people are at work, they often have to show each other what they have done.

Making mistakes is an inevitable and necessary part of all real learning. It just isn't possible to really learn anything without making mistakes. In fact, it could be argued that, as we learn 'by consequence', we learn most of all from our mistakes. When I described people learning how to use a word processor we saw that, to really learn, we must test our hunches; and when we do that, we will probably make as many incorrect as correct responses. If so, it would surely help learning if we could foster a classroom climate in which learners feel able to make mistakes, can talk to each other about them, and hence learn from them.

Of course, there are occasions when it might be helpful for a teacher to point out a mistake directly – perhaps in a laboratory or a workshop, where not pointing out a mistake might put someone in danger. But it is a good idea to point out mistakes quietly and tactfully. Otherwise an attempt to prevent an accident might precipitate one.

None of the above is intended to suggest that a teacher should not be demanding. There is no contradiction between being demanding and not being too critical. If poor work has been done, I don't think it should be accepted. But instead of criticizing it, it is surely much better to point out how it could be improved.

When I have done that, I have found that learners have looked annoyed, upset, stimulated, sheepish or concerned. Either their work has then improved, or they have gone off in a huff. I don't think such outcomes can be escaped. There is a bottom line to everything. Teachers have a duty to their community as well as to their learners.

One more detail may be worth mentioning.

When I first corrected written work, I used to use a red pen. I was a teacher in a school then, and as I was teaching English as a foreign language I had to correct an awful lot of mistakes! After a year or two, the sight of all that red ink on a learner's work would bother me. I'd ask myself how I would feel if I saw all that red ink over a piece of work I had done. So I switched to green. Before long I came to dislike green, too. Over the next few years I experimented, and finally settled on any blue or black pen that was handy.

At first I corrected all mistakes, but after a year or two I realized that most of my pupils hardly looked at my corrections. Doing all that work was obviously a waste of time. In fact, I realized that what I was doing was what *they* should be doing! So I corrected fewer errors, and told the pupils who made a lot of them that they would have to check their work more carefully if they hoped to improve. In short, I realized that people learn much more from disciplined practice than from being corrected.

Sometimes I used a pencil and invited my pupils to rub out anything they did not like. Some of the younger ones did. Some rubbed out everything I had written! But their work often improved, too.

In more recent years, when I have been marking the written work of adults, I have kept to the same general approach, with this addition. If I think a learner has gone off the track, or hasn't grasped what I think should be grasped, I ask a question. And if I feel I must point out a mistake, I try to indicate the direction in which a better answer might be found. I also try to find something to acknowledge. Not sounding like a teacher is also helpful. And now I almost always use a pencil.

So much for criticism. Now for Rosenshine and Furst's positive findings.

CLARITY AND ENTHUSIASM

The first item on Rosenshine and Furst's list is: 'being clear'. Not many people will be surprised to hear that it is helpful to have teachers who are clear, but it is difficult to know just what one must do in order to be clear.

Four factors seem to come into it:

1.   having a thorough knowledge of one's topic;
2.   the ability to see to the heart of the matter;
3.   the ability to see the matter from a learner's perspective; and
4.   the ability to explain the matter simply.

The first item is obvious. The second and third items are probably related to one's personality. The fourth calls for a few practical suggestions.

Teachers who are clear use simple language. They use fresh, striking, and real-life analogies (more on that in the next section). They also often begin with a concrete example; better, a concrete problem.

Where a technical term needs to be introduced, they will first use an everyday word with an equivalent meaning. This establishes a context. They will then use the technical term, and perhaps the everyday term immediately after. Next it might be helpful to define the technical term more closely. In this way, slowly, the appropriate schemata are established.

Teachers who are clear illustrate frequently. Having made a theoretical point, they follow it with a practical example. This has the effect of clarifying the point. It also helps the learners to remember it.[3] In illustrating like that, good teachers do not get lost in details. They always come back to a central path, and frequently show us where we are on it. Now and then they retrace their steps, and remind us of the places we have visited. They also remember to tell us where we are heading. In short, they never lose sight of the main point.

Teachers who are clear are systematic, and to be systematic one has to prepare. Also, teachers who are clear do not make their knowledge obtrusive. They do not flood their learners with a mass of knowledge but keep most of what they know in reserve.

Here are a few additional suggestions on how to be clear:[4]

*   A short, well-known word is better than a long obscure one.
*   Use a concrete noun in preference to an abstract one.
*   Use verbs rather than nouns where possible.
*   Wherever possible, provide an illustration from life.
*   Use everyday talk, not book talk.
*   Talk in a personal, rather than an impersonal, way.
*   No matter how theoretical a topic, always attempt to tie it to a practical issue.
*   Pause now and again; give yourself time to find the most suitable way of saying what you want to say.
*   Have as few detailed notes as possible; use headline notes.
*   Do not talk for more than six minutes at a time.
*   Enable (not just encourage) the learners to participate.

Concerning that last item, readers may like to consider the following research.

Leavitt and Mueller arranged for an instructor to teach a class how to draw a geometric figure under four different conditions:[5]

1. when the instructor spoke while hidden behind a screen;
2. when the instructor spoke while visible;
3. when the learners were able to say 'yes' or 'no' in response to the instructor's questions;
4. when the instructor and learners were able to talk freely to each other.

Here are their main findings:

(a) The learners were able to draw the figure most accurately under condition 4.
(b) The learners felt most sure they had drawn the figure correctly under condition 4.
(c) Teaching under condition 4 initially took longer than teaching under condition 1; however, as more lessons took place, less time was required to teach under condition 4, while condition 1 continued to take about the same amount of time.
(d) The learners preferred condition 4.
(e) When the instructor began by using condition 1, 2 or 3 and then changed to condition 4, the learners' comments were often aggressive. It was as if the learners were only now able to express the hostility they had felt when they had had to learn under conditions 1, 2 or 3. However, when the instructor began by using condition 4, the learners' comments tended to be friendly.

The second item which these researchers list is 'being enthusiastic'. Most people like an enthusiastic teacher. But there may be a problem here. Consider the following personal experience.

I was once chatting to some friends, and one of the people present was a girl of seventeen. A few days later she passed me some notes she had written during one of her lessons that week. Here they are:

> If only she would stop talking. She has such an excited voice. A sort of path with no end. It's unfair. She is learning all the time. Her eyes are shining with the pleasure of it. She is exploring, thinking, expressing herself, hearing her own ideas. How lovely for her. She must enjoy teaching.
>
> Wow! She has just asked a question! I wonder what it was? Silence now. I expect everyone has, like me, kind of stopped listening. Everyone is so used to just sitting and listening that, when it's their turn to say something, they feel lost. She has just looked at me and is probably thinking: good girl, writing notes . . .
>
> John is sitting next to me. He is bored, frustrated, breathing heavily. Playing with his pen. Rolling it from side to side. I wish I could write him a letter. God! She has just asked him to give an example of something! He probably never heard a word. He says, 'I don't know.' Dog eyes. She smiles at this and says, 'You're not doing enough background reading for my lessons, John.' I suppose that's the only way to really learn anything.
>
> I wish she would shut up. She is talking more slowly now. I suppose she thinks she was talking too fast before. Soon I'll be outside, won't have to listen to her voice.

That was a pupil. Readers may like to compare her comments with those of Simon Stuart, a teacher:

> As a boy and master I have observed a kind of law whereby the teacher who speaks for long periods induces a corresponding deafness in the class; but the most painful aspect of it is that the deafness not only spreads with the duration of the lesson, but intensifies with the excitement, the self-preoccupation, the earnestness or even the brilliance of the teacher.

A few lines further on:

> it will be found that in his enthusiasm the teacher is making an assault upon the active prin-
> ciple of the class, ignoring their energy and giving no scope to their rivalry; instead, he
> induces an outward passivity (easily mistaken for interest and compliance) and an inner
> resistance (uneasily ignored). If he does not learn to amend this situation it can become a
> vicious circle in which the excessive activity of the master induces resentment in the pupil,
> while the resentment forces the master to close off his awareness of the pupils' feelings
> which have become too painful for him to observe.[6]

Unfortunately, some people seem to be drawn to teaching because they have a need
to talk. They seem to have a need to be out front, to be seen to displace air.

Here is Winnicott:

'It is easy to picture a person with a great need to give, to fill people up, to get under
their skin, really to prove to himself or herself that what he or she has to give is good.
There is unconscious doubt, of course, about this very thing.'

I felt very uncomfortable when I first read those words. Was I reading about myself?
I felt a little better when I read the next paragraph:

> No doubt the normal drive to teach is along these very lines. All of us to some extent need
> our work for our own mental health, the teacher no less than the doctor or nurse. The nor-
> mality or abnormality in our drive is largely a matter of degree of anxiety. But, on the
> whole, I think pupils prefer to feel that teachers do not have this urgent need to teach, this
> need to keep at arm's length their own personal difficulties.[7]

Quite a few people seem to think that teaching is a matter of giving a performance,
and some people seem to be drawn to just this apparent requirement of the job. And
if teaching is like performing, then inevitably the teacher will have the leading role. But
if learning requires active engagement, then the idea that teaching is like performing
must be a mistake.

Does all this mean that teachers should not be enthusiastic? Obviously not. But it does
suggest that enthusiasm is a subtle matter.

If I think about the best teachers I have had, it comes to me that their enthusiasm was
not for hearing their own voices. They tended to be mature people. Their enthusiasm
wasn't even for their particular subject; it was more for learning in general. And mostly
they expressed enthusiasm indirectly. They showed it through their general sense of
commitment and integrity. And they seemed to have the confidence that what they were
doing was worth doing, and worth doing well.

Teachers of this kind convey a sense of purpose. Administrative tasks bore them.
They get them done as quickly as possible to get back to the lesson. Nor do they ask
their learners to do routine jobs to fill in time. When they ask their learners to do
something, it is because they believe that it will help them to learn something, and is of
some consequence.

These teachers tend to be quietly energetic. But they can get excited, and when they
do, it has the effect of switching learners on. In short, a good teacher's enthusiasm is
for the task at hand, and not at the expense of the learners.

VARIETY IN TEACHING

The next item listed by Rosenshine and Furst is 'using a variety of approaches'. The importance of variety in teaching was discovered indirectly by a researcher named Kounin.

Kounin initially set out to discover why some teachers have orderly classes while others have shambles.[8] It is often believed that having an orderly class is related to a teacher's personality. But even if that is so, one would like to know just what it is that such teachers actually do which helps them to maintain order.

After observing a great many teachers teach, it finally dawned on Kounin that having an orderly class was not really a matter of a teacher doing anything in particular. It was more a by-product of good teaching. It seems to me that this, in itself, is a most interesting finding.

Having decided that an orderly class is a by-product of good teaching, Kounin of course realized that he now had a new problem: he had to discover what constitutes 'good' teaching. After more research, Kounin and his colleagues came to these tentative conclusions.

They found that teachers who had orderly classes were what they called 'withit'. That is, they knew just what was going on in their lessons, and they also had the confidence to respond directly to it. For example, if two children were fighting and one was whispering, these kinds of teachers did not deal with the one who was whispering. They dealt with the ones who were fighting. And they did so in a thoughtful and direct manner.

Just as important, these teachers were good classroom managers. For example, they did not begin an activity without first ensuring that the class was ready for it. Nor did they initiate one activity and then go off on a tangent with another. Or, if they wanted a group to do something, they did not get bogged down dealing with an individual.

These teachers did not rely on what Kounin calls 'prop-activities'; that is, they did not waste time worrying about things like collecting pencils in a certain order, or asking the children to sit straight. They focused on the learning task at hand.

A second set of Kounin's findings relate to the way these teachers taught.

The first thing Kounin's data showed was that these teachers did not talk too much. Instead, they engaged their learners in a wide variety of activities. This variety wasn't just in the content of the lesson. For example, they varied the challenges which they posed: first one kind of task, then another. They also varied the social configurations in the class: sometimes the learners worked individually, sometimes in groups, and sometimes the whole class worked together.

These teachers also varied the teaching/learning methods they used: sometimes the teacher talked, sometimes the learners talked to the teacher, sometimes the learners read, sometimes they wrote, sometimes they did practical things, and sometimes the learners discussed things in small groups. All in a purposeful and organized way.

Although this research was done in schools, and although I now teach adults, I have found Kounin's findings very helpful. There isn't a lesson I teach, when I don't remind myself to introduce some variety. I don't mean just variety in my voice or the topic, but all the varieties Kounin lists. And I find that this is appropriate no matter what the age of the learners, the nature of the subject, or the length of the lesson. I try hard to introduce a change at least every half-hour, frequently more often.

Consider how this relates to what we know about attention.

Research on very young babies shows that, when a new smell is presented to them, they turn to it with interest. But after a time, they 'switch off'. To use more technical language, they become 'habituated'.[9] Then, when a new smell, even a weaker one, is presented to them, they show renewed interest. After a time, they pay no attention to that either. It is as if a stimulus is blocked from awareness after it has gone on for some time, no matter how novel it is in the first instance. This happens in all the sense modalities, and it must be caused by an internal biological mechanism.

The above is also true of adults. For example, all kinds of noises might be apparent. At first, we will be aware of them. But, after a time, we will not be – unless there is a change. Then we will notice the change. If the new noise goes on for some time, we will stop hearing that, too. This may be related to the fact that, for many thousands of years, when our ancestors lived in the wilds, a steady input of noise (or movement) did not convey that anything of importance was happening. It was only when there was a *change* that we became alert, and perhaps said to ourselves, 'Food!' or 'Danger!' It is certain that, to this day, we become more alert when there is a change in input.

If so, responding to change, but losing interest in what is the same, is functional and genetically driven. It follows that when learners don't pay attention it may be because they are getting too much of the same thing.[10]

Of course, there is a limit to the amount of variety one can have in a lesson. One can have small-group discussions, teacher input, a video film, individual work, role-play, and a few other activities. I mention this because I have found that, once I have introduced variety into my lessons, some learners get restless when there isn't more variety. Previously, when they were taught only didactically, they did not expect any more. Now they want variety all the time. In response, a teacher can remind them that real learning isn't the same as entertainment; it requires work.

The next item on Rosenshine and Furst's list is 'good questioning'. As this is such a big topic, it will be discussed later in the book. Here we will move to the next item, 'being task-orientated'.

This means that it has been found that learners make progress when they have a teacher who uses the time available mainly for study purposes. That finding is hardly surprising: the more time we actually spend studying, the more we are likely to learn. Unfortunately, we have all had teachers who spend a great deal of time announcing administrative matters, talking about their latest car or pet, and collecting pencils in a certain order.

But that can't mean that a teacher should never crack a joke or tell a story. We like it when a teacher sometimes diverts us like that. But the bulk of the time in a good lesson is surely spent doing work.

This may be a good place to remember that learners vary in the amount of time they need to learn something. It may be that what we call a 'bright' person is better called a 'quick learning' person; and someone we call a 'dull' person might be better called a 'slow learning' person. After all, because some people can walk faster than others, it does not follow that the others can't get to the same destination a while later.

The next item on Rosenshine and Furst's list is 'being indirect'. As there is quite a lot to say about this, a new section is needed.

INDIRECTNESS

'Indirectness' in teaching is difficult to describe directly. When I draw attention to this item in a lesson, I stand up. As I do that infrequently, I hope that doing so might create a bit of extra interest. Then I tell the following story, drawing very roughly on a board from time to time.

I say, 'Imagine our topic for today is "The Nature of Responsibility". I could give you a talk on that topic, or I could introduce the topic to you indirectly via a story. I'd like to introduce the topic to you indirectly, so here is a story.

'Once upon a time there was a village, and through its middle there flowed a swiftly moving river. At its narrowest point, about here [pointing], there is an old stone bridge. On the lower side of the river, near the bridge, about here, there is a house in which live a couple called Adam and Eve.

'One evening Adam says, "They are showing a cowboy film in the village hall this evening. I think it's called *Midnight Cowboy*. Let's go and see it."

'Eve says, "Not another cowboy film!"

'Adam says, "What's the matter with cowboy films? I like cowboy films!"

'Eve says, "I know. But not another cowboy film. We saw . . ."

'And so the talk between the two goes.

'At 8.15 Adam stalks out of the house and heads unhappily towards the village hall. At 8.45 Eve walks out of the house feeling miserable. She goes to the bridge and sees the village idiot standing near the left-hand parapet, about here.[11]

'Eve has known this man for as long as she can remember. He is part of her village landscape. He hangs about, drooling, vacant, entirely harmless. Yet, that evening, Eve suddenly remembers what she has forgotten for years: that it has been said that this man will kill a woman one night. It is the kind of thing typically told in a small place to enliven a humdrum existence. But, that evening, when Eve catches sight of the man in the half-darkness, her heart misses a beat. She detours widely around him, and does not respond to his garbled greetings. Once across the bridge she hurries up the hill on the other side of the river.

'Near the top, on the outskirts of the village, about here, lives Michael. He is an agent for a company. He is unmarried and light of foot and mind. Eve has known him since they went to the village school together. She has always found him rather attractive. At nine o'clock she is at his door.

'At 11.45 Eve suddenly realizes just how late it is. She leaves in a hurry and runs down the hill. Near the bridge, in the half-darkness, about here, she sees the village idiot. She could have sworn he had been waiting for her all this time. When he sees her, he seems to lurch. Almost in a panic, Eve turns to her right and takes a path along the river. She looks back, can hardly see a thing, but feels she is not being followed. In fifteen minutes she is at the ferryman's door.

'The ferryman lives in a shack outside the village where the river broadens into a lake, about here. He makes a sort of living taking combine harvesters and other wide things across the river on his old barge. It takes Eve ten minutes to get him out of bed. When he eventually opens his door, he scowls and pretends he does not believe her story. When Eve persists, he asks for £20. When Eve says she has no money with her, he shuts the door in her face.

'Eve walks back to the village telling herself she is crazy. There is an occasional lap of water from the river. It is a sound she usually likes, but now it seems ominous. It is very dark. The trees along the path seem sinister. Feelings of regret, longings for home, snatches of conversation with her husband alternate with thinking how unreal her present circumstances are. She feels deeply relieved when she enters the village, but the moment she approaches the bridge she catches sight of the village idiot. Mouth dry, she turns to the nearest door.

'She knows who lives there: David, the village schoolmaster. She has known him, too, since childhood. He is kindly and generous and a bit ineffectual. And because he is a little too fond of her, she keeps him more distant than she would really like. It is well past midnight when he opens his door, but he smiles with pleasure to see her standing there.

'The moment she is inside Eve blurts out her story. David listens sympathetically. Then, one shoelace still undone, he looks up, red-faced, and says, "You spend the evening with Michael, and you come to me to take you — "

'Something gives in Eve. She turns and rushes out.

'I cannot tell you what happened next. All I can tell you is that Eve is found the next morning, strangled, lying under the bridge. Actually, the exact details of her death do not concern us. What we must decide is who is responsible for her death.'

I have spoken for perhaps five minutes. As I come to the end of the story I slide into my chair. I have enjoyed taking on the role of performer for a change. The students look a mixture of amused and bemused. I say, 'Well, Simon, what do you say? Please get us started.'

Quite often, once the learners have begun, it is difficult to stop them.

Who was *responsible* for Eve's death?

At first, the speakers tend to put the blame on Michael, Adam, David, the Ferryman – or men in general. Some suggest Eve. Others the whole village. One or two get caught up with deciding who is likely to have committed the murder, rather than who is responsible for it. Others remain silent. Perhaps they sense that, when we speak about such things, we may say more about ourselves than about the nature of responsibility. But if the discussion continues for long enough, almost everything – from a definition of sanity to the notion of free will – is touched on. As the discussion continues, I remind the learners that we are also considering 'indirectness' in teaching.

It seems to me that indirectness in teaching is extremely important. In being indirect, a teacher is by definition not supplying an answer. Instead, the teacher is pointing in the direction in which an answer may be found. In this way, when a learner comes upon an answer, that learner will experience it, not simply hear it. And, of course, it does not matter whether the topic is cooking or calculus.

Being indirect is an ancient teaching device; it was practised thousands of years ago by the Prophets in biblical times. Consider the teaching: 'It is easier for a camel to go through the eye of a needle, than for a rich man to enter into the kingdom of God.' We have become used to that sentence. It no longer startles. If anything, it tends to slide through the mind. If we think about it at all, it tends to sound childish.

But just what is 'the kingdom of God'? And why the implicit reference to money?[12]

If we can imagine ourselves hearing that sentence for the first time, and at a time when camels were the usual means of transport, the sentence may begin to nag. If it does, that is partly because the teaching is indirect. It hints at an answer.

That sentence also invites us to compare things which, normally, we would not compare. Learning is often a matter of comparing. We compare that which we do not know with that which we do know. A child may ask, 'Why does an electric light go on when we flick a switch?' A parent or teacher may answer, 'It's like turning on a tap.' Good teachers help their learners to compare. They intuitively go about things indirectly. Only later will they draw an electric circuit, and note the difference between it and the way water reaches us.

A comparison of this kind is called an 'analogy'.[13] Good teachers have a knack for thinking up clear and striking analogies. When a teacher uses an analogy, learners are not told what a thing is; they are encouraged to consider what they already know and to expand on that.

When a teacher is indirect, the learners are also encouraged to 'imagine' something – to picture something in their mind; to view it from a variety of angles. That is what we always do when we have to decide on a course of action. It is something which creative scientists and artists frequently do. And the more possibilities we can imagine, the more is our course of action likely to lead to a positive outcome.[14]

The word used above is 'imagine', not 'fantasize'. Imagination differs from fantasy in that, at its best, imagination is rooted in reality. Imagination is very important in all 'real' learning. It helps us to make connections; to move from what we know to what we do not know.

Readers may also have noticed the power of a story to convey a lesson.[15] Perhaps we take in a story containing facts, better than a bare string of facts, because a story has a human element. Learners are, after all, human. It is certainly much easier to remember a group of words when one embeds them in a meaningful sentence than to attempt to remember them on their own.[16]

Of course, one does not use indirectness in isolation. When teaching is imaginatively practised, a whole range of approaches is employed. One of the many defects of the transmission method is that it is unimaginative.

This brings us to Rosenshine and Furst's next item.

GIVING LEARNERS AN OPPORTUNITY TO LEARN

The title of this section may sound odd. Don't all teachers give their learners an opportunity to learn? If one is trying to teach as well as one can, one might be forgiven for thinking one is trying to help others to learn! But perhaps teaching has to stop before learning can begin?

Here is an illustration.

The teacher in this section teaches anatomy, in a school of radiography. He could just as well be a teacher of underwater hairdressing in a school of mermaids.

The first time I saw this young man teach, he stood in front of his class of twenty-five learners. They sat behind their tables, and ranged in age from nineteen to thirty. They looked a pleasant enough bunch. The teacher, sandy haired, not much older than his students, announced the topic, and began to speak.

He held up a bone, and noted that it was pointed here, and concave there. He explained why the shapes were as they were, and gave a name to each part. About fifteen names to one bone! On a table in front of him he had his notes; the topic is highly factual and he did not want to leave anything out. His voice was pleasantly modulated and he had a friendly manner. Occasionally he seemed a little unsure of himself. That did not seem to matter. One sensed his students liked him.

While he spoke, the students sat and listened, took notes, fingered pens, sat and listened, looked at illustrations, looked at the teacher, looked at each other, looked out of windows, took notes, and sat and listened.

Occasionally the teacher went over to a skeleton hanging in a corner and explained how the present topic fitted into the total anatomical structure of the human body. He made several sketches – one looked like the rigging on a sailing ship – and he wrote up lots of terms. It was like learning a new language. At several points he passed bones around the class. Quite often he repeated something, especially if he thought there might be a question on it at the next exam.

The students sat and listened, took notes, and looked at the teacher. Very occasionally one of them asked a question. Sometimes they whispered. Once or twice they teased the teacher. When they did, a ripple of good-natured laughter went around the room. Quite often they sat a bit vacantly as he cleaned the whiteboard.

And so it went – for an hour and a half.

These were pleasant young people, and they sat and listened quite attentively. But after the first half-hour their attention often wandered. After all, they had been sitting in those seats for the past three hours, and how much information can anyone take in by just sitting and listening for hours at a time?

That was the first lesson I observed. On my sixth visit this is what I saw.

In his previous lesson, this young teacher had asked his students to study half a dozen pages in preparation for today's lesson. He began by saying a few words of introduction, then divided the students into groups.

He took one group to the whiteboard and gave them a list of instructions. These required them to draw certain bone structures from memory and to label each significant part. The next two groups he took to the other side of the room, where he had prepared some fluorescent screens. On to these he now clipped X-ray photographs, and he asked the students to draw and describe in their notebooks what they were seeing.

He took another pair to a corner where there was a table. He told one student to lie on it and the other to palpate the recumbent one; and both were to tell each other exactly what they could feel. He also gave them a checklist which required them to identify, on a person's body, the bones and muscles that constituted the topic of that lesson.

In front of two other groups he placed a pile of what to me looked like very similar (plastic) bones. He asked them to identify in writing which of the bones fitted the topic of today's lesson, and on what basis they had identified them.

The other groups in the room he set similar tasks.

Then he sat down. For the next thirty minutes the room was a hive of purposeful activity.

After the students had settled to their various tasks, the teacher moved around. He checked that work was being done, he answered an occasional question, and he encouraged people to persist. On on occasion he expressed his displeasure when it became apparent that one of the learners had not prepared for this lesson, and he did not do this very well. He clearly hadn't had much practice in such a thing for his previous teaching hadn't required it. But it was clear, from the way the other learners were acting, that this teacher had, between that first lesson I have described and this one, managed to encourage a new kind of attitude.

At another point he shared a laugh with a pair of learners who were palpating each other. Mostly he didn't say much. When a group of students had finished a task, they exchanged places with another group who had finished theirs.

After about half an hour, all the students were finished. The teacher then gave out a worksheet. The dozen questions on it required the students to respond with a combination of factual recall and analytical reasoning. The questions covered the work that had been done so far.

The students answered the questions briefly in writing, again in informal groups. Sometimes all the students in a group had the answer pat. Other times they discussed what they should put down. It took them about ten minutes to complete the work. In the mean time the teacher sat to one side.

When most had finished, the teacher asked for their answers. These were read out quickly, compared, and in this way checked. The teacher commented only when necessary.

By then about an hour had passed, and this teacher had not done much that would conventionally be called teaching. Yet considerable learning had taken place. Next, this teacher introduced a new topic, but that is not my concern here. What I can report is that, for the hour just described, I did not see any students look bored, and I believe that this must have been due, at least in part, to the fact that they had been given 'an opportunity to learn' rather than only being taught.

To sum up this section: good teaching is a matter of periodically turning that which is to be learnt into a tractable task or problem, of the right size and complexity, so that one's learners will be intrigued, able to cope with it, and hence learn.[17] Readers may notice how this approach is based on life, and also that it relates closely to the earlier chapters on learning.

Good teachers are imbued with the problem-setting approach. To them, teaching is largely a matter of 'problematizing'. Even when they are simply explaining something, and find themselves talking for more than a few minutes at a time, they feel uneasy. They know that no one can learn that way. So the next thing they do is to ask a question.

For example, a teacher may have been explaining the structure of muscles for a few minutes, and has now got to the point where he is saying, 'And so we see that a muscle consists of a large number of fibres, and that each fibre is enclosed in a tissue called endomycium.'

At that point a fire alarm will go off in that teacher's head! The next thing he will say is not, 'And a bundle of these fibres is enclosed in what we call perimycium, and the whole muscle itself is enclosed in epimycium.' The fire alarm will prompt him to turn his next statement into a question. He will say, 'If you now look at that photograph, what else can you see about the way those fibres are organized?'

A good teacher will not act like that occasionally. His whole lesson will be imbued with a questioning approach. And this will not be intended to test anyone, or to retain attention, but to encourage an active, reflective and participative orientation. But that is best done, not by endlessly asking questions, but by giving the learners 'an opportunity to learn'.

Giving learners a suitable task or problem through which to learn – rather than merely practise – seems an easy enough thing to do. But anyone who has tried such an approach knows it is not that easy. Finding tasks or problems of the right size and complexity throughout a lesson is difficult. One has to know how to encourage the learners to get to work, to divide the class into pairs or groups, to help generate an atmosphere in which work is done in a relaxed but purposeful way, and to know what to do when the work is completed.

This approach requires considerable thought, lots of preparation, and reasonable resources. However, once the investment has been made, it can be used again and again. Such an approach also relieves a teacher from having to teach a whole class for the whole of each lesson, and that enables a teacher to help individuals as the need arises.

My own observations have shown me that teachers seldom succeed with this approach when they first begin to use it. The first difficulty is to stop teaching. The second is to see 'problematizing' as a way of teaching. Both require more imagination and sense of classroom management than 'teaching by telling'. A certain kind of interaction with learners is also required. This will be considered in a later section. However, when this approach is mastered, it affords most teachers and learners far more satisfaction than teaching by only telling.

I have heard some teachers say that their learners don't like problems. I have usually found that these teachers don't like problems either. They like solutions. And as that is what they like, they think that that is what their learners like. When these teachers set a problem, they do so without much faith that it will work. That communicates itself to their learners, and then these teachers find that their learners don't like problems either.

Having written so much about setting problems, I should perhaps emphasize that none of what I have said is to advocate 'learning by discovery' or 'student-centred learning'. Like most other catch-phrases, these are trite. What I am suggesting is that learners should be enabled to tackle that which they need to learn in a direct and carefully structured way. That isn't a 'method'. It is an approach. It follows that setting learners a plain task is often just as useful as setting them a problem.[18]

The tasks teachers can set differ from subject to subject. Teachers could get together, according to the subject or level which they teach, and show each other examples of the learning materials they use. Such meetings could be very useful. But I have found, both from my own teaching and from having observed many other people teach, that it is best to produce one's own materials.

This can consist of a text or drawing one has devised oneself, or material taken from another source and suitably modified. It may consist of no more than a diagram, an incomplete list, or two photocopied paragraphs followed by a question one has devised oneself. The material should never consist of mere photocopied pages. Not only is that illegal, such material seldom fits really well into one's own teaching. Interestingly enough, it has been found that learners do best on courses which their teachers have developed themselves.[19]

Quite a few courses are based on a textbook. A textbook tends to be a rehash of other people's work, and it usually attempts to cover a whole topic. There is a danger that a course based on a textbook will foster parrot learning. Like a dictionary, a textbook is occasionally useful for looking something up, but using it as one's main source of learning is like using a dictionary to learn a language. A good course is one where learners are encouraged to consider a variety of materials. These should include original sources, real-life situations, material a teacher has devised, and an occasional textbook.

In my own classes I ask student-teachers to bring in learning materials which they have themselves produced, and to tell us how they have used them in their classes. The following then often happens.

A woman who teaches computing will bring in a worksheet intended to help her students to learn how to organize a sub-directory. She will pass copies around, and tell us how she uses it. A man will then call out, 'That's interesting. I could use that idea for a worksheet on ways to classify types of handles in pottery . . .'

I have seen many surprising connections made in that way. They reinforce my belief that the important thing is to understand principles. When one does, one can adapt them to one's own circumstances. Those are some of my favourite lessons. The students themselves demonstrate and make concrete the way theoretical principles can be applied to varying practical circumstances.

TEACHING A FACTUAL SUBJECT

Some readers may have found the material on learning and teaching discussed so far quite interesting. However, they may also have thought that it does not lend itself to the kind of teaching which they do. They may agree that things like variety, indirectness, group work, discussions and worksheets have their uses in some lessons, but not with the kind of subject or learners which they teach.

They may teach a factual subject, like mathematics, geology, electronics, accountancy or production engineering, and in such subjects the important thing is to convey information.

Such readers may also agree that many learners could get just as much out of reading a good textbook as from listening to a teacher. But, they would add, many learners don't read textbooks: they come to a class expecting to be given information; and it is the primary job of a teacher to give such information.

These readers would probably agree that it is important for learners to have practical experience. But that comes later – in a lab, or a workshop; or when learners are out at work. It makes no sense to put them to work immediately if they don't know anything about a subject.

I hope that is a fair summary.

Let us continue this discussion by taking a concrete example. Let us take a highly factual subject like law, and let us say that it is our job to teach a group of learners a specific law: the law which determines who may, or who may not, give evidence. Clearly there is no room for discussion here. The law is the law. We may consider it fair, or unjust or whatever. But if we are teachers, our first job is to ensure that our learners know that law. In any case, how can we decide whether a law is just or unjust unless we have first carefully studied it?

Let us also be practical. Let us say that we have twenty-seven serving police officers in our class. And it is our job to teach that piece of law so that those officers will be able to take intelligent account of it as they go about their daily work.

Continuing to be as concrete as possible, let us examine the actual law. Here it is, copied out of the relevant legislation. I invite readers to read as much of it as they can without falling asleep. We can then consider how anyone could teach such material effectively:

(1) In any proceedings the wife or husband of the accused shall be competent to give evidence –
(a) subject to subsection (4) below, for the prosecution; and
(b) on behalf of the accused or any person jointly charged with the accused.
(2) In any proceedings the wife or husband of the accused shall, subject to subsection (4) below, be compellable to give evidence on behalf of the accused.
(3) In any proceedings the wife or husband of the accused shall, subject to subsection (4) below, be compellable to give evidence for the prosecution or on behalf of any person jointly charged with the accused if and only if –
(a) the offence charged involves an assault on, or injury or a threat of injury to, the wife or husband of the accused or a person who was at the material time under the age of sixteen; or
(b) the offence charged is a sexual offence alleged to have been committed in respect of a person who was at the material time under that age; or
(c) the offence charged consists of attempting or conspiring to commit, or of aiding, abetting, counselling, procuring or inciting the commission of, an offence falling within paragraph (a) or (b) above.
(4) Where a husband and wife are jointly charged with an offence neither spouse shall at the trial be competent or compellable by virtue of subsection (1)(a), (2) or (3) above to give evidence, in respect of that offence unless that spouse is not, or is no longer, liable to be convicted of that offence at the trial as a result of pleading guilty or for any other reason.

A typical piece of legislation. How does one teach such stuff? How could anyone use research findings on effective teaching – like the value of indirectness and giving learners an opportunity to learn – to teach this kind of material?

The usual way is for a teacher to explain it. As a teacher would understand the jargon, she would be able to translate it into more straightforward language. She would also be able to give real-life examples to illustrate how this law works in practice. Here and there she might ask a question, or invite a contribution from a learner. Finally, at the end of a lesson, she might administer a test to assess how much learning had taken place. But mainly the teaching would be by telling.

Here is how a past student of mine went about teaching the above material in a different way.

This man had a law degree and worked for a police training establishment. Once inside the classroom, and past the usual salutations, he spent five minutes introducing the topic. Then he divided the learners into small groups, and gave out two sheets of paper. One of them reproduced the legislation presented above. The other contained the following:

Read the following case, and after discussion in your group, answer the questions below it.
One day a Mr Ness comes home with a car radio, shows it to his wife, and boasts it has been given to him by a friend who had stolen it.
That evening Mrs Ness catches her husband having sexual intercourse with their fourteen-year-old niece who is staying with them while on holiday.
A few days later Mr Ness is charged with 'dishonest handling' and with 'unlawful sexual intercourse'.

Questions:
1. Is Mrs Ness competent to give evidence against her husband for
(a) 'dishonest handling'
(b) 'unlawful sexual intercourse'.
And:
2. Is Mrs Ness compellable to give evidence against her husband for
(a) 'dishonest handling'
(b) 'unlawful sexual intercourse'.

It does not take more than a minute to see that, when the questions are read together with the legislation, the legislation soon comes to life. That is because, in trying to answer those questions, the learners must restructure the material so that it fits into their existing schemata. In other words, by turning his lesson into a question, this teacher has based his teaching on an understanding of learning.

I can report that in this particular lesson those students got to work, and in about twenty minutes of reading, forming hunches, and discussing their answers among themselves, they answered those questions. The teacher then asked them what they had, and when the answers were read out there were more opportunities to clarify whatever it was necessary to clarify.

Notice also that, in going about things like this – in being 'indirect' and in 'giving opportunities to learn' – the students are helped to understand the *implications* of that legislation. That will enable them to apply it in differing circumstances.

Another approach is to divide the students into groups, give them the material to be learnt suitably edited, and ask them to write questions on it. The questions are then distributed among the various groups, and the group which has formulated a particular question is asked to approve the answers given. As an alternative to group work, a teacher can ask students to work singly on a worksheet. When they have finished, they can be asked to exchange their answers and to discuss them.

In preparing a worksheet, it is essential to choose a suitable text, or, as I suggested earlier, to write it oneself. A worksheet should contain clear directions, the relevant information, and a few questions. It should be written in a simple and direct way: commonly used words, short sentences and simple grammatical structures are best. The questions should be worded so that they require understanding as well as recall, and half a dozen are usually enough. And the whole exercise should be as lifelike as possible.

Research has shown that a reader retains the information given in a text better when the text is interspersed with questions, and when the answers to those questions are later supplied. In other words, here, too, we see that learning is helped when a reader is actively engaged.[20]

It takes some time to get these things right; I seldom get a worksheet right the first time I use it, no matter how long I have spent preparing it. I often have to use it several times in class, and amend it in the light of the learners' responses, before I am reasonably satisfied with it.

I believe that a particularly important aspect of the above lesson is this. In most establishments, a teacher will first teach 'theory', then give the learners an exercise so that they can get some 'practice'. In this lesson that convention is ignored.

In the lesson just described, the teacher announced the topic of the lesson, then gave the learners 'practice' *immediately*. That is, he enabled the learners to tackle that which they needed to learn *directly*. Such an approach follows life. Perhaps I could use an illustration from repairing a car again.

Sometimes I have to carry out a repair which I have never done before. The evening before, I get the repair manual out and begin to read the relevant procedure. After about ten minutes of examining text and diagrams, I usually find I am unable to follow the directions. I feel I have to have the actual thing I must repair before me. So I put the manual aside till the next morning.

Next day I put on some old clothes, open the manual again, and soon I am touching this and that on the car. And so it goes: references to the manual (i.e. the theory), followed by examination and manipulation of the faulty mechanism (i.e. the practice). Then I have to go back to the manual (theory), and then back again to the actual mechanism (practice), the two flowing in and out of each other. Anyone who has carried out a like task will have had a similar experience.

This is an unsophisticated example. Consider next the following finding from medical education.

In most teaching hospitals, students are first taught basic medical science, then clinical practice. But in some establishments a training programme has been devised in which the two are integrated. When one such programme was evaluated, it was found, among other things, that whereas students on a conventional programme tended to become increasingly cynical about the value of basic science studies, students on an integrated programme increasingly appreciated their value.[21]

Perhaps 'theory' and 'practice' are commonly taught separately, not because it has been established that such a separation aids learning, but because of administrative convenience and the dead hand of habit. In the medical training course noted above the integrated programme consisted of a series of medical problems. These were so organized that, in solving them, students had to acquire a knowledge of basic science.

The lesson in law described earlier shows a single instance of such an integrated programme. In another instance, the teacher could have given out the case study, placed copies of books which held the relevant legislation on a table in a corner, and invited the students to get to work. In the above instance, he passed out photocopies of the relevant legislation, in this way saving the students time. But the principle remains the same: the material to be learnt is given to the learners in the form of a problem – and they are invited to tackle the material to be learnt *directly*. In that way, theory and practice are integrated.

Worksheets are common in teaching, but they tend to be used for mainly revision purposes. That is, a teacher will first explain a topic (i.e. present the 'theory'), and then pass out a worksheet (i.e. give the learners some 'practice'). In the above lesson, the worksheet is not used for 'practice'. *It is used as a medium of instruction.* As a result, the teacher did not dominate the lesson with explaining before or after the 'practice'.[22]

The same kind of thing can be said about demonstrations. Teachers usually demonstrate before they invite their learners to tackle a practical task. Occasionally that is helpful. Mostly it isn't. Such an approach often inhibits learners as we seldom learn much when we watch someone. It is much better to tackle a practical task directly. If we don't manage it very well, we will want to observe an expert doing it. That way round, we will have the beginnings of an idea of what is required, and that will make our observation of an expert far more searching.

There are occasions when it may be necessary for a teacher to demonstrate first, as when not doing so may place someone in danger. But it is surely important not to stretch this requirement to cover situations when it would be perfectly safe to encourage learners to try a task themselves.[23]

If one takes this kind of an approach, classrooms become as much as possible like workrooms, for both theoretical and practical subjects. There is a tendency in that direction already in some educational establishments that have maths or language 'workshops'. Learners can walk into one of these and practise, with or without the help of a tutor. The trouble with some of these workshops is that they are adjuncts to the 'real' lesson. A good lesson already is a workshop.

In the lesson described above, the worksheet took the form of a 'case study', and was used as a medium of instruction, not for revision purposes.

A 'case study' is a real-life description which requires learners to solve a problem. The problem is often stated in the form: 'If you found yourself in this situation, what would you do?' A realistic and imaginatively stated case study helps learners to test and consolidate their existing knowledge, and often also helps them to see how their knowledge needs to be extended.

Case studies can be used to teach any subject from public administration to auto-vehicle maintenance. The section in which I discussed the importance of indirectness, and told a story about Adam and Eve, could very easily be presented in the form of a case study.

If the subject is auto-vehicle maintenance, and if the topic of 'braking' has just been completed, a case study on that topic could read: 'What would you do if a customer brings in a car you serviced last month, and complains that one of the front wheels keeps seizing up? It so happens that, when you serviced that car, you replaced not only all the shoes, pads and wheel-cylinders, but also the master cylinder.'[24]

The important thing is to give a case study to the learners, ensure that the necessary manuals or models are available, say as little as possible, and let *the learners* work on it in pairs or small groups. Few tasks generate better discussion than a well-thought-out case study. Such discussions enable learners to test, clarify, modify and expand their knowledge.[25]

When the learners have finished, the teacher can ask for their answers. There is no need for a 'reporting back' stage. On no account should a teacher stand at a flip-chart and note the important points as they are called out! A case study is for the learners: the more teaching, the less learning.

Where a practical task is being taught, it is best to outline what is to be done, provide the materials required to do it, and then let the learners get to work. They can be asked to work singly, in pairs or in small groups. It is most important for a teacher not to elaborate. Doing that takes the intrinsic reward of doing something well, and on one's own, away from the learners: the more teaching, the less intrinsic reward for the learners.

Occasionally there will be a key element in a task over which learners get stuck. One way to help a class in such circumstances is to tell just one of the learners about it. That element will then be conveyed from that one learner to all the others, but it is unlikely to be conveyed smoothly. At such moments teachers tend to feel that they must 'make things clear'. If they can resist that urge, they will find that, as the bit of information is passed from one group to the next, a good deal of discussion is generated. That helps to clarify it.

A misunderstanding can sometimes arise and remain. At such times a teacher must of course intervene. But it is helpful to give learners as many opportunities as possible to rectify their misunderstandings themselves. That is surely a powerful way to learn.

Practising teachers sometimes say that the approach suggested here takes much longer than 'teaching by telling'. That magic phrase about the need to 'cover the syllabus' is used. Common sense suggests that teaching by telling should take less time than using a worksheet. But is common sense correct here?

Consider first that there tends to be a great deal of redundancy in all explaining. We never state one fact after another. There is always some embellishment. It is typical to hear a teacher say, 'You have all probably heard of Thorndike. He was one of the early experimental psychologists who made a significant contribution to educational thought. He worked at about the same time as that famous Russian psychologist Pavlov. But unlike Pavlov, he was one of those who. . . .' These embellishments, especially the fatuous name-dropping kind, take up valuable time.

Consider next that, in any class of two or more learners, one learner will always know more than the other. Yet, to be clear, an explanation must be pitched so that all can understand. This means that, in explaining something to a group, a teacher will say a good deal that some of the learners already know.

Consider also that the more factual a subject, the less it lends itself to 'teaching by telling'. How boring it is to have to listen to something straightforwardly factual for an hour at a time!

To the above, I can add a personal observation. In many years of observing teachers it has been my consistent experience that the approach described in this chapter usually takes *less* time than 'teaching by telling'.[26]

But perhaps it is important to add the following.

Readers may have noticed that the learners in the above lesson were not simply told to 'go and find out'. That really would take a long time. The very essence of the approach suggested lies in this: that the teacher saves the learners a lot of time. In this kind of lesson, the teacher has to contrive things so that the learners can find out for themselves. But efficiently, systematically, and with as few redundancies as possible.

Finally, it may be worth remembering again that, when teachers 'cover the syllabus' in class, they do exactly that. As learning requires active engagement, the learners then have to cover the syllabus at home. If so, it would surely be helpful to teach in a way which enables the learners to cover at least some of the syllabus in class.

PREPARING A LESSON

I have read quite a bit of research on teaching, but I have not come across any findings which suggest that learners are helped to learn when a teacher prepares before a lesson. Perhaps we don't need any such findings! I have certainly found that I absolutely must prepare, even if I have a topic to teach which I have taught many times. That is not only because it is important to keep abreast of ever-growing knowledge, and changes in emphasis, but to ensure that I have a reasonably clear idea of what I hope to achieve before I walk into a classroom. So in this section I am unable to cite much 'objective' evidence in support of what I say, and must trust that readers will find what follows sensible.

We all know that careful preparation is important in many tasks, and with some tasks the necessary preparation can take longer than the actual task. Repainting a window frame is one example, and I think that teaching a topic for the first few times is another.

Teachers must also usually prepare for more than just a single lesson. They often have a whole syllabus to teach, and they must ensure that they have it sensibly divided into the available lessons. Beginner teachers usually find doing that far from easy. A beginner does not usually know how much can be achieved in any one lesson, and that isn't something one can learn from a book. It is something which one can only learn through practice.

When preparing to teach a topic, I find it helpful to think of it in terms of a 'Teaching Programme'. A good programme consists of three elements:

- a set of lesson plans;
- one or more assessments to help determine what the learners have learnt; and
- an evaluation to help find out what went well and what needs improving in the programme.

On some courses – like non-vocational adult evening classes – there may be no need for an assessment. Even so, a teacher could suggest that the learners might like to try one. A few imaginative assignments, among which the learners could choose, can help to increase interest. The learners could tackle one of these at their leisure, and a teacher could comment on (not grade) it in an encouraging way. I have had some experience of such classes, and I have found that the learners who act on such a suggestion are always later happy to have done so.

In the rest of this section I should like to comment on each of these three items in turn, and I begin with lesson plans.

I prefer to use a lesson plan which looks like this. (I have filled in some of the spaces to illustrate how the plan works.)

Class: . .   Topic: . .   Time: . .

Aim: To explain the use of 'objectives' in teaching.

Objectives: By the end of this lesson the learners will be able: (a) to state the origins of the idea of objectives; (b) given a simple topic, to write five behavioural objectives for it using appropriate wording; (c) to list three advantages and three difficulties with this approach; (d) to write two expressive objectives correctly.

Timing	Learner activity	Teacher activity	Resources
9 a.m.	listening	introduce topic	board
9.05	listening and responding	describe objectives	handouts
9.15	discussing and writing objectives in small groups		worksheet

Timing	Learner activity	Teacher activity	Resources
9.30	examine work of others in class		
9.35	listening	note advantages and limitations	
9.40	general discussion		
9.50	listening	describe expressive objectives	
9.55	writing expressive objectives in groups		
10 a.m.	end of lesson (to be continued)		

How will learning be assessed? By listening to the way the learners frame their objectives.

Readers will notice that the plan begins with an aim. A beginner teacher, especially, will find it helpful to spend a few minutes jotting down the aims of a lesson. That can help to focus one's attention. It is then easier to do the necessary reading, calculating, practising or whatever, in preparation for that lesson.

After that comes writing a list of objectives. An 'objective' – as that word is used in education – refers to what a teacher has decided the *learners* will be able to *do* by the end of a lesson. That is, an objective refers to the learners' activity (not the teacher's), and it refers to what they will be able to 'do' (not, for example, 'understand'). It takes lots of practice before one is able to write clear objectives, but listing objectives, in the way indicated, can help to clarify what one hopes the learners will learn during a lesson.

The form then shows a number of columns. The first one should help a teacher to time a lesson. The next two are the most important. The first, and largest, draws attention to what the *learners* will be doing. I have found that using this kind of form has the effect of directing a teacher's attention towards the learners. The strange thing about teaching is that it is often such a demanding activity that one tends to be both very aware of one's learners, yet also liable to forget them.

Readers may notice that in several places in the above plan the teacher is not doing anything. This is natural if one believes that teaching must often stop before learning can begin. The converse is surely true: it does not follow that anybody is learning because somebody is teaching, even teaching well.

The third column does not require comment.

The fourth column is there to help remind a teacher what materials will be required for a lesson. In the case of a teaching aid, it is essential to check that it works *before* a lesson. It is very frustrating to discover that a bulb has burnt out just as one is about to use an overhead projector. One tends to become flustered, a great deal of time can be lost, and learners can be very critical about such a lapse. One dud bulb can spoil a whole lesson!

The form ends by asking teachers how they will know that learning has taken place. That question is intended to remind one that a lesson is useful to the extent that the learners have actually learnt something, that is, changed. Of course, it isn't always easy to determine just what learners have learnt unless one tests them. But that cannot mean that there is no point in asking oneself what learners have learnt in the course of a lesson. Readers may agree that, in the lesson plan example, a teacher should be able to get at least a rough idea about whether learning has taken place.

Having considered lesson plans, we can now consider assessments; that is, how a teacher, and the learners, can find out whether the learners have learnt what they are supposed to have learnt. A well prepared teaching programme will contain two or three assessments, based on the objectives stated in one's lesson plans. Assessments can take various forms. Common ones are a set of practical or theoretical problems, an essay, a multiple-choice test or a project.

The third item, in a good teaching programme, is an evaluation. By this is meant some kind of tool to help a teacher to find out how well the total teaching programme has worked. Here is one example of an evaluation which teachers could ask their learners to fill in:

'You have just completed a course on . . . (say tentmaking or teaching). I (or a course team) would find it very helpful if you would respond to the following questions.

'1. You studied the following topics. Please give a mark, out of five, to show how useful you found each one, by putting a circle around the appropriate number. (1 = low, 5 = high.)

Motivation	1	2	3	4	5
Learning	1	2	3	4	5
Teaching	1	2	3	4	5
Resources	1	2	3	4	5

   (etc.)

'2. A variety of teaching methods were used. Please give your reactions to them by jotting down a few comments.

(a) lecturing
(b) group work
(c) private study
(d) practicals

'3. You were asked to do three assessments. Please note your reactions to each one.

(a) a multiple choice test on . . .
(b) an assignment on . . .
(c) a practical task.

'4. You were asked to do the following reading. Please give a mark out of five to show how useful you found each one.

Tentmaking through the Ages	1	2	3	4	5
Tent Construction: Materials, Techniques, Marketing	1	2	3	4	5
The Small Business	1	2	3	4	5

   (etc.)

'5. Please give your overall reaction to the course.'

The above is merely an example. I would not want to suggest that it is the best possible one. An evaluation can take various forms, and teachers must work out what best suits them. I would only suggest that it is useful to have an evaluation, as a part of each teaching programme, to help one to improve on it.

All of this may sound a little contrived, especially the use of a lesson plan, and I do not want to suggest that a lesson plan is something one should slavishly follow. A lesson plan is useful because it enables one to rehearse a lesson. That can help one to see it as a coherent whole; and that can help one to be more flexible. It so happens that I have used the lesson plan outlined above, and I found it was far too ambitious. The next time I taught that topic I cut the contents by about half. Having the lesson plan allowed me to do this more easily.

It is also far easier to allow oneself to go in all kinds of directions, during a lesson, when one has a clear plan than when one has only a general idea in the back of one's head. A plan provides points of reference to which one can always return.

I find I am seldom able to stick to a plan, especially when the learners become interested in a particular point and want to pursue it. But if I have a plan, I am able to draw attention to what has not been considered in a later lesson.

At this point, readers may like to consider the following. In research into the way encounter groups function, it was found that:

(a)   the more a group leader used structured exercises, the more effective did the group members find him or her;

(b)   the more a group leader used structured exercises, the less did the group members progress;

(c)   optimal results were achieved when just the right number of structured exercises were used.[27]

Encounter groups are not classroom groups, yet there may be a lesson here for teachers. If there is, it is that, though some learners seem to equate a carefully structured lesson with excellent teaching, too much structure seems to inhibit learning.

After one has written lesson plans for some time, the process becomes internalized. One then always has a model lesson plan in one's head. Even so, I have found it very important to make at least a rough plan for each of my lessons. That helps me to rehearse the lesson, prepare the necessary materials, and orientate myself during the lesson. It also serves as a record of things done and not done from one lesson to the next.

I have no objective evidence to draw on, but I believe that the kind of planning outlined above helps the learning and teaching enterprise. I have been teaching for many years, but when I have not prepared for a lesson in roughly the way just described I tend to be flustered. That can make for a lack of focus, which is unfair to both the learners and the teacher.

EFFECTIVE TEACHING AND A CONSIDERATION OF LEARNING

The last item on Rosenshine and Furst's list is: 'making structuring comments'. That is, research into teaching suggests that learners are helped when a teacher periodically summarizes what has been done, and points the way ahead. For example, a teacher may have explained something, or there may have been a discussion, or the learners may have completed a task. When such a point in a lesson has been reached, it has been found that learners are helped when a teacher makes a structuring comment.

But perhaps a word of caution is in place here.

In summarizing, a teacher may convey the idea that a topic is now closed; that everything which needs to be said has now been said. Of course, that is never the case. Also, something left a little unfinished – perhaps with a hint of what's to come – may be better remembered than something finished.

Secondly, when a teacher summarizes, he or she may inadvertently convey that a topic can be summarized in only that way. But of course, there are many ways of summarizing. One way of making a topic our own is to summarize it. This suggests that it may be helpful for teachers to encourage their learners to do some of the summarizing themselves.

I try hard to remind myself to make structuring comments in my lessons from time to time. Most learners seem to find it helpful to be given these signposts as they push their way through the thickets of a new topic. I also try to remember that a signpost is a signpost, not a guidebook.

All of Rosenshine and Furst's findings – except good questioning – have now been reported, and there may be some readers who feel that their findings leave out several important factors in teaching. For example, their list does not include anything about the need for teachers to know their subject really well. But these researchers cannot be faulted here. They state explicitly that their research is into the teacher 'behaviours' which affect student progress.

It may also have been noticed that these researchers do not refer to the personality of the teacher. Many people feel that a teacher's personality is an important factor, and I do, too. But again, Rosenshine and Furst cannot be faulted here, because their research is into teacher 'behaviours'.

It may be worth noting some other things which Rosenshine and Furst do not mention in their review of research into effective teaching. For example, it is often said that a teacher should not have 'distracting mannerisms'. By that is meant that teachers should not do things like jingle coins or stroke their hair. But there is no mention of this nugget in their findings. Nor is there anything about the need for teachers to 'motivate', 're-inforce', have clear 'objectives', use 'visual aids', engage in 'task analysis', or apply appropriate 'assessment procedures'. It may be true that these aid learning, but there does not appear to be any *evidence* that this is the case.

Notice also that Rosenshine and Furst have nothing to say about classroom 'skills' or 'competences'. This may be because these terms became the flavour of the times after their research had been published, or it may be that the qualities I have described do not lend themselves to such descriptions. Nor do these researchers have anything to say about such skills as being able to stand at a blackboard at a certain angle, or to produce transparencies which are clear and colourful. Again, there does not appear to be any *evidence* that learners make progress when their teachers have such 'skills'. The ability to do these things is probably useful, because not being able to do them may be distracting. But these kinds of abilities are unlikely to be the ones which differentiate between effective and ineffective teaching.

Aside from the practical help a teacher may have gained from the past few chapters, the findings presented may also have implications for the appraisal of teachers. There is considerable discussion at present about the need for teachers to be appraised annually. I have seen many checklists of desirable teaching behaviours, but the items included are seldom based on any *evidence* which shows that they affect learning. If teachers are to be appraised, perhaps the items discussed in the past few sections could be used. That would ensure that such appraisals were based on at least some tentative evidence.

I came across the research on teaching presented in this chapter several years after I had begun to form the understanding of learning presented in Part I of this book. In other words, the research on learning, noted in Part I, and the research on teaching, noted in this chapter, were done quite independently. However, notice how the two complement each other. For example, the finding noted just previously – that learners make progress when their teacher makes structuring comments – complements what was noted in a previous chapter about the importance of pattern, and the way in which 'facts' gain a meaning from their context.

Or consider how the finding that giving learners an opportunity to learn complements the work of Carroll and Mack on the way people learn how to use a word processor. Notice also that giving learners an opportunity to learn ties in with what was noted earlier about the need for learners to be actively engaged. Consider also how giving learners an opportunity to learn relates to the effect of intrinsic rewards, the importance of experiential learning, and the need for personal involvement.

Or consider indirectness, and how this relates to the finding that telling learners an answer prevents them from experiencing it, and from being able to transfer their learning to only marginally similar tasks. Or consider indirectness and the phenomenon of insight. Or how indirectness helps learners to make connections, and how this connection making deepens their understanding of the meaning of a subject.

Readers may also have noticed that the material on learning, presented in the first half of this book is coherent: it seems to make a pattern. And if the material on teaching presented so far dovetails with the material presented in the first half of this book, then there is a larger pattern.

It took me several years to see these patterns, and I discover more as the years pass. Whenever I do, I feel a sense of pleasure. It is like cutting up some timber to build a porch, and finding not only that the roof fits but that those dimensions are even right for a garage that is added later.

Rosenshine and Furst urge us to consider their findings tentative. That is only proper. But I believe that their findings are given added strength by the way in which they are complemented by the material on learning presented in Part I.

It is quite possible that the 'fit' which I seem to see is no more than wishful thinking. Readers must evaluate these things for themselves. But there is one thing I have often mentioned which must be right, and it is that whatever teaching approach is advocated, it must square with a coherent description of learning.

Chapter 8

Classroom Interaction

CLASSROOM COMMUNICATION

Most people would consider that the way a teacher communicates is an important matter. As a result, one of the topics commonly taught on teacher training courses is 'Classroom Communication'. It is then usually treated as if it were a skill (or a competence), that is, something one learns by considering its salient points, followed by practice until one knows how to apply it.

But a moment's reflection suggests that learning how to communicate effectively may not be primarily a 'skill'. A skill is primarily something we do. But how well we communicate must also depend, for example, on how interested in other people we really are. If so, learning how to communicate more effectively may be more a matter of learning how to change as a person, to some extent, rather than simply learning how to do something.

Consider the following example.

Among other things, Carl Rogers discovered that clients make progress in therapy when their counsellor has, among other things, what he called 'unconditional and genuine regard' for them. By this he did not, of course, mean that a counsellor *has* to show each client such regard. That is impossible and hence absurd. He meant that, *when* a counsellor has such regard, then a client may be helped to make progress. It follows that when a counsellor does not have such regard – as is often the case – a client is best advised to go elsewhere.[1]

However, at some centres, when people come for training to become counsellors, they are given instruction on how to *show* unconditional and genuine regard!

Whether I show or do not show *genuine* regard cannot depend on what I do. Ultimately, what I do reflects who I am. Hence another central concept in Rogerian therapy is 'congruence'. That is, that counsellors are able to help a client to the extent that their behaviour accurately reflects the way they actually feel. It follows that, to become an effective therapist, one must first learn what one really feels. That sounds absurd, but in previous chapters I tried to show that this this may be extremely difficult.

There are even courses on 'The Advanced Empathic Response'!

The increasing use of that word 'skill', and more recently 'competence', is perhaps no accident. When it comes to the personal, there is often a sense of unease. The personal is often fraught with risk. Perhaps the growing use of such words is an attempt to objectify, and hence depersonalize, that which is deeply personal.

I do not believe that it is helpful to compare communicating in a classroom with the 'skill' (or 'competence') required to mill a crankshaft. To communicate is to relate. Learners are people. Learners are not bits of metal which can be placed in a lathe and 'skilfully turned'. If they are normal, they won't respond for very long to anyone's 'skills'; they will respond to who we are. In short, I don't think that effective communication depends primarily on acquiring 'listening skills', 'social skills' or any other kind of skill or competence.

The way teachers communicate in a lesson surely conveys much more than facts or ideas. It conveys the kind of people they are, and how they feel about other people. It also conveys the kind of attitude towards learning and teaching they have, and the kind of values they hold. If that is roughly so, it may be more helpful to consider 'communications' as the outward manifestation of everything that goes on in a lesson, rather than a subject in its own right. Whatever the case, that is how I would like to consider this topic in the next few sections.

CONSTRAINTS ON PARTICIPATION

I believe it is safe to say that the majority of teachers like their learners to participate. When learners do, teachers feel that they are showing an interest; and if being actively engaged is important in learning, then the learners' participation must be desirable. However, although schoolteachers sometimes complain that their pupils talk too much, those who teach older learners often say that they do not get as much participation as they would like. The odd thing is that the moment those learners leave a classroom, many of them talk a good deal.

The last observation suggests that it may be a mistake to begin the topic of 'learner participation' by discussing how to encourage it. It may be better to begin by asking what inhibits participation. Readers may remember that I adopted the same approach when discussing motivation. What follows is a partial list of factors which, I believe, affect participation.

1. The first constraint on participation must be the transmission method of teaching. There is surely a contradiction between, on the one hand, believing that it is a teacher's primary job to transmit information, and, on the other, expecting participation.

Years of observing teachers at work has suggested to me that, although many would like their learners to participate, they do not really listen to them when they do. This is not because they are insensitive, but because they believe that their primary job is to 'cover the syllabus'. Learners sense this and respond accordingly.

2. Even when a teacher would welcome participation, it is obviously not something that can be forced. It can only be invited; and that invitation will be accepted to the extent that the recipients feel that the invitation is sincere and made for a good reason. But the problem goes further than that. For example, a teacher might be perfectly sincere in his or her wish for participation, yet undermine his or her genuine desire for it by an equally strong need to shine.

3. Learners feel encouraged to participate when they sense that their teacher will not evaluate them each time they speak. I am not, of course, suggesting that teachers should always agree with their learners. Only that learners will be encouraged to participate if they feel they are not going to be evaluated each time they open their mouth.

4. Learners will feel encouraged to participate when they sense that their teacher does not need to be talking all the time. Unfortunately, there are some teachers who are so convinced that their primary job is to convey information that, in spite of themselves, they are like a coach who never passes the ball.

5. Learners will feel encouraged to participate if they sense that their teacher has what is commonly called a democratic sense of values. That is, that, at bottom, all humans are of equal worth in the general scheme of things. Such a teacher will seek to treat all learners, of whatever age or kind, with a dignity which is theirs by right. None of this is to suggest that teachers should jettison their ultimate responsibility for what goes on in a classroom. Only that, having established essential boundaries, learners will feel able to participate when their teacher encourages as much freedom as possible within those boundaries.

6. A teacher who values participation will also try to make each lesson a collaborative venture. Such a teacher will try to be an authority, not an Authority; and will be pleased, at times, to become a participator in the learners' activities.

7. Lastly, I believe that learners will feel encouraged to participate if they sense that their teacher is genuine, more warm-hearted than cold, and more genial than dour.[2]

Those are some of the general factors which can affect participation. Now for some concrete suggestions.

In many years of observing teachers, the most common exchange between teacher and taught I have heard takes this form:

 1 *Teacher*: asks question
 2 *Taught*: gives two-word answer
 3 *Teacher*: evaluates the answer ('right', 'yes', 'good', 'no')
 4 *Teacher*: repeats learner's answer
 5 *Teacher*: elaborates – and continues speaking.

I do not know what readers will make of this exchange. Whatever else it does, it kills real participation stone cold dead.

I have suggested that we speak most readily to a person when we sense that that person will not evaluate us. That must be especially the case when we speak in a classroom. Classrooms contain teachers, and most people feel uncomfortable when they are asked a question by someone who is in a position of some authority, as teachers are. Perhaps more importantly, classrooms also contain other learners, and many are much more worried about their reactions than about the reaction of a teacher.

In other words, when teachers generate the sequence:

teacher's question
learner's two-word answer
teacher's evaluation of the learner's answer

– that is, when teachers do that which is most characteristic of many teachers – it is precisely then that they most inhibit learners' participation.

Whenever I have made this suggestion to practising teachers some have protested. They have said that, unless they say whether a learner's answer is correct or incorrect, neither the learner who has spoken nor the other learners in the class will know whether an answer is correct or incorrect.

How true is this?

Consider first that the majority of questions teachers ask tend to be relatively simple. Consider second that, when learners answer a question, they must feel reasonably secure that their answer is correct. If so, what is gained by saying an answer is correct? Participation is surely more likely if an answer is acknowledged with a smile. At this point readers may recall a previous section on intrinsic and extrinsic rewards.

What if a learner's answer is incorrect?

Where a participative atmosphere exists in a class, another learner is more than likely to correct a mistake. If that does not happen, a teacher could always ask a learner who has made a mistake how he or she had got to that answer. In doing that, a learner who has made a mistake would not only discover that he or she has made one, but also why it is a mistake.

So far I have drawn attention to the first three steps in the five-step sequence noted above. What of the fourth step, repeating an answer?

Whenever I have suggested that this, too, inhibits participation, some practising teachers have protested. They have said that repeating a learner's answer 'reinforces' it. Even if that is so, surely such 'reinforcing' inhibits participation? Imagine you and I were talking. How would you feel if, every time you said something I considered correct, I repeated it? You would think me either condescending or an imbecile. I believe you would also very soon stop talking to me.

The five-step sequence noted above begins with a question. Many teachers would probably say that they ask a question either to test knowledge, or to encourage participation. With regard to the first reason, I think it would be safe to say that, if a question is asked to test knowledge, it is unlikely to encourage much genuine participation.

What about questions which are intended to encourage participation? Teachers probably believe that they ask some of their questions for this reason, but many years of observing teachers has suggested to me that it would be more correct to say that quite a few teachers ask questions to retain their learners' attention.

That would not be surprising. Whenever we talk for more than a few minutes at any one time, we tend to fear that our listener may have switched off. If so, it is hardly surprising if a teacher, who has talked for more than five minutes, should ask an occasional question in the hope that this will encourage continued attention. But such a question must be a poor way to encourage genuine participation.

Most teachers probably do not analyse their asking of questions in the way just described. Most probably ask questions in the way they do because that is how they were asked questions when they were learners. I feel reasonably sure that this analysis is correct because, over the years, I have heard the five-step sequence described above repeated hundreds of times – by teachers who have become convinced that it inhibits participation. In discussing their teaching after a lesson, these teachers often say, 'I know I'm still repeating their answers. I can hear myself doing it! It's ridiculous. But it's very hard to get out of the habit.'

And because teachers often ask questions and repeat answers as a kind of reflex action, learners find themselves having to play a game which can be called 'Guess the Answer the Teacher Wants'. As it is often difficult to guess the answer another person wants, one is forced to produce short, vague and childish ones.

Quite often, these will not be the answers a teacher wants. When teachers ask a question, they usually know which answer they want. When they get it, they are pleased. When they do not get it, they go on asking till they get it. A learner's contribution is seldom seriously explored because many teachers are concerned with 'covering the syllabus'.

If teachers are in this way concerned, they are not able to listen to their learners' answers properly. And if their questions are mainly intended to retain their learners' attention, then the actual answers which they get will be less important to them than the fact that someone has answered. Learners notice this, and answer – or do not answer – accordingly.

In schools, when a teacher asks a question, many children wave their arms whether they know the answer or not. If they are picked on, and know the answer, they give the usual two-word reply. If they do not know the answer, they mumble – or pretend they have forgotten it.[3] They do this because they know it is their attention, not their answer, which many teachers want. Older learners sense this and stop responding altogether.

If there is some truth in the above, there is reason to fear that younger learners in particular may see the act of responding to a teacher's question primarily in terms of gaining that teacher's approval. Responding to a question may then have the effect of destroying rather than fostering considered reflection.

Unfortunately, these patterns of behaviour are reinforced by the learners. Learners respond, or do not respond, because they have also become conditioned to such a state of affairs. So a style of interaction is often generated in a classroom which neither teachers nor learners really want.

CLASSROOM TOPOGRAPHY

Having drawn attention to some constraints on participation, I shall now try to make some suggestions on how participation may be encouraged.

Traditional classrooms are so arranged that the learners sit in rows and face in one direction. In schools, there may be anything from five to fifty learners in one class, usually sitting in rows behind desks. In other establishments smaller classes may be the rule. In these, the learners sometimes sit in a semicircle behind movable seats. In many colleges there are anything from 20 to 200 learners in one class. Here the learners usually sit in rows.

All these arrangements have one thing in common: the teacher is placed opposite the class. A class so arranged that the learners sit in rows and face a teacher generates at least three basic results. It

- conveys the impression that it is the teacher who is responsible for what goes on in a class;
- creates the expectancy that the teacher will do most of the work;
- brings about lines of communication going mainly from the teacher to the taught.

These effects are made even stronger when teachers stand. When teachers stand, they:

- convey the idea that they are in charge;
- convey the idea that they are the active one, especially if they move about;
- suggest that the learners are insubordinate and passive;
- can make the learners feel simultaneously resentful yet bored;
- may undermine some of the beneficial effects of group work;
- may frustrate the development of a sense of social cohesion in a class.

Perhaps the worst aspect of the above is this: when teacher and taught face each other in two parts of a room, a sense of opposition may be created. I would have thought that few things could undermine participation, even productive learning, more than that.

Another important effect of a teacher facing a whole class is that it encourages the belief that, in order to learn, one needs a teacher.

Sometimes, when I see a class for the first time, I begin by asking the learners what they would do if I just sat there and did nothing. After a pause, somebody will say that he or she would talk to a neighbour. Others say that they would doodle or read. Others say that they would wonder what I was up to. When I ask what would happen after that, some learners say that they would ask me what I intended doing. Others say that they would complain, or leave the room, or even the course. When I ask how they would feel while all this was going on, they say they would feel surprised or annoyed.

My aim in asking these questions is to try to illustrate the extent to which we tend to believe that learning is something that follows from being taught.

Very young learners, say those below the age of twelve, do need a teacher in order to learn many things (clearly not everything). But even when mature people have learnt a great deal on their own, they often do not consider this real learning. Hence it is common to hear people complain about not having been sent on a course. They seem to believe that it is necessary to be on a course in order to learn. Most classrooms reinforce this myth by the way they are laid out.

I was once on a course in which there were about 160 students. We took three subjects each term, one of which was compulsory. The other two could be chosen from the half-dozen on offer. For the compulsory subject, we all met in a large hall once a week. We sat in long rows facing the teacher, who gave us a lecture.

In the first term the compulsory subject was 'Perspectives', and it was taken by a man. He would come in, say hello, begin talking, and usually spend five minutes introducing a topic. Then he would report either two conflicting points of view, or one controversial one. He would cite the evidence on which these things were based, and then he would stop and say, 'What do you think?'

He would smile and wait for a response. Somehow he managed to convey that he would be interested to hear what somebody might like to say.

And soon somebody would say something.

This teacher would listen thoughtfully, nod his head as if to say he understood, smile his appreciation, look round the hall, wait, and then another student would say something. When half a dozen people had spoken, this teacher would nod his head, thank the last speaker, and say that the next point he felt he ought to bring to our attention was . . .

He would continue speaking for another twenty minutes, then stop and invite a comment. All in the way I have just described. And get it. From a crowd of 160 learners, very few of whom knew each other!

Three weeks after we had begun, I found myself saying something in response to one of this man's questions. When I had finished, he nodded, smiled his thanks and said, 'Yes, Eric. Incidentally, you may know that Weber made more or less the same objection. But what do you think has been said in response to that?' And he looked around the hall expectantly.

I sat there flabbergasted. How on earth had that lecturer known my name? Never, but never, had that man and I ever met. And this was only the third time I had sat in that hall.

In the next few minutes I worked out the only possible way he could have known my name. During the next break I mentioned the matter to some fellow students, and we agreed that this man must have gone through the 160 application forms my fellow students and I had sent to the institution, and matched and memorized the photograph and name on those applications.

I mention this man for two reasons. One, to show that it is possible to gain participation in a lecture hall with 160 learners sitting in rows in front of you. And two, to suggest that such an ability requires a certain kind of teacher. That is, a teacher who teaches first people, and only then a subject.

However, even this teacher was unable to encourage interaction among his learners. How could he, when what they saw was either him, or the back of a score of heads?

In the lesson just described there was participation. But the lines of communication went only from teacher to taught and back again. There was very little communication between the learners. Such interaction is very difficult if the learners are unable to face each other. But we have seen that discussions can aid learning.[4] For a genuine discussion to take place, a classroom must be arranged so that:

- the teacher does not occupy a prominent position;
- the learners are able to see each other's faces.

Where the numbers allow, a suitable arrangement is for the learners to sit in a circle, the teacher a member of that circle, and the tables or desks making a block in the centre. That way the learners can sit around the tables, and place writing and reading materials on them.

Where small desks (or chairs with a writing-arm) are in use, they can be placed in a circle. However, such an arrangement creates an empty space in the middle, and some learners say they find talking across a large empty space inhibiting.

Where the numbers are too great for sitting in a circle, learners can be invited to sit in groups of three to five around a room. Most discussions will then be in small groups. One can encourage a whole class to take part in a general discussion using such an arrangement because learners will spontaneously turn their chairs to gain the most suitable position at any given time. I find I can work best with from fifteen to twenty-five learners, but I am quite happy to work with twice that number if necessary.

I have often worked with teachers who have begun to adopt the approach suggested in this book, but who have hesitated to rearrange the seating in their classrooms. Sometimes they have shared a classroom with colleagues who have not been exposed to the kind of approach suggested here. In such circumstances, I have seen such teachers labour in vain to raise the level of learner participation. Then I have seen some of them make a break, rearrange the room along the lines suggested above, and the results have been remarkable. It is as if the learners had been liberated to participate.

I have also known teachers who have reached a stage when they have felt the need to relocate fixed fittings (like lab benches or electric sockets) to get rid of rows of desks. Making such a change is extremely difficult. An electric socket can be as stubborn as an administrator. But once such fittings have been moved, and the seating arranged as described above, the change in the class has been remarkable.

A square room is best because it is difficult to create a circular seating arrangement in an oblong room. With a big class, say over thirty learners, having a big room is most helpful. It enables a teacher to encourage groups to form in the corners and in the middle when such an arrangement is likely to help learning.

Not every establishment has decent-sized rooms, but a great deal can be done with whatever accommodation is available. The biggest problem is habit, not accommodation. Changing the seating arrangement in a classroom, to facilitate participation, seems to be the most natural thing in the world to do once one has done it.

Unfortunately, many classes consist of so many learners that interaction between them is impossible. These classes often meet in so-called 'lecture theatres'. Such places were commissioned by people who knew nothing about learning. They based their ideas on a notion of teaching that is, literally, medieval. Lecture theatres generate theatre-like expectations. One expects a Performance in them. They force a teacher to take on the role of an entertainer; and they encourage learners to believe that learning has something to do with being entertained. So learners sit back and expect the equivalent of a TV documentary with its beautiful images, resonant commentary, subtle music, reassuring expertise, slick superficiality and an illusion of learning.

As most teachers are unable to reproduce the pheno-barbiturate world of the TV documentary, the learners soon switch off. Most teachers sense this and become either cynical or resigned. A few have a flair for showmanship and manage to evoke enthusiasm. That is probably better than resignation. But neither kind of teaching will generate much 'real' learning.

Many establishments already have lecture theatres, so scrapping them raises questions of cost. So did scrapping slavery. Lecture theatres have their uses. It is good to be able to listen to an invited speaker sometimes: it can be interesting to listen to someone who has made a significant contribution. After all, ideas have to come from people. Only people can dream up the idea that humans are essentially machines.

As learning requires work, it is best done in rooms that lend themselves to being worked in. Such rooms should have coat-pegs and colourful posters on the walls. They need a few cupboards and some movable chairs and tables. They need windows, reasonable lighting, a board to write on, and heating in the winter. But none of this is intended to suggest that learners should sit in circles, groups, rows, or in any particular way for the whole of any lesson. Only that the topography of a room has a powerful effect on the level of participation in it.

ENCOURAGING PARTICIPATION

In this section I should like to make a few more suggestions on how one might encourage participation. Perhaps the best way to go about this is to describe some episodes from my own teaching. That might provide practical illustrations which readers can examine for both mistakes and advantages.

I try to get into a classroom a few minutes before a lesson. If there are about fifteen of us, I arrange the seating in a rough circle. If there are two dozen of us, I arrange the seating in a square with all the tables in the middle. If there are more of us, I arrange the tables and chairs in clusters so that the learners are able to get into small groups. I also try to ensure that the room is reasonably tidy.

I begin the lesson by sitting down, usually in a different place each time. I do this to convey that I am not going to put on a Performance; that I may be the teacher, but that the lines of communication can go in any direction. Then I say hello and smile. Then I say something original, like something about the weather, or how nice it is that the end of a week is coming.

I begin like that to try to suggest that, although I may consider the lesson to come very important, I realize that the learners might not think so. After all, they may have other things on their minds! A few pleasantries before a lesson also allows the learners to get settled, and may act as a bridge between the classroom and the outside world.

If such a beginning does not help to focus attention, I look around and try to sense the mood of the class. There may be a concern which needs to be dealt with. Occasionally, I try something a little unusual. I bring out an odd object, or pass out a gum-drop. Other times I say something mildly provocative. The last thing to do is to launch straight into details.

Then I invite general comment.

Sometimes there are comments, and sometimes there are no comments. Sometimes somebody will mention a recent experience which has illuminated something we examined in a previous lesson. Other times somebody will say that they found a book or an assignment boring or interesting. Somebody may suggest we consider a different topic, or tackle our present topic in a different way. Other times somebody may ask a question. Occasionally one of the learners will launch into something, and this might evoke so much interest that a good part of the lesson gets taken up with it.

The value of these comments varies greatly. Some people make them to sabotage a lesson, others to move things along. Either way, I believe it is helpful to make a space at the beginning of each lesson to enable learners to say anything they may have on their minds.

Next, I might make an administrative announcement, or ask for suggestions about future lessons. Other times I ask whether the learners would like a 'free group discussion period' during the week (i.e. a period when they can discuss anything they like) with me absent or present. As I am usually asked to leave at such times, it is hard to say exactly what takes place in these periods. What I can report is that the learners seem to use them productively for discussing such things as assignments. The fact that it is the learners themselves who organize these periods is productive in itself.

Once administrative matters are out of the way, we tend to do one of two things: either we do a revision of the previous lesson, or I introduce a new topic. We do a revision for these reasons: no matter how thoroughly a topic may have been examined in a previous lesson, some learners may not have understood it very well.[5] A revision may also help to build bridges between a previous lesson and the coming one. And a revision may aid someone who has been away.

A revision goes like this. Very briefly, I remind the learners of the topic of the previous lesson. Then I give out a worksheet with a few questions on it. In choosing questions, I try to remember that theory is most useful to the extent that it helps intelligent practice. I ask the learners to answer the questions briefly, in writing, after discussing them with a neighbour, or in a small group.[6] I make it clear that this is a revision, not a test, and that I shall not ask to see anyone's answers.

As the learners work, I sit to one side. When people are learning it seems best to keep quiet. When they have finished, I ask if anyone has got stuck. Sometimes a learner will say something and a brief discussion may develop. Occasionally I may chip in to clarify a point. Other times nobody wants to say anything. I am usually happy to leave it at that. The learners have had a chance to check their answers with each other, or to ask me. The question-sheet will show them what they know and do not know, and it is now up to them to act accordingly. This part of the lesson takes from five to fifteen minutes.

Next I outline the topic we are going to consider in today's lesson. Readers may remember my comments in a previous chapter about how things get their meaning by the way in which they fit into a pattern. In introducing a topic, I try to convey that pattern. I do that sitting, and it usually takes from three to five minutes.

Then I draw attention to a few of the most salient facts of today's topic, or I report briefly what various researchers have claimed. I happen to enjoy a radical approach, so I often mention one. In reporting a matter, I try not to be too personal. I try not to get in the way of the topic, but I am not at all sure I manage that. I believe in the need for objectivity, but I also believe that a good teacher will sometimes convey strong emotions. The kind I have especially in mind include an awareness that the simplest things are often the most mysterious, that genuine scholarship is something to esteem, that there is an excitement about discovery, and that there is a very great pleasure to be gained from understanding something.

I also think it best to introduce a controversial position in the name of the person who first made it. Insights and discoveries are made by *people*, usually in a specific context, and often allied to personal needs. Learners are people, too, and I have found that they are more likely to make these insights their own when they are introduced to them in this way.

When one of the learners attacks a position I have outlined, and no one speaks for it, I try to defend it in the originator's name. I also try to remember that a position is most likely to gain acceptance if opposing ones are also mentioned.

Much has been written about my subject of teaching, and I have read quite a bit. But I have found it best to make my knowledge unobtrusive. If I don't, I risk swamping the learners. It is important to know one's subject really well, but I think most of what a teacher knows should be kept in reserve. I have found that learners are more switched on by empathy than expertise. This part of a lesson takes from five to fifteen minutes.

Then I give out brief reading material on the topic. That may consist of an article I have shortened, or two paragraphs from a book I have photocopied. Sometimes the material is in the form of a list or a diagram. To this material I usually add one or two questions.

I don't just pass this material out. I try to 'sell' it. I say something like, 'I think you will find this material interesting. I came across it by chance . . .' I mean such things sincerely, and I believe such personal touches are helpful. There is often a kind of residual resistance in every class, and a little wooing, and a little good humour, can help to counterbalance such a tendency.

I pass this material out, sometimes exchanging a pleasantry with a learner as I do so. Then I ask the learners to respond to the questions briefly, in writing, after consulting a neighbour, or having a discussion in a small group. Such exchanges help the learners to clarify their understanding, make for variety in a lesson, and provide scope for social inclinations.

Other times, having introduced a topic, I dictate a one-sentence question and invite the learners to jot down an answer. I encourage them to discuss their answers among themselves first. Of course, I don't ask to see these written answers. I believe inviting learners to jot down an answer sometimes is more likely to generate thought than always throwing out a question for verbal response. Also, that way, all the learners will be engaged, not just the usual vocal few.

Speaking in general terms, I could summarize the approach I have outlined above by saying that I try to 'problematize' the topic. That is, rather than give the learners straight information, I ask them to answer a question, either on the basis of their experiences, or on the basis of descriptive or research material they have been asked to consider. And in trying to answer that question, they clarify their understanding of it. In teaching, this approach can pose difficulties. The main problem, in a subject like teaching, is to see that there are some very serious problems, rather than merely a difficulty in applying a 'skill'. That is less the case in a subject like medicine or car mechanics.

Instead of handing out a text, a teacher could hand out a set of calculations, a series of slides or a piece of equipment, followed by a question. Of course, the material should be intrinsically interesting. After that, the important thing is to sit back and let the learners get on with the task at hand. To this day, I find doing that difficult.

Sitting there, doing nothing, for periods ranging from five to twenty minutes at a time, still somehow seems wrong. I feel I ought to be doing something! Isn't that what I am paid for? But mostly I now manage to resist the urge to get in there and do something. That gets easier from year to year as my conviction grows that the only way of really learning something is to grapple actively with it.

When the learners have finished, I suggest we consider their answers. Of course, I always sit. Sometimes I do not have to do much. I ask one learner to get us started, she gives her answer, and a discussion may then develop spontaneously among the learners. If it doesn't, I invite a learner by name to comment on the answer we have just heard.

As that learner speaks, I try to listen as well as I can. When he has finished, I don't comment (or evaluate or repeat), and I don't say 'yes' or 'aha'. All these will draw attention back to me. Instead, I try to show that I appreciate that contribution. Perhaps I nod and smile. Then I look around to try to convey that I'd be pleased if someone else spoke.

In most discussions the teacher is the centre of attention. That is the case even if he or she does not want to be. Most learners are conditioned to seeing a teacher in that way. They tend to see a teacher as a figure of Authority, and they tend to want confirmation for what they have said.

Getting confirmation is important. We all need what might be called 'authentication'. The trouble is, when a teacher keeps confirming, the learners tend, unconsciously, to see the topic of the lesson as somehow 'belonging' to the teacher. They may then see it as something 'out there', something which has little to do with them personally. When that happens, the material of the lesson seldom becomes 'real'.

So quite often I don't comment after a learner has spoken. I acknowledge the contribution with a friendly nod, then glance around expectantly. If no one speaks, I invite another learner by name to speak. Quite often, especially when the learners and I are new to each other, when that person speaks, the comment will be directed at me, or spoken quietly. In reply, I say I fear not everyone has heard. That is usually enough to encourage that learner to address the whole class. I nod again, and look around expectantly. I try to show I would be pleased if someone else spoke. I often wait quite a long time like that.

I have found that many learners find such behaviour on the part of a teacher unusual. The more outspoken ones sometimes say that they don't understand what I am up to. Some call it a 'laid-back' approach. Others suggest that I am playing a game and wonder when I am going to come clean. A few say that they find me manipulative. Others say that my silences disturb them, or that they find me discouraging. Some say that they want me to tell them if they are right or wrong.

I am always troubled by such comments. I say I am not playing any game. I add I am behaving in the only way that now makes sense to me; that I'd prefer to hear another learner's reaction to my own; that the lesson is as much theirs as mine. I urge the learners to read some of the material which has influenced me, and I give names and titles.[7]

In the following weeks it sometimes becomes apparent that a few of the learners have done just that. I can see this from the way they sometimes smile in class and participate more. It is now these learners who argue with the ones who want me to be more directive.

Very slowly, after I have used this approach for a few weeks, most learners get used to my not commenting immediately after a learner has spoken. Increasingly, they themselves comment on what someone has just said. Increasingly, too, they don't wait for me to say anything. They bring up points themselves. I find I can encourage such learner-to-learner exchanges when I turn my head, or simply sit back and let things take their natural course.[8]

The approach suggested above is far removed from the one often called 'questions-and-answers'. In this, the teacher stands out front, and by a process of judicious questioning attempts to elicit answers from the learners. The most obvious characteristic of this approach is that it is teacher-led. The learners remain essentially passive, there tend to be few learner-to-learner exchanges, and the learners will tend to be hazy about where they are going. If there are more than three of them, they will spend most of the time listening to comments directed to another person. The main effect this has is to create frustration and boredom.

But I had better add that I quite often find that the approach I have outlined does not always encourage maximal participation. Sometimes I do all of the things I have outlined, and the class remains glum. I worry about this, sometimes mention my worry to the learners, and then I often find that they shake their heads and urge me not to worry so much! As I've done all I can, I have to accept their word for it. I find that the best thing to do then is to move on to the next part of the lesson.

No matter what the seating arrangements, many learners will tend to take the same seat in each lesson. They have a right to do that, of course. The trouble is, if they do, they tend to find themselves in the same group in each lesson. That makes for limited experiences. So I encourage the learners to take a different seat now and again. Many hesitate, but soon most of them do move.

Sometimes I ask one of the learners to chair a discussion. To signal the switch, I exchange places with that learner. I have found that most learners act very well as a chairperson. Even unlikely seeming ones often rise to the occasion and show qualities I had not noticed before. I find, when I act like that, more participation is liberated than when I remain 'in charge'. Quiet learners in particular tend to participate more. It also gives the learners more responsibility for what goes on in their lesson. I believe that has valuable implications for behaviour outside the classroom.

Sometimes I leave the room once a discussion has begun. I do that partly to signal that it is the learners' lesson, and partly because I have repeatedly found that more people participate when I leave than when I remain. When a teacher is present for a discussion, many learners seem to feel that there isn't much point in discussing anything, because the teacher knows all the answers anyway.

Some readers may consider that, as my learners are adults, I can allow myself to leave them. But schoolteachers have told me that, when they have sometimes left their pupils in this way – but remained near the class – it is their colleagues, not their pupils, who can be a problem. They seem to believe that, for people to learn, they have to be taught.

Every teacher knows that in any one class there will often be several different understandings of a given fact. It is obviously not enough to state a fact loud and clear to ensure that it is understood. In the sections on perception I tried to show why that is so. A discussion enables learners to find out whether they have understood something.

People who teach a factual subject sometimes say that they can see the point of having a discussion in a subject where it is possible to have a difference of opinion, but not in a subject where facts have to be learnt. I have already tried to show why such an objection misses an important point. The main reason for encouraging a discussion is not so that opinions can be exchanged, but to clarify understanding.

It is also well known that, when humans face a problem, they tend to form a hunch (or hypothesis) very quickly about what the solution might be. They also tend to look for things which confirm their initial hunch, and ignore things which contradict it. Apparently, it often takes a good deal of time, and considerable information to the contrary, before a person will drop a mistaken hunch.[9] A discussion in which the learners genuinely participate is far more likely to aid the process of clarifying hunches, and considering new ones, than anything a teacher might say.

Teachers who try to facilitate participation encourage their learners to frame hypotheses out loud. Then, when somebody responds, these hypotheses are tested. As time passes, learners begin to question their own hypotheses. In this way, they absorb a mode of thinking without even realizing that it is happening.

Most teachers would probably agree that it is important to have some evidence for believing whatever it is that we believe. It may be possible to remember facts by listening to a teacher, but it is impossible to learn how to come to a valid conclusion in that way. To come to a valid conclusion, one must have the repeated experience of weighing up the available evidence.[10]

What exactly constitutes 'a valid conclusion'? I don't think it is easy to answer that question. Perhaps it would be roughly fair to say that a valid conclusion is something which is consistent with what has gone before, or is open to rational debate, or is based on the best available evidence.[11] One of the things which I most frequently find myself asking during a discussion is, 'What is the evidence for that?' After a time, this phrase becomes a sort of in-joke. When a learner makes a largish claim, another learner will often say, 'Ah, but what's the evidence for that?!'

Here is an illustration.

One learner might say, 'Too much salt causes heart disease.' Another might respond with, 'How do you know?' The first speaker will probably say, 'But everyone knows that!' The second speaker might reply, 'Yes, but is that *evidence*?' It seems to me that to want at least tentative evidence for an assertion is one of the most important things that anyone can learn.

Another way of putting the above is to suggest that one of the ingredients in 'real' learning is dialogue. In the course of a dialogue, learners often discover that things are seldom the way they first appear to be – that learning is, to a considerable extent, a matter of having to discard first assumptions and grope for new ones. That can make learning and teaching quite an anxiety-provoking business.

Another feature of a good discussion is that it enables learners to relate the facts under discussion to their own experiences. One will typically hear a learner say, 'Yes, but I couldn't do it that way because . . .' and another learner might then say, 'But how would it be if you . . . ?' In this way a topic stops being merely a classroom exercise. It begins to take on possibilities in the real world.

Occasionally, I have found it helpful to be more personal during a discussion. Our topic may have been 'motivation', and the discussion may have continued for some time and become rather aimless. I might then say, 'Here we are, talking about motivation in the abstract. But what about here and now? How about you, Susan? Do you feel motivated right now?'

Sometimes quite powerful discussions can be generated in that way. Learners will say how frustrated, bored or involved they feel. That can lead to an examination of the circumstances which have caused such feelings.

One way to organize a discussion is to divide the learners into groups, and to give each group a different question to consider. When the groups have finished, a spokesperson announces the conclusions of the group. As this is being done, the teacher notes the main points on a flip-chart. These points are then discussed by the whole class in 'a plenary session'.

I believe that this approach has merit in subjects such as management training, where the aim is not so much to acquire new knowledge as to refine and extend the knowledge one already has. I doubt whether this approach generates much learning in most classrooms.

When this approach is used in a conventional classroom, opinions tend to become confused with evidence, and the balance between studying something and discussing it tends to be weighed towards mere discussing. Most of the ideas thrown out will be put on a flip-chart, and, in the nature of things, some will be half-baked. Teachers will hesitate to point this out, partly in order not to offend the speaker, and perhaps partly in deference to the present fashion which holds that, as long as learners are encouraged to express ideas freely, learning will take place.

But anyone who knows anything about significant learning knows that that isn't simply a matter of acquiring facts or exchanging opinions. It is also a matter of being able to think critically, to require evidence, to see relationships, to defer judgement, and to try to state things accurately. To learn these things is to learn a *discipline*. This awareness – that a subject is also a discipline – is often absent in such discussions.[12]

Such discussions can also be very time-consuming because many points tend to get discussed twice, once inside one's own group, and then by the whole class. Further, if each group has considered a different question, the learners never seriously consider more than a fraction of the material to be studied. And if the teacher does the usual flip-chart act, he or she will tend to dominate the lesson.

Group work and discussions have been fashionable in some educational circles for many years, but they can be overused and misused. I believe that it is fair to say that discussions are most useful after the learners have had a chance to study new material, as a discussion can help to clarify it.

Group work and discussions can easily go wrong. The same speakers may do most of the talking, and important points may be raised and not given the attention they deserve. Sensitive learners may hold back for fear of being considered pushy, and thoughtful ones may want more time to consider the issues raised.

Among younger learners, a discussion can become rowdy; among older ones there is sometimes one person who will bury a topic under a rubble of irrelevance. These things are not easy to deal with. Too much intervention on the part of a teacher may inhibit participation; too little may cause some learners to feel they are wasting their time.

Rowdiness I'll deal with later. With the learner who talks too much, I have found it best to suggest in a friendly way that others be given a chance to speak. As for irrelevance, it is obviously important to distinguish that from misconceptions.

When a discussion has gone on for some time, it often becomes apparent that the attention of the learners has wandered. At such times I believe it is important for a teacher to intervene. I try to gather strands together, and to restore a sense of purpose to the group. A good way of doing that is to introduce a new activity.

I believe that periodic discussions are most important in learning. But I don't always find them easy to encourage. No matter how thoughtfully I have tried to conduct a lesson, it sometimes falls flat. Nobody says a word. I have a few more things to say about such failures in the next section.

PROBLEMS WITH PARTICIPATION

Many teachers will have had the experience of preparing a lesson really well, intending to have a discussion at one point, and then finding that the discussion falls flat.

One or two learners may say something – and then the discussion fizzles out. Perhaps the teacher has been *too* keen to have a discussion – after all, it's not something which can be forced. Perhaps the teacher has been too keen to make a point. Perhaps the learners had a test in a previous lesson. Perhaps something else happened that day. But a silent class can be deceptive. Provided that the learners have had some *direct* access to the material to be learnt, a good deal of learning can take place without anyone saying anything. Sometimes, weeks after a seemingly unsuccessful lesson, a learner may say something that shows the teacher that the lesson has been successful after all.

When learners have had direct and suitable access to lesson material, it will register somewhere. When that happens, the learners are just as likely to discuss it outside a lesson as in it. We consolidate our learning best when we are able to use our knowledge practically, and that usually happens long after a topic has been considered in a lesson.[13]

But sometimes discussions don't seem to develop in a certain class at all. When that continues for some time, I feel uneasy. In response, I try to be friendly but not too personal. I say, 'Our discussions haven't seemed to get off the ground lately. I wonder why?'

Then I sit back and wait. Obviously, the last thing to do is to make a speech about the need for participation! If I have managed to put the matter fairly, and if I am patient, I usually get a reply. One of the more outspoken learners will usually say something: it may not be complimentary, but it may clear the air. Discussions may then get under way again.

The above is with adults. With children I have taken the same tack, and it has sometimes worked.

And sometimes it has not. When that happens, I ask if something is wrong. That is a more personal kind of thing to do, but participation is a personal matter. When learners participate, they signal that they are willing to collaborate.

So I ask what is the matter. In reply, a more outspoken learner may say that they are bored. Or that they can't see the point of what we are doing. Or that they are tired. Or that they are fed up with something. Sometimes a learner will say something critical about my teaching. I am often hurt by such replies. Sometimes the comment has been more than critical, and I have then sometimes felt so bad I have wanted to give up teaching. But, as time passes, I have come to see that occasional attacks like these are inescapable. Genuine participation will only develop in a class when a teacher is reasonably open, and that involves some risk.[14]

So I listen to these comments, and I say I'll think about them. I do think about them, and occasionally I feel I have learnt from them. More frequently I sense that the comments are not really what they appear to be. They are often expressions of the resentment or anxiety inherent in being a learner. Other times they are intended to test a teacher. I'll have more to say about that in the next section.

Sometimes there is good participation in a class, but not by all the learners. Some sit there and hardly say a word. These quiet learners seem to be of two kinds. One kind consists of those who prefer not to speak, but who do not seem to dislike discussions. The second kind dislikes discussions.

The first kind tends to be shy, or prefers to work alone. These learners can produce both good and poor work. The same holds for those who participate. In short, it has been my experience that the extent of a learner's participation has little to do with the kind of work he or she otherwise does.

When the timetable allows, I speak privately and informally with every learner in my classes. To those who don't speak much in class, I say I have noticed that they don't say much. I add that I would value any contribution they might care to make. Some reply that they have always been shy about talking in public. Others say that by the time they are ready to say something, somebody has already said it. The thing that these learners most frequently say is that the ones who participate seem so very much more intelligent and articulate than they are.

In reply, I say I have often heard learners say such things. I add that I have often felt that way myself. I try my best to listen and to reassure. Later, in class, I sometimes call on these learners by name if I sense that they might like to say something.

Such an approach sometimes helps. Other times it does not. Some people have a dread of self-disclosure. Others find it difficult to assert themselves enough to take part in a discussion. Others have a poor self-image and stay silent for fear of saying something that might lower their self-esteem even more. Others stay silent to indicate their aloofness. Some learners only speak when certain other learners are absent.

It is difficult to know what to do in such circumstances. A teacher must certainly try to encourage these kind of learners to participate. If one does not, and they continue to remain silent, they may begin to assume the role of being 'a silent one'. That role is then reinforced with each passing lesson. If that goes on for long enough, it becomes almost impossible for that learner ever to participate.[15]

But if one has been sympathetic, and done the best one can, there comes a time when a teacher must let such things rest. There is only so much one can do. It is also true that some people gain just as much from listening as from talking. And learners of whatever age have just as much right not to participate as to participate.

So much for the first group.

The second group consists of learners who positively dislike discussions. When I have asked them about it, I have found that they want an unambiguous delivery of lesson material. They believe that this will help them to pass their next exam. Their approach is strictly instrumental. They come to study in order to obtain a qualification. Notions like 'personal development' or 'self-expression' irritate them. And if you say that simply listening to a teacher is unlikely to generate much learning, you irritate them even more. They don't like discussing things!

This experience of mine is corroborated by the work of several researchers. One of the earlier and best, Lauren Wispé, reported research in which she found that learners tend to fall into three groups: 23 per cent who like discussions; 51 per cent who do not; and 26 per cent who tend to be satisfied with whatever kind of teaching they get.[16] These proportions probably vary, but I have found that the general tendency is usually there.

Wispé notes that learners' preferences in this respect tend to be very strong. She found that those who like direction want more of it, even when they are getting a great deal of it. And learners who like discussions tend to want more of them, even when they are getting a great many of them.

When Wispé considered the personalities of these learners, she found that the ones who like discussions tend to be academically able, and fairly secure and independent individuals. Those who dislike discussions, and prefer a more didactic approach, tend to be academically weaker, and appear to be less secure individuals. She also found that the latter kind of learners tend to be 'very critical' of lessons, instructors and fellow-learners. They even expressed 'hatred' of an open approach. On the other hand, the learners who prefer a more open approach, including lots of discussions, tend to express themselves as 'moderately favourable' towards lessons in general.

Such findings suggest that, no matter what a teacher may do, some learners will be unhappy. In response, Wispé suggests that it might be an idea to match learners with teachers. That is, let the learners who prefer a didactic approach have teachers who prefer that; and let the learners who prefer a more open approach have teachers who prefer that.

This seems a sensible solution, but it raises many questions. For example, is the aim of teaching no more than helping learners to acquire knowledge? Shouldn't a teacher also try to encourage learners to evaluate knowledge? Can that be done by 'telling'? In any case, we have seen that the transmission method of teaching does not rest on anything known about the way humans actually learn.

I have found such research findings helpful. But, rather than accommodate my teaching to the possible inclination of some of my learners, I have persisted in encouraging discussions when I have thought that they would help learning. When I have acted like that, the majority of learners who initially expressed resentment at time 'lost' in discussions have increasingly taken part in them. That begins to happen especially when I draw attention to the research findings noted above.

The attitude of some of these learners then becomes ambivalent. On the one hand, they participate more in my classes, and encourage participation in their own; many even become highly successful at encouraging participation in their classes. But, in discussing my teaching, and that of others who encourage participation, they continue to be critical about things like 'time lost', and the absence of 'clear objectives'.

This suggests that participation is not just a technical matter. I noted earlier that it is probably related to things deep in one's personality.[17] It is as if the learners who are critical of discussions can see their educational value. But, having an authoritarian personality, they feel uncomfortable when someone in a position of some authority, like a teacher, is not authoritarian.

Humans are complex creatures! It isn't surprising if learners are sometimes ambivalent or hostile towards their teacher. Coal miners have to put up dirty conditions, bus drivers with an occasional traffic jam, and teachers with the vagaries of human nature. It could be worse.

From the above, it may appear as if I am suggesting that an absence of participation in a class must be due to something inside a teacher, or inside a learner. There is another possibility.

Most teachers teach because they want to, and the majority probably feel that the material they teach is worth teaching. But their learners may not think so. They may be there because they have to be there.

In developed countries, pupils attend school ultimately because the law forces them to do so. Older learners often attend classes because they have been sent. Many others attend, not so much because they are particularly interested in a subject, but because they wish to obtain a qualification which will enable them to earn a living.

A good deal of schooling is not simply a matter of acquiring useful knowledge. It is also about winning a kind of hurdle race which determines who gets what of the national cake.[18] Many learners are prepared to put up with course material which they consider irrelevant, and with teachers whom they consider boring, in order to take part in that race. But, under such circumstances, it isn't surprising if some of them are reluctant to participate. In short, teachers work in a system which is to some extent coercive, and coercion does not encourage participation.

It is also the case that quite a few learners, no matter what their age, come to an educational establishment for mainly social reasons. The lesson material tends to be a secondary matter. They are primarily concerned with things like who they are sitting next to, and who they hope to meet during the next break.

It is hard to know to what extent such factors inhibit participation. My own experience has been that, once inside a classroom, and provided that the teacher has some insight into how participation might be encouraged, many learners will be prepared to participate. Perhaps that is because participating is usually more interesting than not participating.

The extent to which learners participate varies from country to country. I have no systematic evidence, but it has certainly been my experience that, in some countries, learners participate more readily than in others. After all, you can travel for hours by public transport in England, and people sitting close to each other may not say a single word, so it is hardly surprising if that also sometimes happens in an English classroom. Go back far enough, and child-rearing practices will probably come into it.[19]

This chapter has been about some of the problems teachers may have when they try to encourage participation. The next two sections will be about more serious difficulties.

DIFFICULT LESSONS 1

In the past few sections I have tried to outline what I have called an 'open' approach, an approach in which there is as much participation as possible. Although such an approach may have some strengths, it also involves some risks; and in the last section some of the results of taking such risks may have become apparent. It is certainly the case that when I look back on my own teaching I can remember many painful episodes, and readers may find it helpful if I describe some of these.

We don't usually discuss our failures except with close friends. Perhaps that explains why I have not come across many books on teaching which describe what it feels like to have a bad lesson.[20] One book in which there are such descriptions is by Wittenberg. It did me good to read what she wrote. As I noted above, I have had many bad lessons, and she helped me to understand why some of them have made me feel so bad.[21]

When I began to teach, I used to think it was my fault when I had a bad lesson. Now I am not so sure. After all, not every learner is a paragon of virtue. And if we think about the world around us – from the way some people drive cars to the way the people of one race sometimes treat the people of another race – we remember that humans do not always behave in a rational manner. Unfortunately, the irrational nature of much human motivation is seldom discussed in the current literature on teaching, especially the teaching of adults.[22]

In my own years of teaching, I have often noticed how full of quirks and difficulties a great many learners are. Especially adult learners. And of course teachers, too. And classrooms are not neutral places like parks. They can produce a great deal of stress. But it is probably best to begin with simple difficulties.

Every teacher knows that one sometimes has a bad lesson because one has not prepared for it. Life being what it is, one then pays. But anyone who has taught also knows that to teach well is very difficult, so it isn't possible to get it right each time. Always one is dealing with the most complicated things on earth: other people! So it isn't surprising if some lessons go wrong. In view of these circumstances it seems best not to blame oneself too much when a lesson goes wrong, but to try to use the occasion to learn something from it.

A typical difficulty teachers have is that, when they teach an examinable subject, they are often tugged in opposite directions. Teachers are in the business of trying to help their learners, but they must also try to safeguard the needs of their community. It does not matter if they are teaching children, doctors or electricians. Always teachers must try to reconcile their wish to help their learners achieve individual competence with the need of their community to have competent practitioners. An effective teacher is a person who manages both tasks most of the time. But that isn't always easy, especially in today's climate when so much emphasis is placed on 'meeting the needs of the *individual*'.

Another difficulty teachers sometimes have is that the more they offer, the more some of their learners seem to want. Provide variety in lessons, and some learners will want more variety. Pass around lots of handouts, but ask to have the longer ones back, and one learner is sure to complain that they are not allowed to keep handouts – while others complain that they are given too many! Give out a guide for doing assignments which is into its seventh rewrite, and someone is sure to say that it isn't clear.

Such reactions are especially common among learners who are used to a didactic approach. When a more open approach is introduced, some learners respond in the same way that some people respond when they get their first taste of democracy. Their demands run beyond the bounds of the possible.

I remember here an occasion when the college in which I then worked carried out a market survey. One of the questions asked students what they thought of the building. The range of responses was amazing. What to some people was 'pleasant', to others was 'smelly, tatty, dirty'.

Another problem teachers have is that they personify a figure of some authority. That is the case no matter how old the learners, or how much a teacher tries to foster a spirit of independence. Learners bring their attitudes into every classroom, and some people's attitude to any kind of 'authority' can be very negative. But that is hardly surprising, for not everyone has had the good fortune to have had decent parents.

The above is most easily seen in the area of assessment. If a course is examinable, the teacher must indicate whether the learners have reached a satisfactory level of competence or not, even when the teacher is not responsible for the final grade given. This inevitably makes some learners feel vulnerable, and that can make some of them aggressive.

Some learners turn their disappointment with their difficulties inward; others, the extra-punitive kind, take it out on a teacher. They will complain bitterly about not having been given enough time, about things not having been explained properly, about how boring they have found lessons, how irrelevant most of the material has been, and how only the teacher's word seems to count. They will be biting, even savage in their criticism. That can hurt!

One way of dealing with such difficulties is to teach with another teacher. Unlike most other professions, teaching is usually done by a single individual. When two teachers can work together in a class, the kinds of difficulties noted above might be more easy to deal with.

But team-teaching also has its difficulties. If two teachers are to work effectively together, they must collaborate closely beforehand. That requires a lot of time. They will also have to have similar orientations and enjoy each other's company. It isn't easy to find someone with whom one can work that closely.

Other times it may be more appropriate to call bluffs. Many years ago, when I was working in a school, I had a pupil in one of my classes who caused many problems. One day I found myself saying to him, in a friendly way, that I believed he was causing difficulties because he was scared he couldn't cope with the lesson material; that playing up was his way of taking the easy way out; and that I believed he could cope – if he were prepared to take the risk. He laughed and played up some more. But to my surprise there was a subtle, and then a marked, change in him. He began to work, and both his behaviour and his learning improved.

When I feel that things have become difficult in a certain class, I sometimes suggest that some learners might like to work on their own. I say this in a friendly way, and don't mention any names. I also say that it isn't in my power to excuse anyone from class, that any learner who so wishes should feel free to go to the library during my lessons, and that I'd be glad to offer suggestions about reading material. I add that I won't be offended if anyone leaves.

When I have done this, a learner has very occasionally chosen to work on his or her own. Mostly he or she has later asked to come back. Of course, I agree. Perhaps that learner missed the company of the other learners. The main effect of suggesting that learners might like to work on their own is to clear the air. And if certain learners would prefer to work in this way, why not? After all, they may then produce better work.

Another difficulty is that teachers can pose a threat to their learners. All real learning implies change, and change, as we all know, is difficult. That can be a serious problem in some subjects. For example, in my subject of teaching, one is unlikely to evoke much hostility if one suggests that a teacher must remember not to talk to a blackboard when addressing a class. The obvious usually goes down quite well. But consider the likely effect if you suggest that teaching has to stop before learning can begin.[23]

The non-obvious tends to cause some hesitation, disbelief, even resentment. At the very least, we are seldom indifferent to the new. Quite a few learners seem to resent anything that probes, that challenges the accepted view; but teaching is often a matter of suggesting that the obvious is not so obvious after all. Hence, the better the teaching, the greater the possible threat. No wonder Socrates and Jesus died in the way they did.

Another difficulty in teaching a subject about which people have had some experience, such as teaching, is that many people will feel that they are reasonably knowledgeable about it. After all, the students will have had at least ten years' experience of teaching! So a common response to subtle research can be 'so what' or 'fancy that', both, in Haste's memorable phrase, 'reflecting processes of assimilating new material into existing schemata with the minimum of cognitive disturbance'.[24]

In nearly every class I teach there are one or two learners whose faces fall whenever I try to go beyond the obvious. As long as we are talking about something relatively straightforward, most learners seem content. But the moment someone struggles to get past the obvious, a grimace of boredom is likely to appear.[25] I am particularly struck by this when the comment responsible for creating the dissonance isn't my own.

Looking at those bored faces, I feel a sense of despair. I wonder whether my understanding of teaching is wrong after all. I decide I must be a poor teacher. I rack my brains to try to find a better approach. I often decide that the only thing to do is to stop teaching altogether. Perhaps I should simply make myself a resource. Leave it to the learners to ask for what they want. After all, they are adults.

Next day I am not so sure. Is everyone generous enough to acknowledge a contribution? Is everyone interested in the new? And if learning implies change, does it follow that every person will want to learn – even if responsibility for the learning is passed to him or her?

Consider an example taken from the world of art.

As is well known, the group of painters commonly called Impressionists have had a powerful effect. Not only were many later painters greatly influenced by them, they also influenced all the decorative arts. They have taught all of us to see in a new way, so it seems fair to call them 'teachers'. Here are some comments by contemporary critics of theirs, the first writing in an influential newspaper:

> The impression made by the impressionists is that of a cat walking over the keyboard of a piano, or of a monkey that has laid hands on a paintbox.

> Cézanne can only be a bit of a madman, afflicted while painting with delirium tremens. . . . In truth, it is only one of the weird shapes generated by hashish, borrowed from a swarm of absurd dreams. . . . No audacity can surprise us. But when it comes to landscapes, M. Cézanne will allow us to pass in silence . . . ; we confess that they are more than we can swallow.[26]

Are people less bigoted today? Are we all keen to expand our understanding? Does everyone strive to be self-aware? Does every troubled person go to a counsellor?[27]

Consider the following comment by a thoughtful woman: 'I've been accused at times of being a bit of a masochist, because I always wanted to know . . . But always I would rather know, whatever it costs. But, then, in my family, not knowing went as far as madness . . . I knew what a good experience should be about and so I looked for it. But for other people there may be different needs.'[28] What has repeatedly struck me is that the people who most readily agree with such sentiments are often the ones who act most strongly in opposition to them.

Here is a last example of a difficulty I have encountered in teaching. Because I do not always comment on what a learner has just said, but try to convey my interest by listening carefully and encouraging others to respond, I have been told, by a few learners, that they feel I do not value their contributions. That has happened even when I have valued a certain learner's contributions – and told him or her!

At such times I find myself wondering, yet again, to what extent I am responsible for what is happening in a class. Some of the learners seem to believe I have attitudes which I do not have. Teaching in this open way can turn a teacher into a kind of screen on to which the learners seem to project some of their own attitudes. It has certainly sometimes felt to me as if a hornets' nest has opened up.

DIFFICULT LESSONS 2

It is well known that, when people find themselves in a group, some of them may come to act in a way different from how they usually act when on their own. An early analysis of this tendency is to be found in Freud's comments on the work of LeBon.[29] These writers made three broad observations:

1. A group consists of a number of people. This may make the people in it feel much stronger than they normally do; and this may also make them feel much more able to express, and to act on, their wishes. Wishes, for their part, may be conscious, and

unconscious; and an important difference between the two is that unconscious wishes are often repressed because some of them are anti-social. After all, it is during the process of socialization, in our early years, that we learn that we cannot always have everything we want.

2. Another effect of being in a group – and allied to the previous one – is that the individuals in it will often fall in with what appears to be the common aim. This tendency has been termed 'contagion' – that is, when the sentiments or acts of a few members affect the whole group.

3. One of the most striking effects of being in a state of 'contagion' is that the people so affected may perform at a level far beyond that which they would normally achieve as individuals. Such actions may be both moral and immoral, brave or cowardly, sublime or bestial.

One could summarize these points by saying that being in a group can have the effect of making us feel much stronger, but also less socially responsible. Inhibitions may be lifted, and we may regress to a more primitive level of behaviour. And all of this can have both dire and beneficial consequences.

Most practising teachers will have had ample opportunities to observe such tendencies. They will also know that the most effective way of responding to unproductive forms of group behaviour is by genuinely listening, then by cheerful reasoning, and then, if those do not work, with unobtrusive and quiet firmness.

Teachers who practise an open approach are much more likely to encounter group reactions – both productive and unproductive – than teachers who practise a didactic approach. The former are also much more likely to become aware of various undercurrents in a class. There will usually be some approval, some hostility, some indifference, and lots more that is difficult to fathom. A consideration of group dynamics may be helpful here.

For example, in observing groups at work, Bion found the following.[30]

A group is usually doing something. The group may consist of a bunch of children trying to decide what to do next; a committee trying to decide a course of action; a dozen managers trying to decide policy; or it may be a class of students discussing a topic. The surface features of the situation may be reasonably clear. But when people get together in a group, all kinds of undercurrents may also be generated.

One kind of current is generated by those who have a yearning for a charismatic leader. In a class, there will usually be a few learners who want the teacher to clear up all ambiguities. If they get such a leader, they are pleased. If not, they are disappointed, and show it.

But most teachers are not charismatic, and the best have no wish to be. They are mature people who don't have an itch to shine. They prefer their learners to shine. Nor do they want to clear up all ambiguities. On the contrary; they deliberately create manageable ambiguities which will enable their learners to grapple directly with lesson material, and hence 'really' learn it.

Another kind of current is generated by those who attack or run away. Experienced teachers will not be surprised by such an observation. Most classes contain some learners who are inclined to help things along. But there are often a few who prefer to find fault, and there are many ways of sabotaging a lesson.

A third kind of current is generated by those who jettison the group, and pair off when things don't go well. One manifestation of this can be seen when two learners work together to undermine a teacher. A teacher may have said something, and one of the learners will typically say, 'As Rachel was saying, it isn't *always* like that. You have to take a broader view. It's simplistic to say . . .' That teacher probably did not remotely suggest that things are 'always' any kind of way; and the last thing he or she did was to make things 'simplistic'!

The most characteristic feature of such behaviour is that it is often motivated by factors below conscious awareness. But to suggest such a thing is likely to antagonize the participants even further. In any case, classes are not encounter groups, and teachers are not therapists. Perhaps it is enough if a teacher is aware of such possibilities. He or she might then be in a better position to deal with them. For my part, I have found that an awareness of such tendencies has helped to reassure me that what is happening in a class may not be caused by anything I have done or said.

Such an awareness also helps me to see that occasional attacks on me are inevitable. In part, they may be a test of my ability to cope with them. So I try to listen to complaints as carefully as I can. I say I'll think about them, and continue with the lesson. I do think about them, and I try to get right what might be wrong. And sometimes I feel hurt when I realize that a criticism was unjustified.

But the hurt usually passes in a day or two. Next time I see that class, I try saying something wry or mildly amusing. If one lets things blow over, most things do blow over. If I act like that, a bad atmosphere in a class will sometimes lift. Learners who have never spoken may even chip in. But it is impossible to escape attacks if one adopts an open approach. An open approach invites all kinds of contributions, and not all of them are likely to be helpful. The alternative is to go back to didactic teaching. That way one is safe. The angry learners then hide their hostility and express it elsewhere.

Occasionally, when I feel I have got into a rut with a class, I try to compare myself with an actor who has got himself into a rut playing a part for a long time. Such actors have been known to try to imagine their role in a new light. It is not that I believe that teaching has much to do with performing, but I do sometimes try to imagine myself taking a new approach with a class. Sometimes that has helped to improve things.

There is one sure way of having disciplinary problems. It is to expect them. If one goes into a classroom expecting to have problems, one's manner will tend to be seen as antagonistic. That will elicit a like response. If one walks into a classroom cheerfully, responses are more likely to be cheerful. I speak from experience!

Doing the various things noted above with a difficult class has sometimes helped, and sometimes it has not. I once had a learner who not only complained bitterly about my teaching in front of others, she did not want to leave my class either! She upset me, but she also puzzled me. In spite of her virulent complaints, it was obvious she was learning a good deal. But it felt strange to be with her because I could not recognize myself in most of what she said. Concepts like 'projection' kept floating into my mind. In spite of several private talks with her, I never managed to get to the bottom of what was happening. But then, that is hardly surprising.[31]

Unlike anything I have read in the books on teaching that have come my way, I have sometimes had a learner in a class who seems bent on destroying our lessons. He or she has seemed so angry! With school pupils, there may be accepted sanctions a teacher can use. With older learners there may not be. Having an aggressive learner in one's class can be painful. I have sometimes felt like walking out. But that's the last thing one should do.

On such occasions, I have half expected the other learners in a class to help me, but that hasn't usually happened. No matter how badly a single learner may behave, the others seem to find it difficult to take a teacher's part. Teachers should not expect such help, and should not seek it. Learners expect a teacher to cope.

Occasionally, I have felt that a class almost enjoys my discomfort when I am attacked by a learner. It is as if the class had a need to see me in the hot seat for a change! There is often some anxiety in learning, and there is often one person in a group who will express the anxiety the others may be feeling. It is then important for a teacher to respond to the group's attitude, not to the learner who is expressing it. Otherwise that one learner may be made a scapegoat for the rest.

However hostile a situation may have become, it is never helpful to get into a slanging match. A teacher has a professional role to play. But as I see it, a role isn't something behind which one hides; it is rather something which helps one to avoid contaminating the professional enterprise with the merely personal.

During difficult moments, I have often found myself wondering whether I shouldn't perhaps be completely open. Perhaps I should confess that I feel hurt and inept. After all, I teach adults. They must know what it is like to feel like that. Perhaps, if one is open about such things, the learners will sympathize and respond constructively. Although I have often had such thoughts, I have seldom acted on them.

It seems to me that learners have a right to expect to have some faith in a teacher. Being a teacher is a little like being a medical doctor. I have in mind the generally accepted belief that the extent to which doctors are able to help us does not depend only on how much they know, but also on how much faith we have in them. A doctor who confesses ineptitude – rather than occasional ignorance – is unlikely to help us much. In short, I believe that the extent to which we should disclose our feelings to a class should be governed by the extent to which we believe that such disclosure will aid the total learning enterprise, not just ourselves.[32]

So in a difficult situation I count to five, try not to take the matter too personally, and try to get on with the task at hand. Humour can be a great help at such times. I find it easier to write this than to be funny at a difficult moment! But when I have managed it, I have always found it a great help.

With an especially difficult learner, I try a friendly approach first. I ask him or her to come for a chat. I try to be quietly myself, not some authority figure. And when I have done that, some learners have opened up, and all kinds of difficulties have been aired.

When I began to teach, I used to find such an experience encouraging, even flattering, and I tried my best to help. But I discovered later that it is best not to go too far in that direction. Not only can this process become extremely time-consuming, it can also become highly complex. Here is a very brief illustration.

Most people would agree that a counsellor should be supportive; and many people would agree that a teacher should sometimes be demanding. The trouble is, it isn't easy to be both. There is sometimes a contradiction between trying to be a counsellor and trying to be a teacher. For such reasons, and many others, it may be best to refer a learner with a particular difficulty to a counsellor. However, I believe it is essential to find time to chat quietly with such a learner.

Sometimes that is enough to clear the air. Sometimes it is not. I then try to convey that it is my job to get certain things done; that this is a part of an organizational endeavour; that there is a limit to the amount of difficulty any organization is able to tolerate; and that, if that learner pushes too hard, I and the organization will have to act in order to protect this endeavour. In short, and in a non-threatening way, and if suitable with a touch of humour, I try to persuade that learner to be more realistic.

Very occasionally one may find that one has a particularly aggressive learner in one's class. With that kind of learner, it is obviously best to avoid situations which are likely to generate aggression. What does not work is appeals to reason. This kind of learner seems to respond best to a calm, respectful and professional manner. All one can do is to play things by the book.

Occasionally I have had a class – more exactly, a few individuals in a class – whom I have found an ordeal no matter what I have tried to do. Such a situation has been made worse when I have known I will not get any help from higher up. In fact, I cannot remember a single instance when the two problems have not been present together. When I have known that I have the support of colleagues and superiors, I have had the confidence to tackle difficulties with a mixture of consultation, good humour, steadiness and self-reflection. Where I have known I do not have such backing, I have been unsure. That has always made things worse. These instances have given me the very worst memories of my occupational life.[33]

Superiors can be negative or positive, the same as anyone else. But many have moved into administration because they do not like teaching. If so, they are likely to have ambivalent feelings about teachers, especially teachers who take an unconventional approach.

Nor do administrators have much real contact with learners except when one of them complains. Unfortunately, there are administrators who positively seek such opportunities to show how 'responsive' they are. In a case of serious conflict, it is essential to keep written notes of dates and events. It is also important to adopt a professional approach (rather than a personal one), to be cheerful, to remain calm, and not to be too ready to accept the other person's ground-rules.

There are writers who would consider what I have written above naive, perhaps even destructive.[34] They would say that my calling certain classroom behaviour 'aggressive' is self-indulgent and obscures the real issue. They would say that all systems of knowledge are social constructs; that their main function is to serve the needs of those in power; that the behaviour which I have called 'aggressive' is a justified reaction against a fundamentally coercive social system which uses what passes for 'knowledge' to keep wealth and power in the hands of those who already have them; and they would add that I have understandably been made a target of aggression because I am the unwitting agent of that unjust social system.

Such writers might also maintain that, in labelling someone 'aggressive', rather than 'dissenting', I have devalued, even degraded, a person whose behaviour is functional. Instead of attempting to examine what such behaviour might tell us about the society in which we live, I try to silence it because it threatens my own power. I am aided in this by an army of administrators, psychologists and policemen, all of whom unwittingly act with me as agents of social control. Such alienated behaviour on our part enables those in power to retain their power.

I believe that there is some truth in such a view. But the governing word in that sentence is 'some'. First, there are levels of injustice. There are profoundly unjust social systems in many parts of the world, but, in writing this section, I have in mind countries which have a half-way reasonable social system.

Second, even when a so-called democratic country has an unjust social system (as I believe is often the case), it does not follow that aggressive behaviour towards an individual is directly caused by this unjust social system. I suspect that when a learner acts aggressively towards an individual teacher, that aggression is more likely to be caused by unjust personal circumstances. The way people behave is, of course, always embedded in, and related to, a given social system. But that does not imply a causal relationship between a social system and an individual act.[35]

These are complex matters, and it would be foolish of me to try to unravel them in the space available here. It seems essential to me that teachers should be sensitive to such issues; but that said, I think it is fair to add that, in going about their daily work, both learners and teachers have the right to expect that the people around them should behave in a way which makes personal life tolerable.

I could sum up the last two sections like this. When I began to teach, I used to feel that it was my fault if a lesson did not go well. That made me feel bad. More recently, I have come to see that teachers do not carry all the responsibility for what goes on in a lesson. There is only so much a teacher can do. And if one has done it, that's that. If the worst comes to the worst, the end of a course will always come. Then one can go one's separate ways. In the mean time, one must try to cheer oneself up by remembering classes in which things went better. Teaching has its difficult times, just like any other profession.

TEACHERS ASKING QUESTIONS

The next two sections are about asking questions. They are followed by an overview, and then we have reached the end of the book.

But now a few comments on the kinds of questions which, I believe, are most likely to encourage participation.

I have found that I encourage participation best when I ask a question which conveys that I am attempting to extend an invitation to participate, rather than wanting to test anyone. For example, instead of saying, 'How much is two and two, Ben?', I say, 'Ben, considering so and so, what would you say is two and two?' Print does not convey the tone in which something is said, but readers will know that these two questions tend to be asked in rather different ways. I think that that difference is important.

I prefer to ask a question in the way indicated because I would like to convey that my aim is not to test anyone, or to gain attention, or to assert my authority, but to encourage an enquiring approach.[36]

Learning is surely not the same as playing quiz games. That's for TV. And questions should surely not be seen as opportunities to show who is the brightest of them all. With young learners, teachers might first ask a question which requires the recall of information, but good teachers follow that with a question which requires a reasoned reply. No job in the world can be done simply by remembering facts.

Many research findings lend support to such a view. It has been found that the kinds of questions we ask help to determine the kind of learning that ensues. For example, if learners are asked only factual questions, they tend to process the material to be learnt in a superficial way. But if they are asked questions which require some 'thinking', they tend to process the material more deeply.[37]

What do we mean by 'thinking'?

A question which stimulates thinking is one that helps learners to see links between facts. This helps them to see a pattern, and readers will recall how important that is. Another kind of question which promotes thinking is one that helps learners to see the difference between a symptom and a cause. For example, in teaching history, one might ask students to consider whether Hitler caused the Second World War, or whether he was the kind of person likely to be produced by the conditions prevalent in Europe after the First World War; in teaching child development, one might ask students to consider whether a child's stealing reflects something about the child, or about its environment. Another kind of question that promotes thinking is one which helps learners to see why an inference may (or may not) be justified. And perhaps nothing encourages thinking more than a practical project, especially one which is of an experimental or observational nature, and which comes at the beginning, rather than at the end, of a course.

Good questions probe below the surface. They help learners to discern an underlying structure. That is important because most structures are hidden from casual view.[38] One of the most important results of being educated is that it alerts us to the need to look beyond surface features, beyond the immediately apparent. Perhaps a simple example will help to illustrate what I mean.

Family doctors are often criticized for prescribing medication for every complaint we bring them. They seem to treat us as if we were a chemical exchange system, rather than as 'a whole person'. Tell them you have a sore shoulder, and they are very likely to prescribe a pill. Why don't they consider that we may feel tense? Why do they take such a narrow view? The trouble is, the moment we think about it, we realize that not all of them can be stupid. So why do many act as I have described? Many reasons have been put forward. Here is one.

Consider what happens when we bring in a car for repair. Until quite recently, if a part was faulty, a mechanic would try to repair it. Today a mechanic will usually replace a faulty part with a new one because labour tends to be more expensive than parts. Compare that with family doctors.

Until about thirty years ago, if we went to doctors with a sore shoulder, they would sit with us, talk to us, perhaps even give us a massage! Unless it was essential, they would think twice before they prescribed a medicine, because medicines were expensive. But, as labour increasingly becomes dearer than goods, doctors tend to spend less time with us, and prescribe medicines instead. In other words, a consideration of the underlying costs – as well as other factors – can help us to understand why doctors often act in the way they do.

Beginner teachers sometimes find it difficult to frame questions which require learners to think, especially in the middle of a lesson. If so, they might find it helpful to jot down before a lesson the questions they could ask. Eventually, with practice, one gets used to framing higher-level questions. One then feels embarrassed about asking the childish kind which can be answered with two words.

It has also been found that good teachers seldom need to:

- rephrase their question; or
- answer their own question.

When teachers do these things, there are probably two reasons. The first must be because they have not managed to make themselves clear.[39]

The second reason is more important.

Consider first that when a teacher asks a question, it is usually on the basis of what has gone on before; and the link is clear to the teacher. But it may be unclear to the learners. So they sit there, looking interested, vacant or bored. Teachers are then tempted to rephrase their question, or to answer it themselves. If they do, they are unlikely to help their learners.

Teachers then sometimes repeat the question. If one does, one may manage to wring an answer out of one of the learners. But it will often be wrong. Earlier I suggested that, when that happens, it is a good idea to ask that learner how he or she has got to that answer. If that is done in a friendly way, the learner will explain. A teacher will then usually be able to see where that learner has got to. One can then go there, and help that learner to extricate himself from the thicket in which he is stuck.

In other words, a good question often helps a teacher to enter a learner's frame of reference. It offers opportunities for clarification, not testing. And if one is consistent about that, learners will see how useful the practice is, and will then be more likely to want to participate.

A technique often used in teaching is 'Question and Answer'. In this a teacher attempts to lead the learners to a certain conclusion by asking them a series of questions. I have already suggested that this technique has many disadvantages. It tends to make learners follow a teacher passively, and to make them play the 'Guess the Answer the Teacher Wants' game. It also tends to prevent teachers from exploring the answers which learners offer, because they are usually too concerned with getting the answer they want.

I have often seen this technique used. But, except with the youngest of learners, I have seldom seen it foster participation. On the contrary, it seems to cause resentment and apathy. Teachers sense this, feel bad, but do not usually see what is causing such a state of affairs. Instead, they often conclude that their learners do not want to participate, in spite of their sincere endeavour to encourage it.

When I am about to introduce a new topic to a class, I sometimes wonder whether I should ask if somebody knows anything about it. If one of the learners does, why not encourage him or her to speak? But I increasingly hold back from doing that. I have found, when I encourage a learner to introduce a new topic, that that learner will often not really know it well enough. When that happens, I have to do some correcting. The learner who has spoken may then feel put down, and the other learners may get a confused view. So I have come to see that it is better to introduce a new topic myself, and only then to ask for reactions to it.

I have already made a few suggestions on how a teacher might respond to a learner's answer. As that is such an important topic, a few more comments may be helpful.

Having got a thoughtful, but probably incomplete reply, one can nod and smile, or thank a speaker. As I said, one should not evaluate or repeat an answer. Instead, it is much better to acknowledge the reply in a friendly way, and then to look around. I try to show by my expression that I am hoping for more contributions. Often I am met by silence, especially with a new class.

I think I speak for most teachers if I say that we tend to find such silences troubling. When a silence continues for a little time, many teachers want to say something in order to end it. Many teachers find *not* doing that, but allowing a silence to continue, stressful. The odd thing is that learners hardly notice these silences. They are usually too busy trying to work out a possible answer.

Unfortunately, they are seldom given enough time to do that. Research has shown that the majority of teachers do not wait for more than one second after they have asked a question. If they do not get a response within that time, they tend to

- repeat their question;
- rephrase it;
- ask another question; or
- call on another student for an answer.

If the usual two-word answer comes, they repeat it, then ask their next question – all in less than one second. To anyone who has had an opportunity to observe this process, the main impression conveyed is one of a teacher incessantly talking.

Research shows two other things: that teachers tend not to be aware of this pattern; and that when they do become aware of it, and wait for three or more seconds after they have asked a question, their learners tend to be affected in the following ways:

- the length of their responses increases;
- the number of their spontaneous and pertinent comments increases;
- the learners' confidence when responding increases;
- learners comment more frequently on each other's responses;
- usually quiet learners respond more frequently;
- the learners ask more questions.[40]

So, when there is a silence after I have asked a question, or one of the learners has given an incomplete reply, I try not to say anything. I lean back and wait. More often than not, if I am patient, the same learner will continue speaking, or another will offer a contribution. Again I try to listen as carefully as I can. When that speaker has finished, I express my appreciation through look or gesture, then look around expectantly again.

If no one says anything, and I feel some encouragement may be helpful, I turn to a learner and ask her by name what she thinks. Using names is important. It suggests a teacher is interested in what a particular learner may be thinking. I try to involve as many people as possible, but of course I seldom press anyone to reply.[41]

Another thing I occasionally do, when there is a silence after a learner has spoken, is to laugh, and to say something like, 'It's disappointing, isn't it? You say something real bright, and no one says a thing! It happens to me all the time.'

As learners get used to this approach, they increasingly speak to each other. And when I think it is appropriate, I come in, too. Sometimes I come in because I can't help myself! That usually happens when somebody has said something I consider outrageous. And if I am not too vehement, that might spark off more comment. And so it goes, until I feel no more will be usefully said.

Notice how often this process takes place in everyday life. For example, when two people are speaking, and the first one says, 'Let's meet at the entrance to the supermarket', the second one is very likely to say, 'Do you mean the main entrance, or the entrance in the car-park?' Even in a situation as straightforward as that, a discussion is often necessary to get something clear.

Like most teachers, I am sometimes asked a question. When I am, I usually ask the learner who has asked the question what she thinks. The moment a learner has asked a question, that learner has indicated an awareness that there is an answer. I have found, when I return a question like that, that most learners are able to answer their own question. This suggests that they often ask a question to get corroboration for an answer they already have in their heads. I would have thought that being given a chance to state one's own answer, and finding that it is correct, is the best kind of corroboration.

If a learner can't offer an answer to her own question, I turn to the others in the class and ask what they think. Nine times out of ten, somebody will suggest an answer.

If nobody can answer a question which has been raised, and I can, I mostly do. And if I can't, I (usually) say I can't. I then ask the learner who has asked the question to find the answer for us. After all, it was her question.

In short, I seldom answer a question when it is first directed at me. Instead, I deflect it back to the class. That encourages participation, and I believe it also fosters a spirit of co-operative enquiry.

Very occasionally, when a question is raised, I 'brainstorm': I invite the learners to get into small groups, and to suggest any and every solution that comes to mind. The important thing is to accept every suggestion made, no matter how absurd it may seem.

Answers so obtained seldom result in anything better than what a single student might have suggested. But the process of 'brainstorming,' can have the effect of encouraging participation. However, I think it is very important not to use brainstorming to find an answer when it would be more appropriate to do some study.

Teachers sometimes say that their learners don't ask them any questions, even when they ask them whether they have any. If those teachers are using the transmission method of teaching, that is hardly surprising. Participation does not depend on whether a teacher invites it at a particular time, but on whether it has been encouraged throughout a lesson. Perhaps this comment will illustrate what I meant when I suggested earlier that 'communications' should not be seen as a subject in its own light, but as the manifestation of everything that goes on in a lesson.

There is one question which seldom elicits any response. It is the question, 'Are there any questions?' It usually comes when a didactic teacher has finally stopped talking. It seems to mean, 'I have finished. Do you want me to continue?' If we have had to listen to somebody talk non-stop for an hour, we are usually relieved when he or she has finally finished.

LEARNERS ASKING QUESTIONS

It is usually the teacher who asks most of the questions in a lesson, and we tend to take such a state of affairs for granted. However, it might be an idea to examine that custom for a moment. After all, the answers we understand and remember best of all tend to be the answers to the questions we have asked ourselves. If so, teachers might help their learners if they could contrive things so that it is the learners who ask more of the questions.

Consider research which compares the way young children behave at home with the way they behave at nursery school. This research found that

> teachers were in no position to satisfy the children's curiosity because the children hardly ever asked them any questions. The girls asked their mothers on average twenty-six questions an hour, but they only asked two questions an hour of their teachers. Nearly half the children (fourteen) asked five questions or less during two mornings at school, and a further three children asked no questions at all at school.[42]

These researchers go on to report that 'of those questions that were asked at school, a much smaller proportion were "curiosity" questions and "why" questions, and a much larger proportion were "business" questions, of the "Where is the glue?" type, than was the case at home'. The researchers also note that challenging questions, or questions which suggested a child was trying to understand something, were entirely absent at school.

Why do young children ask many intelligent questions at home but hardly any at school, the place where they are supposed to be doing most of their learning?

These researchers suggest two answers. One: that teachers consider it their job to ask questions and do so; but that, in doing so, they unintentionally convey that it is the teacher who asks the questions. And two: that the kinds of question teachers ask tend to be about what is going on in school; but children's questions at home tend to be about life in general, and it is this which naturally interests them the most.

Of course, it isn't only children who ask questions. Most people, of whatever age, try to find out what is going on around them. Would it be possible to tap this inherent wish to understand, and arrange things so that it is the learners who ask more of the questions?

We know that creative scientists and artists always begin their work with a question. They ask: 'Why is this the way it is?', or: 'How can I express that idea in a fresh and striking way?' The most creative among them are then sometimes able to answer their own question, and these are the ones who become famous.

In other words, the most eminent scientists and artists are not people who know a lot. They often do know a lot. But more important than that, they are people who see questions where most of us do not. (How does one program a computer to ask intelligent questions which no one has thought of asking before?)[43] In short, being creative is firstly a matter of discovering a question.

The trouble with forgetting that there must first be a question before you can have an answer, is that this can have the effect of making you believe that the answer was always somehow 'there', waiting to be learnt. Perhaps that explains why many learners find classrooms rather unreal, for they are often places in which you are expected to learn an answer without first knowing what the question is.

How can we encourage learners to ask questions? Not the kind which ask for clarification about something we have already said, but the kind which children ask their mothers at home. Questions like: why is water wet? why does a cut hurt? why do I look strange in a mirror? (Readers may incidentally notice from these examples that powerful thinking depends, to a considerable extent, on realizing that it is the most obvious things which are the most mysterious.) It would clearly aid learning if we could contrive things so that it is the learners who ask more of these kind of questions. But how?

I am far from sure I know. Perhaps the best thing I can do is to outline how I approach the matter in my own lessons. That way, if I am wrong, readers may be able to see why I am wrong and go on from there.

First, in every lesson I try to show that most knowledge has come about because somebody has discovered a question. I try to show this in one of two ways. Either I invite the learners to say what they find problematic about a certain matter; or I draw attention to the questions that have led researchers and scholars to give us the answers which now constitute that 'subject'. In the latter case, I try to restate those questions so that they are real questions. Then I invite the learners to try to answer them. As some of them do, I try to encourage further speculation.[44]

Second, as the learners begin to see the complexities involved, I outline some of the difficulties and answers which have been suggested. I do that either by giving a short talk, or by handing out brief material for examination. I have already written about the kind of worksheets I use, and how the learners tackle them. I give this material to the learners, do as little explaining as possible, and try to encourage the learners to tackle the material as directly as they can. When I act like this, and the material is of the right size and complexity, it often raises further questions in the learners' minds. I never dictate anything, and I never talk with the expectation that notes will be taken.

Possibly as a result of going about things like this, a few learners often tell me, in the first few weeks after we have begun a course, that, although they have sometimes enjoyed a lesson, they don't feel that they are learning very much. Others say that they have very few notes, and can hardly remember what we have done from one lesson to the next. Because some of these learners are angry or upset when they say these things, I get upset, too.

In response, I try to reassure. I say that our work in class is only an introduction; that whatever real learning is going to take place will take place when the learners get to work on their assignments. Most of the learners seem to find this reasonable, but sometimes it may be for the wrong reason. Many see assignments as tasks in which you reproduce knowledge, and many learnt how to do that at an early age when they discovered that learning is often taken to be the same as remembering.

That brings us to the final factor: how can we foster learning which is more than remembering?

I have tried to answer that question throughout this book. I believe that the last and most important factor is the way assignments are set. In a nutshell, I have come to see that assignments should be seen primarily in terms of learning – not testing.

Assignments become a part of the learning process when the learners are required to do two things:

- learn something which has been carefully specified; and
- apply what they have learnt to their personal or professional circumstances.

I have found, when these two things are done, that learners often produce work which shows that they have, at least to some extent, 'really' learnt. I say 'to some extent', because learning never reaches an optimal level until learners use their learning practically in the real world. But work done for this kind of assignment seems to lay a good foundation. Such assignments often convey a sense of immediacy, of 'felt-experience', sometimes even of personal urgency.

In time, the majority of learners warm to such an approach. But there are always a few who seem to find it confusing. Previous experience has led them to believe that learning is a matter of remembering, and they seem to get upset when they are asked to apply their understanding to the real world.

The approach described above seems self-evident to me. However, as noted, some learners find it confusing, and a few complain bitterly. That happens every year, and every year I am as surprised and dismayed as when it happened the year before. The criticism most often made is that I am not 'clear'. It took me some time to understand what that word 'clear' means when it is used in this way. It means a teacher who 'tells' rather than asks learners to consider a question.

Every year I feel the approach I use must be wrong. The trouble is, I find I can't change back to didactic teaching even when I want to. So I continue teaching as I do, often feeling bad, often feeling clumsy, and sometimes feeling so bad I want to give up teaching altogether. But I continue, deriving some comfort from the understanding of learning I presented in the first half of this book, and occasionally cheered by a word of encouragement from a learner who seems to like what I am doing.[45]

Then, as a course continues, a few learners begin to smile in class. Later, as the course draws to an end, a few even tell me that they have never learnt so much. It is at times like these that I begin to think that perhaps teaching has become learning.

TEACHERS AND PARTICIPATION

The past few sections have been on classroom interaction. It may now be helpful to describe the kinds of difficulties and rewards which the student-teachers with whom I have worked have experienced when they have tried to develop the kind of approach described in this book.

I should like to begin by recalling a lesson I described earlier – the one which I and 160 other learners had to attend, and in which there was considerable participation. While on that same course, there was an elective on cognition, and I decided to take it. There were about fifteen of us in that class. The man who taught it – a specialist in teacher education – began his first lesson by saying that he did not think anybody would learn much if he lectured; that he soon got tired of the sound of his own voice; that he proposed to run his classes in the form of seminars; and that he thought we would all learn more if we discussed things.

For the rest of that term, in that man's class, we mainly heard his voice. That experience strengthened my belief that we tend to speak most about what we would like, rather than what is. Perhaps that is why so much love poetry is about the lady who wouldn't say yes.

I am quite sure that that teacher would have liked more participation, but facilitating participation isn't easy. I have found that it takes several months before most student-teachers are able to manage it; and I think it takes that long for mainly three reasons.

The first is related to the fact that, before one is able to practise a more open approach, one must unlearn a good deal about teaching first, especially the things one has learnt from being a learner. That is difficult. In the discussion of the formation of schemata, we saw that having experienced something, we learn it, and in that way it becomes a physical part of ourselves. That means we can act on it automatically; and what we can do automatically usually feels 'right'.

The second reason a change to a new teaching approach is difficult is that it can't be picked up by listening to a teacher, watching TV, or reading a book. It must be experienced.

The third reason encouraging participation is difficult is that more than developing a 'skill' or a 'competence' is involved. That is, before one can adopt a more open approach, one has to change as a person to some extent. For example, one has to become less directive, yet remain reasonably confident that one's lessons won't fall apart.

Having noted these three difficulties, here are some practical suggestions on how they might be overcome.

Many years of observing and talking with teachers has suggested to me that the following factors help a teacher to overcome the problems involved in adopting a more open approach:

- knowing one's subject really well;
- having a very strong desire for more participation;
- feeling reasonably confident that one's learners will not tear one's lesson apart if one opens it to more participation;
- observing a teacher who uses the approach suggested here and seeing that he or she feels reasonably comfortable with it;
- the presence of someone who is supportive and knowledgeable.

Here are a few further observations on the above.

Teachers obviously have to know their subject really well. If one is unsure about the material one is supposed to be teaching, one is going to be nervous about anything which might show up one's deficiencies. As a result, one will want to keep tight control of a lesson. The best way of doing that is to talk non-stop. Participation is then impossible. It is also difficult to keep having to refer to lesson notes, and to interact with learners.

The second factor is also obvious, but not so obvious, for it implies a certain attitude to others and to life.

With regard to the third factor, I have found that having the confidence that learners won't tear one's lesson apart isn't so much a matter of being able to do anything in particular, but of not being too afraid of anything in particular. Many student-teachers have told me that, until they had actually tried a more open approach, and accepted the possible risk, they were unable to deal with that risk. However, once they had taken it, they found that their fear had been greatly exaggerated. In fact, it was difficult to remember it afterwards.

As to the fourth factor, it helps to observe an experienced teacher practise an open approach because that will provide one with a role model with which one can compare oneself. The importance of this may be gauged by the following. It has been found that simply viewing oneself teach on a video film, in the absence of having a model of good teaching in one's head, does not result in much improvement in one's teaching.[46]

Lastly the fifth factor.

Readers may recall the tutor-librarian named Betty described earlier. When writing about her, I noted that, with a very few exceptions, when I first observe a student-teacher teach, there is seldom much participation in the lesson, even when the student-teacher has expressed enthusiasm for the approach to teaching suggested in this book.

In other words, I have repeatedly found that my 'theory' lessons, on their own, do not produce any significant 'practical' results. So much so, I have come to believe that, when I don't work together with student-teachers (by observing them teach and discussing their teaching with them afterwards) then my theory lessons are largely a waste of time.

But that is exactly what is to be expected if the account of learning presented in this book is broadly correct. Of course, the above may merely indicate that I am an ineffective teacher. But the following observation, by another teacher from a very different discipline, suggests that it may not be my ineptitude which is responsible for the fact that my theory lessons have so little practical effect:

> The belief is very generally held that if only we are told what to do in order to correct a wrong way of doing something, we can do it, and that if we *feel* we are doing it, all is well. All my experience, however, goes to shew that this belief is a delusion.[47]

That comment may sound provocative. It is not intended to be. It is simply the case that the moment one says something that flies in the face of widespread belief and practice, one sounds provocative. I give this quotation here, in part, to remind readers of the material on learning presented in the first half of this book.

When I visit student-teachers, I usually look at their lesson plan before I observe them teach. (As we saw, a lesson plan indicates what the learners and the teacher will do at various times during a lesson.) I have then had the following repeated experience. I will see, from a lesson plan, that a teacher intends the learners to discuss something at a certain point in the lesson; but when I observe the actual lesson, I often find that there is no real discussion in it (usually because the teacher has dominated the lesson).

After the lesson, the teacher and I will have a chat, and it then often becomes painfully apparent that this teacher actually believes that there has been a discussion in that lesson. In short, I have found that teachers often *genuinely believe that they are doing something which they are not doing.*

A sympathetic observer can gently draw the attention of a student-teacher to such a state of affairs. Most student-teachers will be defensive, sometimes hurt, quite often angry. It is then extremely important not to insist. If the relationship between student-teacher and observer is one of mutual respect and some affection, it is enough when something has been mentioned lightly.

Where resources allow, a video of that teacher at work, in a real classroom, and at his or her request, can also help. When viewing such a video after a lesson, a teacher will often say things like, 'I didn't really give that student a chance to answer . . .', or, 'I shouldn't have said anything at that point. . . . It's amazing, I didn't even notice it at the time. . . .' Here, too, a tutor can help by listening sympathetically, and by corroborating *in an unobtrusive way.*

The student-teacher now needs time to reflect, and opportunities to practise in a supportive environment. Some student-teachers prefer to practise on their own, because the more open style of teaching suggested here is risky.

Whatever the details, I have found that it is only when a student-teacher and a sympathetic observer have had *repeated opportunities* for the kind of exchanges noted above that progress is made.[48]

Above I noted my belief in the need for a relationship of mutual respect and some affection between student-teacher and tutor. I did this because I have occasionally found myself working with a student-teacher where such a relationship has not developed. I have then felt unable to make a useful contribution. Fortunately, there has usually been a colleague with whom I can exchange duties, and I have withdrawn.

I should also note that I have sometimes found myself working with a student-teacher with whom a cordial relationship has developed, but whose teaching has remained essentially didactic no matter what I have tried to do. Such a teacher has always told me that the approach to teaching suggested in this book 'does not suit my subject or my learners'.

He or she will say that the learners are too old, or too young, or too inexperienced, or too sophisticated, or too traditional, or too unruly. Sometimes the subject is said to be too factual or too loose. Always the problem is either the subject or the learners. These experiences have suggested to me that the single most important quality required to become a more effective teacher is the ability to consider and reconsider one's teaching honestly. When that is impossible, there is nothing much that can be done.

Above I drew attention to some of the factors involved when student-teachers acquire a more open approach. I should like to add my belief in the importance of the following:

- considering the materials on learning and teaching presented in the earlier part of this book;
- doing assignments which apply the work of Holt, Abercrombie and Rogers to one's own teaching;[49] and
- observing the struggles of myself, or another teacher, to teach in what I have called an open way.

We all know that change is difficult. Nevertheless I have found that a remarkable change often takes place in the teaching of those with whom I have worked. Instead of them talking for most of a lesson, a participative atmosphere develops. Their learners don't spend most of a lesson listening or writing notes, but frequently grappling with and reshaping their understanding of the material they are trying to learn.

That brings a lightness to such lessons. Occasionally, a learner may express some frustration, but these episodes usually pass quickly enough. In general, the majority of learners are much more cheerful, more actively engaged, and much more thoughtful with such an approach, and I have often seen student-teachers beam with the pleasure that this can bring.

Chapter 9

Overview

THE OCCASIONAL LESSON

This chapter contains two sections. In these I describe a number of different lessons, and I do that in the hope that this will provide readers with an overview of the approach to teaching suggested in this book.

The teacher in the first lesson is a young woman named Sara. She is a dietitian in a large hospital, and one of her duties is to give a talk on diet in pregnancy, to mothers who come to this hospital for a weekly antenatal class.

When I first observed Sara teach, she gave the kind of talk which is common on such occasions. She began at 2 p.m. and finished at 3.15 p.m., and near the end of the talk she asked if there were any questions. She was asked one or two, she answered them, and then she smiled and thanked the women present for their attendance. As the women left, I thought Sara had put on a good performance. But I wondered how much her learners had really learnt.

This certainly isn't an easy kind of class to teach. The 'students' have varying levels of understanding, varying backgrounds, and varying needs. It can be difficult to address strangers, and it can be difficult to encourage people who are strangers to talk to each other. It is also difficult to know just what people have gained from attending such a class.

Here is how Sara taught the same topic on one of my later visits.

It is a Thursday afternoon, and we are in a pleasant enough room in a hospital. Sara enters the class a few minutes before the lesson and arranges the seats in a circle. As people come in, she greets them, asks their names, jots these down, introduces herself, and invites people to sit in the circle. As more people come in, she exchanges comments about the weather, where they live, and how they reached the hospital.

Aside from twelve expectant mothers, there is one husband, two student nurses, and me. The nurses and I are introduced as interested in the topic, and for the rest of the lesson we are treated the same as everyone else. Five of the mothers are of Asian origin, two are of West Indian origin, and one of the Asian women appears not to understand English very well.

Sara sits in the circle. When we are all settled, she announces the topic of the lesson: 'Diet in Pregnancy'. She says that many of us will know a good deal about healthy eating, and that she hopes we will contribute our knowledge to the class. Then she asks if anyone would like to ask something.

For a moment there is silence. Sara smiles and waits. Then one of the women says she still suffers from morning sickness. Sara nods, does not say anything, but her face shows she is listening. Several women nod their heads. One woman nods emphatically. Sara asks her if she has the same problem. The woman describes her symptoms, and goes on to say how she has found some relief. Another woman adds a comment. Sara nods, turns to another woman and asks her whether what has been said tallies with her experiences. The woman says something quietly. Sara says she fears the others may not have heard. The woman raises her voice and addresses the whole class. Another woman comes in with a few more comments. Finally Sara reports very briefly what is usually recommended in such a case, and adds that the speakers had themselves made several useful suggestions.

Then Sara says it might be an idea to consider what kind of diet is best for a pregnant woman. She says it has been found that a healthy diet consists of a balanced intake of four kinds of food: calcium foods, protein foods, vitamin foods and energy foods.

Sara has a set of colourful posters on the floor next to her chair. She has made them herself. They have pictures of foods, and under them Sara has written in bold letters to which group they belong. She holds the posters up, and points to the foods. She talks in a cheery manner, without in the least putting on a show. She sounds more like a person chatting than a teacher giving a talk. Her introduction takes about five minutes.

Next she gives out sheets of paper which contain three case studies. The first reads: 'Mrs Patel is a strict vegetarian and has a part-time job. She is a bit underweight and has some problems with morning sickness. Suggest a healthy diet for her to cover three days.'

Sara asks the women to get into groups of three, and to note their recommendations for each case. She places the posters in a line against a wall. She has a few pencils handy for those who might need one.

At first no one moves.

The people in the room smile, look a little uneasy, and move their chairs about an inch. But with a little encouragement, a few smiles, a quietly assured manner, and herself helping to move chairs, Sara soon gets her 'students' to sit in groups of three. What happens next might surprise anyone who has not witnessed such a thing before. After a minute or two of silence, most of the people present begin to chat. And within about three minutes the talk in some groups is lively.

Several things soon become apparent. The Asian woman, the one who seemed to find English difficult, actually speaks it quite well; one of the groups contains a health visitor who is knowledgeable; and the woman who had spoken quietly in the full class is happy to chat in a small group. While the 'students' work, Sara sits to one side.

It takes the learners about six minutes to complete the case studies. Then Sara invites comment. There is no 'reporting back' stage, and no use of a flip-chart to summarize. When one person says something, Sara does not repeat or evaluate it, and she seldom elaborates herself. All through she remains seated in the circle.

Now and again Sara asks a question. When she does, it does not require merely factual recall. Her questions always come after she has reported some information, or after someone has made a statement. She then asks people for their reaction. When someone replies, she uses that contribution for further discussion by asking what someone else thinks. Sometimes she makes a point herself. Often there is enough collective knowledge in the room to supply information and correct misconceptions without her having to say much.

Next Sara begins another talk. She reminds the class that it is considered inadvisable to eat large quantities of certain foods. She mentions over-refined foods, animal fats, salt, sugar and alcohol. She notes that there are good reasons to suspect that large quantities of these are implicated in certain maladies. She cites one or two pieces of research by name and gives their date. She is obviously well read, but her expertise is unobtrusive. Her talk lasts about five minutes. She frequently stops, invites comment, and in this way encourages the active participation of the learners.

Next Sara gives out a worksheet. It contains two 'diets'. Sara asks the learners to examine them and to suggest improvements. Here they are.

> DIET ONE
> *Breakfast*: toast (white), butter, marmalade, fried bacon and eggs, tea and sugar. *Mid-morning snack*: coffee (with milk and sugar), chocolate biscuit. *Lunch*: egg sandwich, potato crisps, ice-cream, Coca-Cola. *Tea*: tea (with milk and sugar), jam tart with cream, chocolate cake. *Evening meal*: fried fish or ham, chips. *Late evening TV snack*: beer, peanuts (salted).
>
> DIET TWO
> *Breakfast*: toast (wholemeal), butter, orange juice, tea (without sugar). *Mid-morning snack*: coffee (black with sweetener). *Lunch*: tinned low-calorie tomato soup, bread roll (wheatmeal), butter, banana, diet Coke. *Tea*: coffee (black with sweetener). *Evening meal*: baked potato, butter, coleslaw salad, coffee (black with sweetener).

Again there is an initial silence. But this time she has to do much less encouraging. Discussions are soon under way while Sara sits to one side.

When the tasks have been completed, Sara invites the people present to form a circle again and to relate the improvements they have recommended. At first no one says a word. Sara makes a humorous reference to her own diet; another woman mentions hers and laughs; Sara turns to the one husband present and asks him what he has recommended; and soon a new discussion is under way.

When it falters, Sara turns to one of the people in the circle and asks her by name what she thinks. (She takes the name from the list she quickly compiled at the beginning of the lesson.) She sounds as if she is extending an invitation to participate rather than asking a question.

In the last quarter-hour Sara gives out a question-sheet containing twenty short items. They cover a good deal of the material discussed so far. One question asks whether skimmed milk contains less calcium than whole milk; another whether a baby is harmed by cigarette smoke in a room; another whether a breast-fed infant can get drunk if its mother drinks a gin and tonic.

Sara invites the learners to answer the questions in pairs, and with a smile promises those who get all the answers right two gold stars. When they have finished, Sara encourages the more outspoken ones to give their answers. The others protest or agree.

Five minutes before the end, Sara gives out a crossword puzzle she has herself devised. The clues and answers summarize the objectives of the lesson. She suggests that the women might like to try it on their husbands when they get home. One clue reads: 'plenty of fibre helps'. The answer is: 'constipation'. There are smiles all round as people leave.

The above is a threadbare description. It does not convey the quality of the many comments these women exchanged, Sara's deft responses, her touches of humour, and especially her thoughtful, encouraging and pleasant manner. Even so, I hope I have managed to show how incomparably better a lesson this was than her first one.

I believe it was better for at least the following reasons.

If we agree that nobody is likely to remember more than a fraction of the information that can be conveyed in one hour, twenty-four hours after they have heard it, it is clear that attempting to convey a great deal of information in such a lesson is a waste of time. In any case, the main aim in such a lesson is not so much to convey information as to encourage a certain attitude. That is far more likely to occur if the clients are able to participate.

Furthermore, people tend to get bored when they have to listen to one person speak for more than ten or fifteen minutes at a time. Some teachers are born entertainers, but most of us are not. Anyway, why should those of us who do not have the gift of the gab assume a role which has no educational value?

Next, unless a learner is given repeated opportunities to speak, there will be no way to check whether any learning has taken place. Nor will there be any opportunities to correct misconceptions.

It is also very easy to assume that learners know less than they actually do. In Sara's lesson, one of the learners (the Asian lady) knew more than might have been expected. Most groups of people have considerable collective knowledge, and unless people are given opportunities to speak, this source of knowledge remains untapped.

But readers will have noticed that this lesson was not based on 'having a discussion'. Most such lessons are fatuous. Sara introduced topics briefly with unobtrusive expertise. She had also prepared excellent learning materials which were simple yet professional, and she invited her learners to consider them in small groups. In this way, scholarship and sociability were combined. As a result, opportunities were created for people to learn new information actively, and to check on whether they understood that information.

Sara may even have managed to help some of the women to become acquainted. That would be a real achievement. In the Western world many mothers tend to feel isolated when they first have a baby. It would be a great bonus to come to such a class and perhaps become acquainted with another woman in similar circumstances who lives locally. Teaching in the way she did, Sara may have managed to encourage such possible contacts much better than if she had taught didactically.

It had taken Sara time and effort to prepare her learning materials. But, having made them, she could now use them again and again. And not only had they helped her learners to learn, they would also serve as useful summaries when the women got home.

Lastly, readers may like to note that Sara achieved what she did with total strangers, and in a single encounter.

There is a tendency in some training circles to believe that content determines method; that the way we teach depends on the subject we teach. A symptom of this can be seen when training programmes are put on for specific occupational groups.

The implications of such a position are serious. One of them is that no general teaching principles are possible except at the simplest level. All through this book I have argued the opposite. The lesson described in this section was on 'Diet in Pregnancy'; an earlier chapter contained a description of a lesson on 'Computer Engineering'. No two subjects could be more different, yet the approach to teaching in both is basically the same. It is the same because it is based on what I believe is a viable theory of learning and teaching.

Readers may also have noticed that the lessons described in this book have all been with adult learners. I have described such lessons because I believe I must provide descriptions of lessons I have actually observed. However, I hope it will be agreed that the approach to teaching illustrated here lends itself not only to any subject but also to most learners.

VARIATIONS ON A THEME

The first lesson to be described in this section is an induction. An induction is sometimes used when one wishes to introduce learners to an establishment. In this lesson the teacher is called Michael and he is a senior instructor at a community education centre. Training schemes for adults, and courses on subjects from art to yoga, are on offer here.

Today a dozen newcomers are to be introduced to the centre. In the past, this had been done by giving them a talk. Later they were escorted around the centre by various members of staff. Today Michael has decided to go about things like this.

We assemble in a classroom, and Michael says a few words of greeting. He gives a brief outline of the centre, then calls on two members of staff to introduce themselves. All this takes about ten minutes.

Michael then says he doesn't think it would be helpful if he were to continue speaking, as those present would soon forget what he has said, and that it might be a better idea to give out a question-sheet. He hands these out, and asks the people present to respond to them in pairs.

He says the questions can be dealt with by looking around, or by asking somebody. He says he thinks two hours are probably enough, and he ends by asking everyone to hand in their completed question-sheets at the reception desk.

I take one of the sheets. The first item asks for the location of three rooms; the third asks what one should do in the event of a fire; and the fifth asks for the names of three members of staff. Here are some of the other questions:

Give your impression of the cafeteria; name two places of interest in walking distance of the centre; state how to make a claim for expenses; give the names of the librarians on duty this morning; suggest the title of a book you would like to see in the library; state what you should do if you cannot come to the centre; write a paragraph to introduce your partner.

It is clear that Michael could have provided answers to most of those questions himself. That is what he had always done in the past. He had talked for about an hour; he had got other members of staff to talk; they had taken parties of people around the centre; and he had always finished with a nagging doubt about the value of what had been achieved.

Doing it this new way, two things were for sure: no one was told what they already knew; and newcomers got to know the centre a little better. He also felt that an independent and friendly attitude had been fostered.

The approach illustrated above can be used for other learning purposes.[1] Learners can be given a list of questions (or check items) and asked to examine a factory, brook, station, library, copse, office, hay-barn, fire-station or any other location. A great deal can be learnt by careful observation. These observations can then be put together systematically in various ways, and learners often feel a much greater sense of personal engagement when they work in this way.

A variant is to supply a set of criteria, and invite the participants to apply them to specific circumstances. I saw a first-class example of this during a training course for park-keepers. They were given a summary of recent regulations on the use of pesticides, taken to a shed in which horticultural materials were stored, and asked to respond to ten questions on whether the manner of storage conformed to the regulations.

For some lessons it might be helpful to use the learners' own questions. In a preliminary lesson a teacher could ask the learners to jot down six questions to which they would like an answer. On the basis of those questions, a teacher could produce a booklet containing a list of the most pertinent questions which had been asked, a few pages of information on the basis of which some of those questions could be answered, and a further page containing a list of sources from which additional information could be obtained. The learners could be given the booklet, and asked to respond in writing to the questions which they had themselves put forward. Alternatively, the class could be divided into small groups, and each group asked to prepare a mini-lecture on one of the questions in the booklet.

Teachers are sometimes asked to give a talk on a specific topic to a group of strangers. That can be difficult, partly because it can be hard to know at what level to pitch one's talk. I have found it helpful to begin by asking the learners what they hope to gain from the talk. When I have consulted the learners like that, I have sometimes discovered what is wanted and what is already known. That way, the learners have also seemed more interested in what is to come.

I have found that I have to be patient if I begin in this way. Not all learners are used to being consulted, and many may be expecting a Performance. Some may also feel uncomfortable about speaking in front of others. So one has to ask one's question, sit back – and wait.

I have found, if I act like that, that somebody is sure to speak. I then don't repeat or evaluate what has been said, and I don't elaborate either. Instead, I acknowledge the comment with a nod or smile, look around, and hope for further comment. When I feel enough has been said, I try to summarize very briefly what I think has been said. Then I ask if I have got the matter right.

More discussion may then develop, and this may continue for some time. I then have to weigh up whether I should encourage the discussion to continue, or to begin my talk. The learners may find a discussion more useful than anything I could say, because it may help them to clarify for themselves what they find problematic about a topic.

Sometimes I have found that such a discussion is getting us nowhere. Some of the participants seem to want to use the occasion to attract attention, others to air a pet idea. When this kind of thing happens, it is obviously best to thank the contributors and to begin one's talk.

After I have spoken for a little while, I pause and invite comment. If I begin in the manner just described, somebody usually comments; and these comments often help to clear up a misunderstanding, or add something which has been left out.[2] It seems to me that such comments are more valuable than using that time to convey more information, for, after all, the learners will forget most of this information a day after they have heard it. Many learners seem to prefer such an approach, perhaps in part because it helps them to get to know each other a little better.

There is always a day when learners and a teacher meet for the first time. Teachers then often wish they could help their learners to get to know each other, as they know that this facilitates communication, and is also welcomed by most learners. There are activities for doing that, and they are commonly called 'ice breakers'.

The following list of activities may be helpful for such occasions.

Ask the learners to get into pairs, and to interview each other briefly. Then ask each person to introduce the person they have interviewed to the whole group.

Invite the learners to give their name (and possibly how they got it), and to say a few words about their interests.

Invite the learners to approach someone in the class to whom they have not yet spoken, and to exchange a few pleasantries with that person.

At one time I used to worry that, if I suggested such an activity, some people might think it artificial. But I have now quite lost this fear. Such activities can help to relieve the sense of awkwardness many of us feel when we first find ourselves with strangers, and most people are pleased when a teacher attempts to do something about this very natural difficulty.

These activities should have about them the feeling of a game, and they should not be too lengthy, too personal or too serious. I have found it important not to force people to speak, and the teacher's contributions should be brief, light and unobtrusive.

Having 'broken the ice', we sometimes wish to go a little further. One way of doing that is to write two or three questions – which can be answered in a few words – on a board. Examples of questions could be: 'What would you most like to gain from this course/meeting/workshop?' 'How would you like people to respond during discussions?' 'Is anything likely to annoy you?' 'Have you any anxieties?'

The participants can be asked to write their responses briefly on a sheet of paper, and to stick it up somewhere in the room. Then everyone walks around for ten minutes to see what people have written.

Learners often worry about whether they will be able to cope; whether the other learners will be brighter than them; and whether the course will be useful. Many welcome an opportunity to air such thoughts in an informal way.

Teaching is usually a matter of helping learners to acquire new information, or to learn how to carry out a task. But teaching sometimes also aims to encourage a certain attitude. One example might be how best to receive a patient in a hospital.

If 'real' learning is primarily a matter of experiencing, it follows that people will learn a new attitude best if they can experience it. Role-play is an approach which can help learners to experience a new attitude.

Here is a practical example.

Many people are now employed (at least in more affluent countries) to care for the handicapped. One of their duties is to feed their most disabled clients, and that probably does not require much training. But it isn't easy to imagine what it feels like to be an adult, yet require feeding. Instead of talking about how a handicapped person might feel in such circumstances, one of my past students (who trains people to work with the handicapped) goes about the matter like this.

She divides her learners into pairs. The hands of one of the pair are tied behind his or her back, and he or she is also blindfolded. The other learner in the pair then feeds the bound and blindfolded one. Roles are then reversed.

When this exercise is realistically carried out, and followed by a discussion, the participants often say what a powerful experience it has been. They mention feelings of rage, frustration, resentment, appreciation, helplessness and relief. It is obvious that none of these feelings can be conveyed so well by a teacher 'telling'. Yet an awareness of such feelings would help a person to take better care of a handicapped person.

In addition to increasing a learner's sense of empathy, role-play can also help people to learn how to follow certain procedures based on a knowledge of important facts. Examples might include preparing a patient for an operation, or approaching a person with a view to making an arrest. As it isn't easy to do these kind of things well when one is new to them, it would be very helpful if one could have lots of practice at them in simulated circumstances. Role-play provides such circumstances.

All the examples given so far have been taken from work with adults. But role-play can also be used with children. It so happens that my maternal grandfather was a scholar and teacher. Among other things, he taught religion, and he did so in part via role-play. For example, instead of always teaching didactically, he sometimes got children to act parts out of the Bible.[3] That must have generated some powerful learning!

Like most things, role-play works best under certain conditions. The following suggestions may be helpful.

1. Teachers sometimes worry that some of their learners may not be happy to take part in a role-play. I have had such worries myself. But I have been so often struck by how readily – even eagerly – most learners are to take part in a role-play that I have now completely lost this fear. That is important because role-play works best when a teacher feels confident about it. Of course, that includes not trying to force anyone to take part.

2. It is probably best to introduce role-play when learners have begun to feel comfortable with each other. However, in some classes it may be an idea to introduce role-play early to help learners to feel more comfortable with each other.

3. In certain circumstances, it may be important to consider the advantages and disadvantages of casting before one begins a role-play.

4. Learners should be prepared for a role-play. Preparation can take the form of some reading or a short talk, followed by a discussion. It can also take the form of prompt cards which a teacher has devised. A prompt card is given to each participant, and on it is written a very brief description of the situation which the role-play will simulate. Each card also has a few words about the character which the holder of that card will act.

5. If possible, all the learners should participate. If there are more than four or five

learners, and there is enough space, the class can be divided into groups. All the groups can then work at the same time in various parts of a room. Alternatively, those not participating can be given a list of questions to answer while observing the role-play.

6. It is helpful to spend a little time organizing the room. This helps to 'set the stage'. In the theatre this is sometimes called 'the suspension of disbelief', and it is generated by things like lights going down and a curtain going up.

7. A teacher's main job is to help organize the role-play. As in most of the lessons I have described, a teacher should do as much of the work as possible before the lesson. Once a role-play is under way, a teacher should not interfere.

8. Participants often stereotype situations or people in a role-play. Teachers can mention this tendency beforehand, or they can allow stereotyping to occur and invite the participants to consider what it implies afterwards.

9. A role-play can generate strong feelings. It is therefore important for the participants to be able to leave their roles behind them when a class moves on to other things. Teachers can help to create a demarcation between a role-play and the rest of a lesson by clearly announcing the end of the role-play. One of my past students managed this neatly by having his police cadets put on hats when a role-play began and take them off when the role-play came to an end.

10. At the end of a role-play a teacher should thank the participants. They have collaborated to make a success of a lesson, and taking part in a role-play is a little like taking part in a play. Unless there is some applause at the end, we may feel deflated.

11. A role-play should be followed by a discussion. The participants should be encouraged to say how they felt during the role-play. If a teacher does this tactfully, and allows for lots of silences, the participants will be able to verbalize their feelings and thereby clarify them.

12. The greatest benefit from role-play comes when the insights so gained are practised in real-life situations; and even more gains are made when one can practise in the presence of a supportive, unobtrusive and knowledgeable person with whom one can discuss one's progress.

Many people teach subjects which do not appear to lend themselves to role-play. Role-play serves certain aims, and it is obviously important to match the methods used with the aims of a lesson. However, a little reflection will often show that a certain topic does lend itself to role-play. Role-play increases the range of things done in a class, and it enables learners to express certain facets of themselves which might otherwise go completely unnoticed.

There are variants of role-play like simulation and gaming. These also enable learners to gain some experience of a situation in a supportive environment. Though these, and role-play, serve limited purposes, such methods are often neglected because of the predominance of the transmission method of teaching. It has been my consistent experience that, when teachers and learners have tried these activities, they have usually found them valuable. Interested readers will find numerous books on them.[4]

Although women do not have to go to university to learn how to have a baby, quite a few like to go to antenatal classes. I described one of those classes in the previous section. Another went like this.

The topic was breast-feeding, and the health visitor who took this class was called Susan. She began the lesson by showing us a video film. It featured three experts talking about the problems that can arise during breast-feeding. We also saw a rather uncertain mother feeding her baby. It took her a couple of seconds to manoeuvre the baby into a position where it was able to get a good suck on a nipple. The experts told us why this was important.

Next Susan showed us some slides. They illustrated the process of milk production in a woman's body. After the last slide, she asked if there were any questions. As there were none, she talked about the care of the nipples, and used a series of glossy charts to do that. (These had been thoughtfully provided by a firm which manufactures baby foods!)

After that she talked about things like bonding, hormones and nappy rash. At the end, she drew attention to the various kinds of bras available. She had a few with her, and handed them around for examination.

As the mothers got up to leave, several thanked Susan for the trouble she had taken. I thought it one of the worst examples of problematizing, medicalizing, and expertising I had ever seen. The most surprising thing about the lesson was the fact that Susan was a particularly bright person. Unfortunately, she had picked up some daft notions about teaching, and they had dimmed her native intelligence.

Four months later I saw her give the same lesson to another group. This time she had asked a woman who had just had a baby to come in. Susan introduced her, and asked her a question. There was nothing remarkable about the woman. She was pleasant, and friendly, and obviously pleased to have a baby; you could see that from the way she handled her infant in a confident and warm way. She answered Susan's question, and a moment later one of the other women asked her something.

For the next half-hour there was a steady stream of exchanges between the mother and the other women. They were all sitting in a circle, so there was no difficulty about that. Occasionally Susan came in to prompt, or to ask a question. Twice she gave some information briefly. Halfway through the lesson the mother and her baby had to leave.

Next, Susan said that the people present might like to discuss what they thought about breast-feeding. As she had now gained some insight into how to facilitate such a discussion, she was able to encourage the women present to address each other directly, and in this way they were able to gain various points of view and clear up misunderstandings.

Occasionally Susan was asked something. When that happened, she first deflected the question back to the group, and answered herself only if that was necessary. As breast-feeding is very much like any other complex but natural human activity, the women present had most of the knowledge they needed from about one hundred thousand years of evolution. What they now mostly needed was a suitable environment in which positive attitudes could be encouraged and misconceptions cleared up.

None of the women thanked Susan as they left, but several stopped to chat. I felt that they had got much more out of this lesson than the previous group had got out of theirs.

Afterword

We have almost reached the end of this book, and I should now like to try to summarize what I have attempted to do in it.

I have tried to present a theory of learning and teaching. It holds that people learn when they discover that they don't know something (which they consider worth knowing), form hunches about a possible answer, seek information, and apply that information to test those hunches. In doing these things they have experiences, and in that way they learn.

As for teachers, their job, as I see it, is to help people to discover that they don't know something which is worth knowing; and then to help them to find answers in a reasonably orderly and satisfying way.[1] It has also been my argument that, for teachers to be able to do these things effectively, they must study a considerable body of knowledge, and have lots of practice in applying it.

Quite a few people might broadly agree with the above, but they might argue that one does not need to have a theory of learning and teaching in order to teach in the way suggested. Indeed, I know from first-hand experience that the principles advocated on many teacher training courses are not that far distant from the ones suggested in this book, but on these courses no theory of learning and teaching is mentioned. I believe that such an approach is fundamentally mistaken, and on at least two counts.

First, I have found that when a person applies a principle without first having made a sustained endeavour to understand on what evidence it is based, that person's practice tends to be unimaginative and superficial. In the case of teachers, such practice also tends to trivialize that which the teacher is trying to teach.

Second, a person who applies a principle without first having made a sustained endeavour to understand on what evidence it is based, is unable to criticize that principle except in a superficial kind of way. Such a person is therefore unable to develop the principle intelligently.

I write at a time when it has become increasingly fashionable to assess knowledge via 'competences'. In this approach, what people are actually able to *do* is the focus of attention – rather than what they appear to know – and readers of this book will immediately see that what I have advocated appears to be in line with such an approach.

However, when one attempts to replace an old approach with a radically new one, one also sometimes replaces an old evil with a new one; and I think that that has happened with the competency-based approach. For an examination of what a person is able to do will seldom indicate how well that person also understands the justification for what he or she is 'doing'; nor is it easy to assess such understanding on the basis of further 'competences'. In other words, instead of trying to tackle the difficult problem of the relationship between theory and practice, the competency-based approach tries to side-step this problem, and in doing that creates a new problem.

I could put the disadvantage of the competency-based approach in another way. It seems to me that the single most important competency that anyone can have is the ability to question the validity of any 'competence'. But it is precisely *that* competence which the 'competency-based' approach undermines, because all the competences one must learn are 'givens'. It is also because they are givens that the competency-based approach is probably the most authoritarian ever devised, especially as it appears to be so transparent and egalitarian.

It is partly because of considerations such as these that, in spite of its dominating position at present, I have not taken a competency-based approach. Instead, I have argued for the primacy of theory, *together* with the need for practical experience. It would follow, even if I am partly right, that all assessments should test both knowledge of theory, and competence in practice.

There has been a great deal of controversy about the nature and validity of theories for many years, but I have found it impossible to get both a discussion of that, and what I have managed to write, into one book.[2] However, I do think a few words are called for.

Whenever we need to do something complicated, like build a house or relieve a persistent pain, we need some knowledge. But the kind of knowledge we need in such circumstances isn't simply a matter of knowing a number of facts. If that were all we needed, everyone could be their own builder or dentist. When we have something complicated to do, we need a deep and integrated understanding of it. That is, we need to be able to see how all the facts of a topic hang together. For that, we usually have to go to somebody who has spent a considerable amount of time studying the matter, and who has had extensive experience of it. To have that kind of knowledge is to have a 'theory' of it.[3]

My argument all through this book has been that teaching is a complicated matter. If it is, if the knowledge to do it well can be compared with the knowledge required to build a house or to relieve a persistent pain, then experience is not enough. We need a theory to guide us in our classroom practice.

If we read a history of the various branches of knowledge, we soon see that we never gain complete understanding of anything. There is always more to be learnt. But such a reading does show that we make progress. We know more about the subject matter of medicine, astronomy, engineering and human development than we knew a hundred years ago. And if we do, it is because the people who have contributed to our understanding have done so by enriching the theory of these subjects.

Another great advantage of theory-building is that it makes criticism easier; and in that way, it also makes progress more likely. For example, we have seen that a theory consists of an integrated series of statements based on some evidence. It follows that, if somebody can show that one of those statements is based on poor evidence, then that statement is probably wrong. It may then also follow that several other statements are wrong. If that happens, we may have to modify our theory, or abandon it altogether.

On the other hand, when we have a series of integrated statements based on evidence it is often possible to find more evidence that will fit the picture we already have. This will then make our theory stronger.

So having only a theory is not enough: one must constantly evaluate one's theory in the light of practice. In that way we constantly refine, modify, extend and change our theory. It seems to me that the kind of knowledge we can gain through this interplay of theory and our practice is likely to be far more powerful – and far less prone to changes in educational fashions – than only personal experience, reflections on experience, and the latest fad.

I used the word 'statement' above. Quite often, when theories are discussed, the word 'fact' is used. But I think it would be a mistake to talk about learning and teaching in that way. Learning and teaching deal with the most complicated things on earth – human beings – and there are too many variables involved in learning and teaching to enable us to talk about 'facts'. For the same reason, I believe it is better to talk about 'patterns' rather than 'laws', when we discuss learning and teaching.

As with all theories, I am sure that many criticisms could be made about the one I have put forward in this book. I can think of several myself, and I should like to mention five.

1. There is nothing about the personality (or the social make-up) of the teacher and the taught here. Many people believe that these can have a strong effect on learning and teaching, and I believe that, too. For example, a teacher who *genuinely* believes that learners can often do better than they themselves believe, and who conveys that belief, is likely to encourage more learning than a teacher who does not have such beliefs. Likewise, learners who feel that they will be able to cope with a task are much more likely to cope with it than learners who do not. Nor is there anything here on the social relations between teacher and taught, or among the learners themselves. These are serious omissions, for we all know that these things can have a strong effect on our learning. I have not included anything on these topics because they are such big ones. I believe they need consideration in a separate book.

2. Another topic not considered here is the context in which learning takes place. That includes things like the economic, political, cultural and social system of a country, as well as the nature of the relationship between the individual and the state. These factors have a very powerful effect on learning and teaching, and if I have not included anything on that topic here, it is again because it is such a big one.

3. A third topic hardly considered is the nature of the material to be learnt, and how it is to be organized and assessed. Yet again these are big topics. I have touched on them here and there, but there has not been room to give them the attention they deserve.

4. Another topic not given the attention it deserves is the ultimate aim of learning and teaching. A teacher's job might be to teach anatomy, bricklaying or music, but most teachers are very pleased when they are also able to help their learners to become more thoughtful, articulate and enterprising people. These things are easily said, but we know that helping learners to acquire such qualities is not so easy. Qualities like these cannot be taught directly. A learner will not become more thoughtful, articulate or enterprising because a teacher says it is important to have such qualities. If real learning requires

experiencing, learners will only acquire such qualities if they have repeated experiences of them. In other words, if learners are helped to develop such qualities, it will not be because of *what* a teacher has taught, but as a result of *how* a teacher has taught.[4]

However, even though I have not been able to consider the ultimate aim of learning and teaching in this book, I would hope that if the approach to teaching I have outlined has a value, it is not primarily because it helps learners to acquire more information, but because it helps them to acquire more information *and* to develop the kind of qualities noted above.

5. Another topic not considered is creativity. Creativity is a quality most of us feel we understand, but it is difficult to separate it out from things like imagination, innovation, artistry and doing one's own thing. As most people value creativity, and as every society needs creative people, it would surely be helpful if teachers knew how to foster it. But the matter goes much further than that. I believe that an understanding of creativity holds the key to an understanding of all real learning.

But I had better stop here. Otherwise I shall begin another book, and readers must be getting impatient to reach the end of this one.

I fear that the theory of learning and teaching I have put forward here has many faults, in addition to the ones outlined above. A great deal of work has been done on the topic of learning and teaching, and I have not managed to consider anywhere near all of it. Nor have I managed to understand all the contributions which I have considered. Learning is a mysterious business, almost as mysterious as life itself. There are also sure to be contradictions and weaknesses in what I have written; and there are sure to be many people who will understand these things very differently from me.

But there is only so much any one person can do. One does the best one can, but eventually one has to stop and accept one's limitations. But in this there is also a virtue, because it might spur someone to come along and suggest improvements.[5] In the mean time, there may be enough here to give a teacher something to begin with.

I write 'to begin with', because a consideration of the materials presented here would obviously constitute only a small part of what is involved in becoming an effective teacher. However, I do know that, when the student-teachers with whom I have worked have considered the materials presented here, they have usually come to see that it is not enough to go into a classroom with a set of objectives, lesson notes and an overhead projector. They have come to see that effective teaching is much more a matter of trying to understand how people learn.

This has many effects. One is to stop one from thinking about teaching primarily in terms of the content of the lesson. Content is important. But when one begins to think about teaching in terms of learning, it becomes obvious that content is only half the matter. The other half is what the learners *actually do* in a lesson.

Another thing that happens, when one begins to focus on learning, is that one often feels disappointed after a lesson. But then, that is common in any creative enterprise. There cannot be many architects, chefs or medical researchers around who are pleased with every one of their endeavours.

It follows that teachers do not improve because they have perfected a skill. Shall we say that Einstein was a 'skilled' mathematician and Cézanne a 'skilled' painter? A person who sees teaching primarily in terms of learning will know that acquiring a skill is a way of playing safe. Almost a path to mediocrity. Being creative is an arduous undertaking.

It is a matter of developing a sensitivity based on systematic study, endless practice and deep reflection. And it is in this way that teaching can become a creative endeavour. And like any creative endeavour, when it succeeds, it does not result in simply helping people to acquire more knowledge, or even a lifelong interest in a particular subject. It can alter the way they see things.

Further Reading

As the notes to this book are quite detailed, readers may like to have a list of works which I believe are especially helpful for a better understanding of learning and teaching.

As it is obviously important for teachers to be aware of more than the practice of teaching, I have added a few books on wider horizons. All are highly readable and many are fascinating. Some of the works listed are quite old. I mention this because I once had a manager who saw books like she did her car: if they were more than five years old she considered them 'out of date'. But with books it's surely what they say that counts, not how old they are.

No books on teaching specific subjects or specific age groups are listed. This is not an oversight.

*   warmly recommended
**   books that should be included in any core study of learning and teaching.

Abercrombie, M. L. J., *The Anatomy of Judgement* (1960). Free Association Books, 1989. This is the best single book I know on the process of learning.**

Augros, R. and Stanciu, G., *The New Biology*. Shambhala, 1987. About the nature of being alive on this planet.*

Bartley, W. W., *The Retreat to Commitment*. Open Court, 1984. On the essential topic of what is involved in being rational.

Bettelheim, B., *The Informed Heart*. Free Press, 1960. Often reprinted. Especially Chapter 4. The writer spent time in a concentration camp and describes his attempts to understand racialism rather than condemn it.

Brewer, I. M., *Learning More and Teaching Less*. SRHE and NFER-Nelson, 1985. Provides a practical demonstration of what the title conveys.

Carroll, J. M. and Mack, R. L., 'Actively learning to use a word processor'. In Cooper, W. E. (ed.) *Cognitive Aspects of Skilled Typewriting*. Springer-Verlag, 1983. Excellent on how people learn in general.**

Donaldson, M., *Children's Minds*. Fontana Books, 1978. Has much of value on how we all learn.

Eiseley, L., *The Immense Journey*. Vintage Books, 1946. Often reprinted. The writer manages to lift the reader's eyes beyond the furthest horizon by writing science like a poet.*

Hebb, D. O., 'Drives and the CNS'. *Psychological Review*, **62**, 1955; reprinted in *Personality Growth and Learning*. Open University Press, 1971. Helpful for a better understanding of motivation.*

Holt, J., *How Children Fail*. Penguin, 1969; revised edn 1987. Especially useful when teaching adults.**

Katona, G., *Organising and Memorising* (1940). Hafner, 1967. On how we learn.*

Kelly, G., 'Man's construction of his alternatives'. In Lindzey, G. (ed.) *Assessment of Human*

Motivation. Rinehart, 1958. Contains highly perceptive comments on the nature of motivation.**

Klapper, P., 'The professional preparation of the college teacher'. *Journal of General Education*, **3**, 228–244, 1959. Contains brief descriptions of lessons, and perceptive comments on them.

Köhler, W., *The Mentality of Apes* (1917). Often reprinted. The best single source I know for a better understanding of understanding.**

Koestler, A., *The Sleepwalkers*. Penguin, 1964. Often reprinted. The subtitle is *A History of Man's Changing Vision of the Universe*. Excellent for indicating how changes in our perceptions come about, and what that might imply for our understanding of learning.

Kounin, J. S., 'An analysis of teachers' managerial techniques'. In Morrison, A. and McIntyre, D. (eds) *The Social Psychology of Teaching*. Penguin, 1972. Much better than the title suggests.*

Krishnamurti, J., *The First and Last Freedom*. Gollancz, 1969. Often reprinted. I don't accept this writer's ultimate aim, but I believe he conveys a way of looking at things which is exceptionally enlightening.*

LeDoux, J. E., 'Brain, mind and language'. In Oakley, D. A. (ed.) *Brain and Mind*. Methuen, 1985. On how much of our knowledge is stored below conscious awareness.

Lynch, J. J., *The Broken Heart*. Harper & Row, 1977. The writer indicates the extent to which we humans are social creatures.*

Mann, R. D., *The College Classroom*. Wiley, 1970. Contains many helpful comments on human dynamics in a classroom.

Marton, F. and Saljo, R., 'On qualitative differences in learning: 1 – outcome and process'; and 'Symposium: learning process and strategies – 2: outcome as a function of the learner's conception of the task'. *British Journal of Educational Psychology*, **46**, 4–11, and 115–127, 1976. These Scandinavians show us a way ahead in educational research and how to report it.

Miller, G. E., 'The contribution of research in the learning process'. *Medical Education*, **12**(3), 28–33, 1978. The writer takes a very close look at conventional approaches to teaching.**

Muir, J. and Gregg, J., *How to Keep Your Volkswagen Alive*. Santa Fe, New Mexico: John Muir, 1969. Many times reprinted. The best example I know of how to write and illustrate learning material.

Nisbett, R. E. and Wilson, T. D., 'Telling more than we can know: verbal reports on mental processes'. *Psychological Review*, **84**, 231–259, 1977. A scholarly source which shows that what we have in conscious awareness is only a fraction of what determines our behaviour.

Oliver, W. A., 'Teachers' educational beliefs versus their classroom practice'. *Journal of Educational Research*, **47**, 47–55, 1953. Sheds light on the nature of that famous gap between theory and practice.**

Peddiwell, J. A., *The Sabre-Toothed Curriculum*. McGraw-Hill, 1937. The first chapter amusingly describes how the material we teach tends to become fossilized.*

Phillips, D. C., *Philosophy, Science, and Social Inquiry*. Pergamon Press, 1987. Discusses clearly the fundamental issues that arise when we do research into learning and teaching.*

Polanyi, M., *Personal Knowledge*. Routledge, 1958. Often reprinted. Shows how all real knowledge is both personal and universal, and to a large extent tacit.

Popham, W. J. (ed.), *Instructional Objectives*. Rand McNally, 1969. A clear and lively discussion of the issues.

Popper, K. R., *The Logic of Scientific Discovery*. Hutchinson, 1959. Often reprinted. A great help for deciding what makes sense and what doesn't.

Postman, N. and Weingartner, C., *Teaching as a Subversive Activity*. Penguin, 1971. I believe the writers make mistakes, but they demonstrate in a lively way that the way one teaches has a greater final effect than what one teaches.*

Rogers, C. R., *On Becoming a Person*. Constable, 1967, especially Chapter 13. Often reprinted. The work as a whole shows why teaching is often damaging, especially when it succeeds.**

Salzberger-Wittenberg, I., *The Emotional Experience of Learning and Teaching*. Routledge, 1983.*

Sherrington, C., *Man on His Nature*. Cambridge University Press, 1940. Often reprinted. About being alive.

Slobin, D. I., *Psycholinguistics*, 2nd edn. Scott, Foresman, 1979. A beautifully written introduction to the relationship between thinking and language.*

Stuart, S., *Say*. Nelson, 1969. On teaching English, and more.

Vogt, E. Z. and Hyman, R., *Water Witching USA*, 2nd edn. University of Chicago Press, 1979. Illustrates well the difference between having an opinion and having tentative evidence, and what follows from that difference.

Vygotsky, L. S., *Thought and Language*. MIT Press, 1962. Often reprinted. An early text but well worth reading.

Watson, J. D., *The Double Helix*. Penguin, 1970. The author describes how he made a discovery and thereby also gives us many clues to how real learning takes place.*

Watts, A., *Nature, Man and Woman* (1958). Often reprinted. A Zen way of looking which helps to make clearer how we usually see things.

Weimer, W. B., 'Psycholinguistics and Plato's paradoxes of the *Meno*'. *American Psychologist*, **28**, 15–33, 1973. Indicates why learning is still a mystery.*

Weizenbaum, J., *Computer Power and Human Reason*. Penguin, 1984. The writer discusses what computers can and cannot do, and thereby tells us something about what we can do.*

West, K. M., 'The case against teaching'. *Journal of Medical Education*, 41(8), 766–771, 1966. A short, clear, penetrating look past 'common sense'.**

Whorf, B. L., *Language, Thought and Reality*, ed. Carroll, J. B. MIT Press, 1956. Often reprinted. See especially the last four chapters, which hint at what may lie behind language.

Wilber, K. (ed.), *Quantum Questions*. Shambhala, 1984. A collection of writings which indicate how highly creative scientists see the world.

Yalom, I. D., *The Theory and Practice of Group Psychotherapy*, 3rd edn. Basic Books, 1985. Group therapy and teaching are not the same, but I believe that teachers will find a great deal of value here.*

Notes

PART I: LEARNING

1 Introduction and Preliminaries

1. An example of the former is John Holt. An example of the latter is Jane Abercrombie. See Holt, J., *How Children Fail*. Penguin, 1969; revised edn 1987, and *How Children Learn*. Penguin, 1970; Abercrombie, M. L. J., *The Anatomy of Judgement*. Free Association Books, 1989; first published 1960.
2. For a discussion of the 'transmission' method see Perkinson, H. J., *Learning from Our Mistakes*. Greenwood Press, 1984. For a description of various approaches to teaching and their implications see Fox, D., 'Personal theories of teaching'. *Studies in Higher Education*, **8**(2), 151-163, 1983. For the best comments I know on the conventional wisdom see Miller, G. E., 'The contribution of research in the learning process'. *Medical Education*, **12**(3), 28-33, 1978; also West, K. M., 'The case against teaching'. *Journal of Medical Education*, **41**(8), 766-771, 1966.
3. See Rutter, M. *et al.*, *Fifteen Thousand Hours: Secondary Schools and Their Effects on Children*. Open Books, 1979. As the writers have no theory to give meaning to their 'facts', I do not believe that teachers will find much else in this book to help them.
4. See Anning, A., ' "Curriculum in Action" in action'. In Hustler, D. *et al.* (eds) *Action Research in Classrooms and Schools*. Allen & Unwin, 1986. This writer urges the need for collaboration between practising teachers and educational researchers. See also Mitchell, P., 'A teacher's view of educational research'. In Shipman, M. (ed.) *Educational Research: Principles, Policies and Practices*. Falmer Press, 1985. A recent publication on research on teaching (Wittrock, M. C. (ed.) *Handbook of Research on Teaching*. Macmillan, 1986) measures 28 × 22 × 5.5 cm, contains 1,037 double-column pages, and weighs 2.75 kilos! It is difficult to imagine a practising teacher reading it. No matter how conscientious the work of the editor and contributors, this raises fundamental questions about the relationship between practising teachers and the academic fraternity. It may be worth adding that, while writing this book, I read several hundred journal papers and many score books on learning and teaching and, to my initial surprise, found the majority unhelpful. (Some of the latter, however, did provide useful references.) For comments on this matter see Bolster, A. S., Jr., 'Toward a more effective model of research on teaching'. *Harvard Educational Review*, **55**(3), 294-308, 1983. The writer's introductory comments are helpful but I cannot see how his recommendation would solve the problem.
5. I am greatly indebted to J. Krishnamurti for helping me to understand this matter a little

better. A good entry into his work is through his *The First and Last Freedom*. Gollancz, 1969, often reprinted.

6. For an amusing illustration see Casey, D., 'The awful nature of change: motivation in hostile conditions'. *Management Education and Development*, **16**(1), 14–16, 1985.

7. I believe there is a tendency to underestimate what is involved in fruitful reflection. The work of those who advocate this in teacher training is obviously based on extensive reading, and the habit of reflection derived from systematic study. Yet these writers often disparage systematic reading and study. To my mind this kind of contradiction, based as it is on a one-sided emphasis on the personal and the practical, leads to a new kind of obscurantism, highly destructive of the whole educational enterprise. For an example of this trend see the introduction to Smyth, J. (ed.), *Educating Teachers*. Falmer Press, 1987.

8. See Hora, T., 'Tao, Zen and existential psychotherapy'. *Psychological Bulletin*, **2**, 236–242, 1959.

9. The 'skills' approach gained prominence as an understandable reaction against merely theoretical knowledge. However, I believe the wholesale application of the skills approach to education has been pernicious, a case of throwing out the baby with the bathwater. I believe that much the same is true of the 'competency' approach, and I return to this matter later. For criticism of the skills approach see Hart, W. A., 'Against skill'. *Oxford Review of Education*, **4**(2), 205–216, 1978.

10. Many of those engaged in the training of teachers seem to accept a great many teaching 'competencies' on no more evidence than that there is some consensus about them. Anyone who believes that consensus makes for good practice should read Trevor-Roper, H. R., *The European Witch Craze of the Sixteenth and Seventeenth Centuries*. Penguin, 1988.

11. As the 'competence' approach is greatly in favour as I write, and as I have some reservations about its applicability to the development of more effective teaching, and as I must restrict my comments, I summarize some of my doubts by noting that giving a student a list of competencies to master tends to:

    • make for doers rather than reflective practitioners;
    • undermine the critical faculty;
    • create an illusion of clarity;
    • foster an atomistic approach;
    • stress product over process;
    • trivialize theoretical underpinnings;
    • give students an answer before they understand the question;
    • nurture an authoritarian impulse (because it stresses the given rather than the discovered);
    • discourage a creative inclination.

    I return to this matter briefly at the end of Part I.

12. For an account which indicates the difficulty of change see Barber, B., 'Resistance by scientists to scientific discovery'. *Science*, **134**, 596–602, 1961.

13. To an outsider, the political left and right in the UK often seem more similar than different, with the left emphasizing individual social needs, and the right individual economic needs (the two sides existing in a kind of symbiosis, with one side stressing the distribution of wealth, the other its making).

14. James J. Gibson attributes this lovely sentence to K. Lewin. See Gibson's fascinating contribution in Boring, E. G. *et al.* (eds) *A History of Psychology in Autobiography*, Vol. 5. Appleton-Century-Crofts, 1967.

15. This is how one scholar describes past attempts to construct a theory of learning: 'Consider the hundreds of theoretical formulations, rational equations and mathematical models of the learning process that have accrued; the thousands of research studies. And *now* consider that there is still no wide agreement, even at the crassest descriptive level, on the empirical conditions under which learning takes place, or even on the definition of learning or its empirical and rational relations to other psychological processes or phenomena. Consider also that after all this scientistic effort our actual *insight* into the learning process – as reflected in every humanly important context to which learning is relevant – has not

improved one jot.' Koch, S., 'Reflections on the state of psychology'. *Social Research*, 38, 669–709, 1971.

16. I refer to the alleged relativism of all theories in several other notes.
17. Huberman, M., 'Teacher development and instructional mastery'. In Hargreaves, A. and Fullan, M. G. (eds) *Understanding Teacher Development*. Cassell, 1992. I take a view rather different from the one expressed by the editors and most of the contributors, but found Huberman's paper most helpful.
18. The most useful work I know on theory building is Popper, K. R., *The Logic of Scientific Discovery*. Hutchinson, 1983. Another helpful work is Lakatos, I. *et al.* (eds) *Criticism and the Growth of Knowledge*. Cambridge University Press, 1970 (especially the papers by Feyerabend and Lakatos). For an application to education see Gibbs, J. C., 'The meaning of ecologically oriented inquiry in contemporary psychology'. *American Psychologist*, **34**(2), 127–140, 1979. The Introduction in Brown, B. B., *The Experimental Mind in Education*, Harper & Row, 1968, has comments on the need for a theory to guide intelligent educational practice. A brief, clear and engaging introduction to the philosophy of science is Chalmers, A. F., *What Is This Thing Called Science?*, 2nd edn. Oxford University Press, 1982. For a clear introduction to the 'scientific method' see Beveridge, W. I. B., *The Art of Scientific Investigation*. Heinemann, 1979. An older but interesting account is George, W. H., *The Scientist in Action: A Scientific Study of His Methods*. Williams & Norgate, 1936. For some criticism of this approach (little of which I find helpful) see Rose, S. *et al.* (eds) *Science and Beyond*. Blackwell, 1986; Latour, B. and Woolgar, S., *Laboratory Life: the Social Construction of Scientific Facts*. Sage, 1979; and Kvale, S. (ed.) *Psychology and Postmodernism*. Sage, 1992. I return to this matter in a later note.

2 Motivation and Learning

1. I am greatly indebted to George Kelly for the orientation taken in this chapter and for much that follows. See his 'Man's construction of his alternatives'. In Lindzey, G. (ed.) *Assessment of Human Motivation*. Rinehart, 1958. Also in Maher, B. (ed.) *Clinical Psychology and Personality: The Selected Papers of George Kelly*. Wiley, 1969. See also Kelly's paper, 'The autobiography of a theory', in the latter publication.
2. The phrase is Kelly's.
3. For an examination of what is implied by viewing learning as a biological process see Chomsky, N., *Rules and Representations*. Basil Blackwell, 1980.
4. I got the idea for this case study from another and regret that I am unable to acknowledge my debt more exactly.
5. There is much research which suggests that, if one would like people to engage in a task positively, especially when change is required, one should encourage them to become involved in the matter, and to decide for themselves how to tackle it. See, for example, Coch, L. and French, J. R. P., Jr., 'Overcoming resistance to change'. *Human Relations*, 512–532, 1948; and Levine, J., 'Lecture versus group decision in changing behaviour'. *Journal of Applied Psychology*, 36, 29–33, 1952.
6. I believe it is Carl Rogers who is most responsible for alerting us to the need to consult learners. I shall be discussing his work in more detail later. This idea first gained widespread currency in adult education in England, and is now beginning to affect all English educational practice. I was first introduced to the idea as a teenager when reading the work of A. S. Neill. See his *Summerhill*. Gollancz, 1962; Penguin, 1968, reprinted many times.
7. A clear and brief introduction to this kind of study is Percy, K. and Ramsden, P., *Independent Study*. SRHE, 1980.
8. Vygotsky, L. S., *Mind in Society*, ed. Cole, M. *et al.* Harvard University Press, 1978.
9. Neil Postman and Charles Weingartner have helped me here and elsewhere. I believe they make mistakes, but see their lively *Teaching as a Subversive Activity*. Penguin, 1971.
10. For a succinct review of the research see Sirotnik, K. A., 'What you see is what you get: consistency, persistency and mediocrity in classrooms'. *Harvard Educational Review*, **53**(1),

16-31, 1983. For a review of primary school teaching in Britain see Bennett, N. *et al.*, *The Quality of Pupil Learning Experiences*. Lawrence Erlbaum, 1984.

11. For most of the research described in the following section I am indebted to Hebb, D. O., 'Drives and the CNS'. *Psychological Review*, **62**, 1955; reprinted in *Personality Growth and Learning*. Open University Press, 1971. See also the paper in the same publication by Hunt, J. McV., 'Using intrinsic motivation to teach young children'.

12. I believe experiments on animals should be humane because I believe violence is indivisible. That is, I don't believe a society can have humane relationships among its people and at the same time be inhumane to animals.

13. I am again indebted to Hebb, 'Drives and the CNS', and Hunt, 'Intrinsic motivation'.

14. I was introduced to Papousek's work by Margaret Donaldson. See her very helpful *Children's Minds*. Fontana, 1978. For Papousek see his rather technical 'Individual variability in learned responses in human infants'. In Robinson, R. J. (ed.) *Brain and Early Behaviour*. Academic Press, 1969. See also Kagan, J., 'On the need for relativism'. *American Psychologist*, **22**, 131-147, 1967; reprinted in Hudson, L. (ed.) *The Ecology of Human Intelligence*. Penguin, 1970. Kagan notes the interesting work of Charlesworth. For more recent comments see Bower, T. G. R., *The Rational Infant*. W. H. Freeman, 1989.

15. None of these comments is intended to suggest that there is a one-to-one correspondence between things in the outside world and things in our brains. For a review of research showing how models of the world become established in our brains see Oakley, D. A., 'Cognition and imagery in animals'. In Oakley, D. A. (ed.) *Brain and Mind*. Methuen, 1985. The evidence Oakley cites questions the belief that knowledge is built up through stimulus-response associations. For further comment see Blake, R. R. *et al.* (eds) *Perception: an Approach to Personality*. Ronald Press, 1951.

16. Tizard, B. and Hughes, M., *Young Children Learning*. Fontana, 1984.

17. I think I am indebted to Jerome Bruner for that sentence. See his *The Relevance of Education*. Penguin, 1974.

18. See Covington, M. V. and Omelich, C. L., 'As failures mount: affective and cognitive consequences of ability demotion in the classroom'. *Journal of Educational Psychology*, **73**(6), 796-808, 1981.

19. The figures are easily found in the relevant material published by the Department of Education and Science in the UK.

20. This comparison is made by Charles Handy. See his *Organising for Capability*, Occasional Paper No. 2. Royal Society of Arts, London, October 1984.

21. A good place to begin on this large topic is Raven, J., 'An abuse of psychology for political purposes?' *Bulletin of the British Psychological Society*, **32**, 173-177, 1979.

22. For interesting comments see Tolley, G., 'The new curriculum: towards the primacy of the vocational'. *Economics*, Autumn 1985.

23. The most vivid source I know for a description of the way a teacher's attitude affects learning is John Holt's *How Children Fail*. Penguin, 1969, revised edn 1987.

24. Here I again draw on the paper by Kelly, 'Man's construction of his alternatives'.

3 The Learning Process

1. A good introduction to the behaviourist position is Lefrancoise, G., *Psychological Theories and Human Learning: Kongor's Report*. Brooks/Cole, 1972. It's even funny! For a brief introduction see Rachlin, H., *Introduction to Behaviourism*. W. H. Freeman, 1976.

2. For an early paper which questions the usefulness of the notion of drives see Diamond, S., 'A neglected aspect of motivation'. *Sociometry*, **2**, 77-85, 1939. For a searching review of the concept of drives see White, R. W., 'Motivation reconsidered: the concept of competence'. *Psychological Review*, **66**(5), 297-333, 1959. White shows how the concept of drives had to be expanded to accommodate more and more evidence till it fell apart under the weight of its own contradictions. See also Segal, E. M. and Lachman, R., 'Complex behaviour or higher mental process'. *American Psychologist*, **1**, 46-55, 1972.

3.   See Skinner, B. F., *The Technology of Teaching*. Prentice-Hall, 1968. Readers who have not actually read Skinner should read this, not so much for the content, but for the machine-like style and hence underlying attitude. Readers might like to compare this with the prose and attitude characteristic of many eminent scientists, as in Wilber, K. (ed.) *Quantum Questions*. Shambhala, 1984.

4.   See Skinner's chapter, 'The science of learning and the art of teaching', in *The Technology of Teaching*. For some critical comments see McKeachie, W. J., 'The decline and fall of the laws of learning'. *Educational Researcher*, **3**, 7–11, 1974.

5.   For powerful critiques of the behaviourist position see: Chomsky, N., review of Skinner's *Verbal Behaviour*. *Language*, **35**, 26–58, 1959; reprinted in De Cecco, J. P. (ed.) *The Psychology of Language, Thought, and Instruction*. Holt, Rinehart & Winston, 1969; Koch, S., 'Psychology and emerging conceptions of knowledge as unitary'. In Koch, S. (ed.) *Behaviourism and Phenomenology*. University of Chicago Press, 1964; Rogers, C. R., 'The place of the individual in the new world of the behavioural sciences', in that writer's *On Becoming a Person*. Constable, 1967; and Weimer, W. B., 'Psycholinguistics and Plato's paradoxes of the *Meno*'. *American Psychologist*, **28**, 15–33, 1973.

6.   See White, S. E., 'The active organism in theoretical behaviourism'. *Human Development*, **19**, 99–107, 1976.

7.   Skinner, B. F., *Science and Human Behaviour*. Macmillan, 1953.

8.   Both these experiments are reported by A. R. Luria in his *The Making of Mind*. Harvard University Press, 1979, p. 125.

9.   Tolman, E. C., 'Cognitive maps in rats and men'. *Psychological Review*, **55**(4), 189–208, 1948. For a most interesting comment see Krechevsky, I., 'Hypotheses in rats'. *Psychological Review*, **39**, 516–532, 1932. I note the date of publication of this paper and feel a sense of awe and affection for all these scholars who have made a contribution to our groping attempts to understand the human condition – with experiments on rats!

10. For a criticism of associationism see Jenkins, J. J., 'Remember that old theory of memory? Well, forget it!' *American Psychologist*, **29**, 785–795, 1974.

11. It is common today to find scholars who claim that a meaning is simply the expression of a certain physical state of the brain, or a derivative of 'a language of the brain'. For comment on this kind of argument see Harris, R., 'The grammar in your head'. In Blakemore, C. *et al.* (eds) *Mindwaves*. Blackwell, 1987.

12. Bransford, J. D., *Human Cognition*, Wadsworth, 1979, p. 254, notes the work of Anita Willis with 'developmentally delayed' children. She found that a behaviour modification approach, in the absence of an attempt to understand what this approach meant for the children, led to poor results. For an example of the simplification and manipulation inherent in therapies based on a behaviourist approach, particularly helpful because it is more sophisticated than many, see Hunt, H. F., 'Prospects and possibilities in the development of behaviour therapy'. In Porter, R. (ed.) *The Role of Learning in Psychotherapy*. J. & A. Churchill, 1968. The discussions that follow this paper, and those between pages 320 and 328, are also helpful.

13. Quoted in Cohen, B. I., *Franklin and Newton*. American Philosophical Society, 1956. For the need to use hypothetical constructs if one is to make progress see Sanford, N., 'Will psychologists study human problems?' *American Psychologist*, **20**, 192–202, 1965.

14. Bower shows clearly, not only that much of an infant's learning cannot be accounted for by the notion of reinforcement, but that his behaviour becomes inexplicable when that notion is applied. See Bower, T. G. R., *The Rational Infant*. W. H. Freeman, 1989.

15. For examples which show that even animals have an 'inner state' see Breland, K. and Breland, M., 'The misbehaviour of organisms'. *American Psychologist*, **16**, 681–684, 1961.

16. For findings which suggest that humans do not hear sentences but the meaning of sentences see Jenkins, 'Remember that old theory of memory?' Also Bransford, J. D. and Franks, J. J., 'The abstraction of linguistic ideas'. *Cognitive Psychology*, **2**, 331–350, 1971; and Bransford, J. D. and Franks, J. J., 'The abstraction of linguistic ideas: a review'. *Cognition*, **1**, 211–249, 1972. Also interesting is Sachs, J. S., 'Recognition memory for syntactic and semantic aspects of connected discourse'. *Perception and Psychophysics*, **2**, 437–442, 1967.

Also relevant is the finding by Keenan and her associates that our ability to remember seems to depend on 'the degree to which a statement conveys information about a speaker's intentions, beliefs, and attitudes toward the listener'. Keenan, J. M. *et al.*, 'Pragmatics in memory'. In Neisser, U. (ed.) *Memory Observed.* W. H. Freeman, 1982. This is an excellent book on memory, and I believe it lends support to the thesis that mental functioning is largely abstract. Some of these findings on memory were anticipated by F. C. Bartlett in his fascinating *Remembering.* Cambridge University Press, 1932. A personal observation may be in order here. I happen to speak a few languages, was once trying to remember a man's name, and could not. Of a sudden, the German word 'Schneider' came into my head. In English this means 'tailor'. I then remembered the man's name; it was 'Chayat' – the Hebrew word for 'tailor'. My younger daughter has sometimes shown that she understands the meaning of a phrase in a foreign language, is sometimes able to use it correctly, yet finds it difficult to translate it into English. See also Frankl, V. E., *Man's Search for Meaning.* Beacon Press, 1962, often reprinted. I am unable to see how behaviourists could account for the kind of material Frankl provides.

17. For much in this section I am indebted to Lepper, M. R. and Greene, D., *The Hidden Costs of Reward.* Lawrence Erlbaum, 1978.
18. For a review of research and detailed comment see Deci, E. L. and Ryan, R. M., *Intrinsic Motivation and Self Determination in Human Behaviour.* Plenum Press, 1985. See also De Charms, R., 'From pawns to origins: towards self-motivation'. In Lesser, G. S. (ed.) *Psychology and Educational Practice.* Scott, Foresman, 1971.
19. See Donaldson, Margaret, *Children's Minds.* Fontana, 1978.
20. Quoted in Dow, G. (ed.) *Teacher Learning.* Routledge, 1982.
21. Their work is noted by Lepper and Greene, *Hidden Costs.*
22. Fransson, A., 'On qualitative differences in learning: iv – effects of intrinsic motivation and extrinsic test anxiety on process and outcome'. *British Journal of Educational Psychology*, **47**, 244–257, 1977.
23. This research is also noted by Lepper and Greene, *Hidden Costs.*
24. I am reporting the work of E. T. Kavanau here. I have seldom seen laboratory findings on small animals with more striking implications for learning and teaching. See his 'Compulsory regime and control of environment in animal behaviour, 1: Wheel-running'. *Behaviour*, **20**, 251–281, 1963. For a review of research on the question of personal control and how it affects a learner's progress see Stipek, D. J. and Weisz, J. R., 'Perceived personal control and academic achievement'. *Review of Educational Research*, **51**(1), 101–137, 1981. Most of this offers strong support for the position taken in this section.
25. Nisbett, R. and Ross, L., *Human Inference.* Prentice-Hall, 1980, p. 129.
26. Noted by Lepper and Green, *Hidden Costs.*
27. I should perhaps own that this is a fancy figure of speech I sometimes use in class, as I never had the pleasure of meeting Albert Einstein.
28. This is the date of publication of J. B. Watson's *Psychological Care of the Infant and Child.* W. W. Norton, 1928; reprinted by Arno Press, 1972. Nobody should adopt a behaviourist approach without having read this work for it is surely important to examine the likely ends before one adopts any means. I believe the mechanistic triteness of this book is its most striking feature. It also seems to me that the picture we get of Watson as a parent, in Cohen, D., *J. B. Watson*, Routledge, 1979, is pathetic and a poor recommendation for his position.
29. This is a huge subject! A good introduction to the social factors which influence the behaviour of learners is Bronfenbrenner, U., 'The origins of alienation'. *Scientific American*, **231**, 53–61, 1974. See also Booth, T. *et al.* (eds) *Producing and Reducing Dissatisfaction.* Open University Press, 1987. For a readable account of some noteworthy schools see Lipsitz, J., *Successful Schools for Young Adolescents.* Transaction Books, 1984.
30. I should like to be able to recommend an introductory book on Gestalt psychology but unfortunately I cannot.
31. For a most interesting comment see Shanon, B., 'The polyglot mismatch and the monolingual tie'. *New Ideas in Psychology*, **2**(1), 75–79, 1984.
32. See Bransford, J. D. and McCarrell, N. S., 'A sketch of a cognitive approach to comprehension: some thoughts about understanding what it means to comprehend'. In Weimer,

W. B. and Palermo, D. S. (eds) *Cognition and the Symbolic Process*, Vol. 1. Lawrence Erlbaum, 1974.

33. These statements are made by the economist Samuelson, and I am indebted to Lars-Owe Dahlgren for them. See Dahlgren's 'Outcomes of learning'. In Marton, F. *et al.* (eds) *The Experience of Learning*. Scottish Academic Press, 1984. See also Saljo, R., *Learning in the Learner's Perspective I & II*. Institute of Education, University of Göteborg, 1979. I feel much in sympathy with these Scandinavians.

34. A study which compares the way beginners and experts view problems in physics concludes: 'experts categorise problems by laws of physics, and novices by surface features'. Chi, M. *et al.*, 'Categorisation and representation of physics problems by experts and novices'. *Cognitive Science*, **5**, 121–152, 1981.

35. Köhler, W., *The Mentality of Apes*. Vintage Books, 1956, first published 1917. This is a central work of interest to teachers, and indeed to anyone interested in learning.

36. See Birch, C., 'The relation of previous experience in insightful problem solving'. *Journal of Comparative Psychology*, **38**, 367–383, 1945.

37. Köhler, *Mentality of Apes*, p. 120. For a searching analysis of Köhler's findings see Schiller, P. H., 'Innate constituents of complex responses in primates'. *Psychological Review*, **59**(3), 177–191, 1952. Schiller also has interesting things to say about the effects of extrinsic rewards on learning. For a detailed discussion of animal thinking and a wide review of the literature see Walker, S., *Animal Thought*. Routledge, 1983. For an account of interesting experiments and their implications see Premack, D. and Woodruff, G., 'Does the chimpanzee have a theory of mind?' *Behavioral and Brain Sciences*, **1**(4), 515–526, 1978.

38. I use the word 'afford' in James Gibson's sense. See his *The Senses Considered as Perceptual Systems*. Houghton Mifflin, 1966. For a helpful comment on the implications of Gibson's work see Mace, M., 'Ecologically stimulating cognitive psychology: Gibsonian perspectives'. In Weimer and Palermo, *Cognition and the Symbolic Process*. Also Reed, E. S., 'James Gibson's ecological approach to cognition'. In Costall, A. *et al.* (eds) *Cognitive Psychology in Question*. Harvester Press, 1987. For criticism see Ullman, S., 'Against direct perception'. *Behavioural and Brain Sciences*, **3**, 373–415, 1980.

39. Menzel found that the chimpanzees he observed learnt to use a pole as a ladder in hundreds of different circumstances, and concludes that his observations 'fail to support the contention that primate tool using can be reduced to certain "innate movement patterns" and that seemingly intelligent performance is the chance occurrence of one of these movement patterns in a situation where it is likely to be reinforced'. See Menzel, E. W., 'Spontaneous invention of ladders in a group of young chimpanzees'. *Folia Primatologica*, **17**, 87–106, 1972.

40. One finding states: 'our experiment demonstrates unequivocally the capacity of rats to store an abstract description of a pattern: they do not merely store a list of the feature detectors fired by an input picture'. Sutherland, N. S. and Williams, C., 'Discrimination of checkerboard patterns by rats'. *Quarterly Journal of Experimental Psychology*, **21**, 77–84, 1969.

41. This is taken from Henri Poincaré's *The Foundations of Science*, reprinted in Ghiselin, B. (ed.) *The Creative Process*. Mentor Books, 1952, p. 37.

42. For some striking examples see Ghiselin, ibid.

43. My comments on the nature of thinking all through this book are strongly influenced by the work of J. Krishnamurti. In addition to his *The First and Last Freedom* (Gollancz, 1969), see his *Commentaries on Living*. There are three series, variously published by Gollancz between 1965 and 1970.

44. Another writer who has introduced me to this way of viewing the world is Alan Watts. See his fascinating *Nature, Man and Woman*. Wildwood House, 1973. Watts and Krishnamurti might be followed by Lao Tsu, *Tao Te Ching*. The best (and most beautiful) edition I know is that by Gia-Fu Feng and Jane English, Wildwood House, 1972. For fascinating and scholarly comment on this approach see Needham, J., *Science and Civilisation in China*, Vol. 2. Cambridge University Press, 1956.

45. Brown, G. S., *Laws of Form*. Allen & Unwin, 1969. See also Hunter, I. M., 'An exceptional memory'. In Neisser, *Memory Observed*.

46. Gittings, R. (ed.) *Letters of John Keats*. Oxford University Press, 1970, p. 43.

47. Readers may like to see the source from which I take this use of the word 'resonate': 'Scholars of old time said that the mind is originally empty, and only because of this can it respond to natural things without prejudice. . . . Though everything resonates with the mind, the mind should be as if it had never resonated, and things should not remain in it. But once the mind has received (impressions of) natural things they tend to remain and not to disappear, thus leaving traces in the mind. (These affect later seeing and thinking . . .)'. Needham, *Science and Civilisation*, p. 89.

48. The position adopted here is very different from that of those who hold that the human mind 'constructs' reality. It is true that the process of socialization shapes our perception of reality to a very considerable extent, but that is a far cry from believing that we construct reality, let alone that there is no 'reality'. I return to this matter in later notes.

49. Spencer Brown writes about this vividly. See *Laws of Form*, p. 95.

50. Carroll, J. M. and Mack, R. L., 'Actively learning to use a word processor'. In Cooper, W. E. (ed.) *Cognitive Aspects of Skilled Typewriting*. Springer-Verlag, 1983. There is a great deal to be learnt from this work. One of its concerns is how manuals should be written. The best manual I have come across is that by John Muir and Josh Gregg, *How to Keep Your Volkswagen Alive*. Santa Fe, New Mexico: John Muir, 1969. Muir and Gregg knew intuitively that a manual has to be personal and interactive, and that humour also helps.

51. It might be argued that the concept of 'reinforcement' provides a better account of learning than the notion of 'hypothesis testing'. For experimental findings and a discussion which suggest the contrary see Levine, M., 'Hypothesis theory and nonlearning despite ideal S–R reinforcement contingencies'. *Psychological Review*, **78**(2), 130–140, 1971.

52. For an excellent description of this process in medical education, and comments on its implications for teaching, see Barrows, H. S. and Tamblyn, R. M., *Problem-Based Learning: An Approach to Medical Education*. Springer-Verlag, 1980.

53. Sacks, J. S., 'Recognition memory for syntactic and semantic aspects of connected discourse'. *Perception and Psychophysics*, **2**(9), 437–442, 1967.

54. Jenkins, 'Remember that old theory of memory?' The implications of Jenkins's paper are much greater than suggested in my text.

55. Craik, F. I. M. and Tulvig, E., 'Depth of processing and retention of words in episodic memory'. *Journal of Experimental Psychology: General*, **104**(3), 268–294, 1975.

56. For some discussion of the words 'meaning' and 'understanding', and the difficulty of defining and measuring the extent to which a learner has 'understood the meaning' of something, see Ormell, C. P., 'The problem of analysing understanding'. *Educational Research*, **22**(1), 32–38, 1979.

57. Elstein, A. S. *et al.*, 'Methods and theory in the study of medical inquiry'. *Journal of Medical Education*, **47**, 85–92, 1972. See also Barrows and Tamblyn, *Problem-Based Learning*. When one compares the findings of this research with that done on children as subjects, it is startling to find how similar they are. It seems that very young children solve problems (e.g. how to balance a piece of wood across a beam) in basically the same way as medical practitioners go about making a diagnosis, that is, by forming and testing a theory. See Karmiloff-Smith, A. and Inhelder, B., 'If you want to get ahead, get a theory'. *Cognition*, **3**(3), 195–212, 1974. See also Bower, *The Rational Infant*. I would claim that findings like these lend support to my belief that people of whatever age learn in basically the same way.

58. Polanyi, M., *Personal Knowledge*. Routledge & Kegan Paul, 1958, p. 101. Polanyi seems to be out of fashion at present. He may have placed too much emphasis on 'the traditional', but I believe there is a great deal of value to be found in his work.

59. Ibid. p. 54.

60. For additional comment on the implication of the concept 'tacit' see Turvey, M. T., 'Construction theory, perceptual systems, and tacit knowledge'; and Franks, J. J., 'Toward understanding understanding', both in Weimer and Palermo, *Cognition and the Symbolic Process*.

61. Holt, J., *How Children Learn*. Penguin, 1970, p. 161. I have learnt a good deal from this writer, but perhaps I should mention what I consider to be two fundamental errors in his work: that children are better off not to go to school; and the emphasis placed on individual needs. The latter appears to be characteristic of many Western writers.

62. A good way to begin considering the place of language in education is to read Labov, W., 'The logic of nonstandard English'. In *Language and Poverty*. Markham, 1970. An excellent introduction to the relationship between thought and language is Slobin, D. I., *Psycholinguistics*, 2nd edn. Scott, Foresman, 1979.

63. A succinct description outlining the nature of language is given by Hockett, C. F., 'Animal "languages" and human language.' In Spuhler, J. A. (ed.) *The Evolution of Man's Capacity for Culture*. Wayne State University Press, 1965.

64. Rogers, C. R., *On Becoming a Person*. Constable, 1967, p. 273.

65. Much of this was of course known to Freud. See his 'The unconscious', reprinted in *On Metapsychology: The Theory of Psychoanalysis*, Vol. 11. Penguin Freud Library, 1984.

66. See Hendrix, G., 'A new clue to transfer of training'. *Elementary School Journal*, **48**, 197–208, 1947; also her 'Prerequisites to meaning'. *Mathematics Teacher*, **43**, 334–339, 1950; and 'Learning by discovery'. *Mathematics Teacher*, **54**, 290–299, 1961. The most perceptive discussion of this matter I know is by George Katona in his *Organising and Memorising*. Hafner, 1967; first published 1940. It is a shame that this work is not better known. For further thoughtful comments see Hilgard, E. R. *et al.*, 'Rote memorization, understanding, and transfer'. *Journal of Experimental Psychology*, **46**(4), 288–292, 1953; Haslerud, G. M. and Meyers, S., 'The transfer value of given and individually derived principles'. *Journal of Educational Psychology*, **49**, 293–299, 1958; Wittrock, M. C., 'The learning by discovery hypothesis'. In Shulman, L. S. *et al.* (eds) *Learning by Discovery: A Critical Appraisal*. Rand McNally, 1966; and Worthen, B. R., 'A study of discovery and expository presentation: implications for teaching'. *Journal of Teacher Education*, **19**, 223–242, 1968. Two further interesting comments are Kersh, B. Y., 'The adequacy of meaning as an explanation for the superiority of learning by independent discovery'. *Journal of Educational Psychology*, **49**(5), 282–292, 1958; and 'The motivating effect of learning by directed discovery'. *Journal of Educational Psychology*, **53**(2), 65–71, 1962. For a thoughtful and practical analysis of what is involved in 'problem-based learning', applied to a university setting but having general applicability, see Schmidt, H. G., 'Problem-based learning: rationale and description'. *Medical Education*, **117**, 11–16, 1983. There are studies on this topic which suggest that expository methods result in learners gaining marks in tests as high as those obtained by learners taught by discovery methods. That is not what is under discussion here. It should also be noted that many of those who have conducted research on this topic appear to believe that teachers can use discovery methods if only asked to do so and given some training in their use. In my experience nothing could be further from the truth. I do not advocate 'discovery' methods or indeed any 'method'. I believe all such labels are trite. I have been much helped by the work of Hendrix, but her samples appear to be small. My attention was drawn to her work by D. P. Ausubel, who is critical of it. See his 'Learning by discovery: rationale and mystique'. *Bulletin of the National Association of Secondary School Principals*, **45**, 18–58, 1961. Lawrence Kubie's 'The psychotherapeutic ingredient in the learning process'. In Porter, R. (ed.) *The Role of Learning in Psychotherapy*. J. & A. Churchill, 1968, is also of interest here.

67. The outlook of a 'liberal' like Rogers, if it emphasizes the needs of the individual, ends up being very similar to the views of those on the radical right, resulting, in my estimation, not only in the neglect of family and community, but also in their destruction and, with that, the destruction of the individual.

68. The most suggestive examples I know are to be found in some of the literature on Zen Buddhism. See for example Watts, A., *Psychotherapy East and West*. Penguin, 1973.

69. For examples of laboratory research into problem-solving see Johnson-Laird, P. N. and Wason, P. C., *Thinking*. Cambridge University Press, 1977; and Wason, P. C. and Johnson-Laird, P. N., *Psychology of Learning: Structure and Content*. Batsford, 1972. For a comment on this approach see Cheng, P. W. and Holyoak, K. J., 'Pragmatic reasoning schemas'. *Cognitive Psychology*, **17**, 391–416, 1985. For a brief introduction see Kahney, H., *Problem Solving: A Cognitive Approach*. Open University Press, 1986. Reading it I found myself thinking that, if a creature from another planet came across it in outer space, the image it would form of a human would resemble a pocket calculator. But then, as Spinoza pointed out, not only God creates man in 'his' own image.

70. See Jerome Bruner's reflections on his research in his *In Search of Mind*. Harper & Row, 1983. For some comment on the neglect of feelings in much psychological literature see Frosh, S., *Psychoanalysis and Psychology*. Macmillan, 1989.
71. The last reason was prompted by a suggestion in one of George Steiner's essays; some of the others were suggested by E. M. Forster in one of his.
72. I have in mind the work of Karl Popper. For an application of it in medical education see Campbell, E. J. M., 'Clinical science'. *Clinical Science and Molecular Medicine*, **51**, 1–7, 1976.
73. See Dreyfus, H. L. and Dreyfus, S. E., 'The mistaken psychological assumptions underlying the belief in expert systems'. In Costall *et al.*, *Cognitive Psychology in Question*.
74. Any attempt at computer simulation of human thinking which ignores the aesthetic dimension is sterile. See Heisenberg, W., 'Science and the beautiful'. In Wilber, *Quantum Questions*; and Polanyi, M., *The Study of Man*. University of Chicago Press, 1959.
75. See Spencer Brown for a fascinating account of the process of discovery in mathematics (*Laws of Form*, p. 95). Nothing could be less like how a computer program works.
76. Readers who find these comments absurd or interesting might like to consider the remarkable opening pages of Harding, D. E., 'On having no head'. In Hofstadter, D. *et al.* (eds) *The Mind's I*. Harvester Press, 1981. I believe the thrust of most of the rest of this book is mistaken.
77. In view of Piaget's eminence, I should perhaps explain why there are no references to his work in these notes. Because of his exclusive focus on cognition and the individual, for years I found his work uncongenial. More lately I came to appreciate the questions he raised, but by then I had almost completed this manuscript. For a helpful comment on his work in this context see Kuhn, D., 'The application of Piaget's theory of cognitive development to education'. *Harvard Educational Review*, **49**(3), 340–360, 1979. For criticisms of Piaget see Phillips, D. C. and Kelly, M. E., 'Hierarchical theories of development in education and psychology'. *Harvard Educational Review*, **45**(3), 351–375, 1975; and Sugarman, S., *Piaget's Construction of the Child's Reality*. Cambridge University Press, 1987. For further comment see Richardson, K. and Sheldon, S. (eds) *Cognitive Development to Adolescence*. Lawrence Erlbaum, 1990; and Carey, S. and Gelman, R. (eds) *The Epigenesis of Mind*. Lawrence Erlbaum, 1991.
78. For a lively account of the development of cognitive psychology see Baars, B. J., *The Cognitive Revolution in Psychology*. Guilford Press, 1986. The interviews with Jenkins and Weimer make for exciting reading and are about the best introduction to the study of academic psychology I know. For a comment on the way cognitivism is a part of Western ideology see Sampson, E. E., 'Cognitive psychology as ideology'. *American Psychologist*, **36**(7), 730–743, 1981. For a general critique of much academic psychology (without the distortions often found in sociological accounts) see Sarason, S. B., *Psychology Misdirected*. Free Press, 1981; also Williams, S. M., *Psychology on the Couch*. Harvester Press, 1988. See also Farr, R., 'The science of mental life: a social psychological perspective'. *Bulletin of the British Psychological Society*, **40**, 1–17, 1987.
79. A recent issue of the *Psychologist* (5, 1992) was devoted to a consideration of the demise of psychology in teacher education. Speaking as a practitioner, and as a person who finds psychological study endlessly fascinating, I could find nothing in it which helped me to understand this demise one mite better. The British Psychological Society (BPS) recently set up a working party which published a report entitled *Psychological Aspects of Beginning Teacher Competence*. Unfortunately, I am unable to find one thing in it which, I believe, would convince anyone that psychology can make a useful contribution to teacher education. This report was published in the Education Section Review of the BPS, **17**(1), 1993. This also contains a contribution by J. T. E. Richardson entitled 'Cognitive psychology and student learning', which begins: 'Paradoxically, contemporary cognitive psychology appears to have little to contribute to the practical enterprise of teaching and learning cognitive psychology itself.' Why the work of academic psychologists has contributed so relatively little to a better understanding of so much, including the process of learning and teaching, seems to me a fundamental question which has received too little attention. The paper by Richardson makes a very welcome beginning.

80. See for example Aitkenhead, A. M. *et al.* (eds) *Issues in Cognitive Modelling.* Open University Press, 1985. I believe that a teacher can read every word of this and, except for Norman's contribution which is critical of much that has gone before, not find anything helpful on learning.

81. Finkelman writes: 'A theory purporting to explain some aspect of psychological functioning is advanced. Experiments are performed to test the theory, with conflicting results. More experiments are performed, each one adding less to any genuine understanding of the phenomenon. Finally psychologists become frustrated (and bored) by their inability to make progress, and study of the issue ceases.' Finkelman, D., 'Science and psychology'. *American Journal of Psychology*, **91**(2), 179–199, 1978. Readers might like to compare the above with the following comment regarding the seventeenth century: ' "Explanation" may perhaps be roughly defined as a restatement of something – event, theory, doctrine, etc. – in terms of current interests and assumptions. It satisfies, as explanation, because it appeals to that particular set of assumptions, as superseding those of a past age or of a former state of mind. . . . All depends upon our presuppositions, which depend in turn upon our training, whereby we have come to regard (or to feel) one set of terms as ultimate, the other not.' Basil Willey, *The Seventeenth-Century Background*. Penguin Books, 1962, p. 10. See also Jerome Bruner's Herbert Spencer Lecture, 'Psychology and the image of man', in the *Times Literary Supplement*, 17 December 1976. Also the same writer's *In Search of Mind*.

82. In 1950 Turing wrote a paper considered a classic, entitled 'Computing machinery and intelligence'. The writer argues that a valid test of computer intelligence would occur if a judge were unable to differentiate between a computer and a human giving a reply, if computer, human and judge were in separate rooms and the human used a typewriter. This paper is reprinted and often discussed in Anderson, A. R. (ed.) *Minds and Machines*. Prentice-Hall, 1964.

83. Sacks, O., *Awakenings*. Picador, 1982, p. 207.

84. See for example Benger, D. A. *et al.* (eds) *Applications of Cognitive Psychology: Problem Solving, Education and Computing*. Lawrence Erlbaum, 1987. The most useful contributions (e.g. by Trowbridge on the best number of learners to each terminal) have nothing to do with cognitive psychology but report straightforward educational research. An even more striking example is Richardson, J. E. *et al.* (eds) *Student Learning: Research in Education and Cognitive Psychology*. SRHE and Open University Press, 1987. There are three kinds of contribution in this: those based on straightforward educational research; those critical of the contribution of cognitive psychology to education; and those based on cognitive psychology. I think most teachers would find some of the first kind useful, some of the second kind interesting, and all of the third kind useless. For an extensive review of the alleged contributions of cognitive psychology to teaching problem-solving see Frederiksen, N., 'Implications of cognitive theory for instruction on problem solving'. *Review of Educational Research*, **54**(3), 363–407, 1984. In its forty pages I was unable to find anything I could use in my classes. For a discussion of cognitivism by a large number of scholars see Haugeland, J., 'The nature and plausibility of cognitivism'. *Behavioural and Brain Sciences*, **2**, 215–260, 1978. Again, I do not think teachers will find anything useful in these forty-five closely printed pages. It seems to me that the general poverty of cognitivism can also be seen in the field of psychotherapy. See for example Mahoney, M. J. (ed.) *Psychotherapy Process*. Plenum Press, 1980. The most interesting contributions (e.g. those by Mahoney, Arnkoff, Neisser, Weimer, and the Maxwells) are all directly or implicitly critical of the cognitive position. Also critical are Coyne, J. C. and Gotlib, I. H., 'The role of cognition in depression: a critical appraisal.' *Psychological Bulletin*, **94**(3), 472–505, 1983. The basic fault of the cognitive model is that it is unable to account for psychopathology. I believe the same is true of family systems theory and social psychology in general. Whatever the case, as these approaches are based on language and cognition, rather than on experience, they run counter to the basic thesis of this book. A notable exception to the general unhelpfulness of cognitive psychology for teachers is the collection by Weimer and Palermo, *Cognition and the Symbolic Process*. I found the contribution by Weimer, 'Overview of a cognitive conspiracy: reflections on the volume', exceptionally helpful. Also interesting is his 'Ambiguity and the future of psychology'. In Weimer, W. B.

and Palermo, D. S. (eds) *Cognition and the Symbolic Process*, Vol. 2. Lawrence Erlbaum, 1982. I did not learn as much from his 'Hayek's approach to the problems of complex phenomena: an introduction to the theoretical psychology of *The Sensory Order*', in the latter publication. This seems to suggest that what we now have in the West – and increasingly in Latin America, Africa and Asia – is the best of all possible worlds. It is interesting that Polanyi, Popper and Hayek – to whose writings Weimer frequently refers – seem to share a basic political and philosophic outlook, perhaps grounded in a reaction to Central European utopian totalitarianism. This might be compared with, say, Lewontin, R. C., 'Organism and environment'. In Plotkin, H. C. (ed.) *Learning, Development and Culture*. Wiley, 1982. An attractively written and produced work in the cognitive tradition is Bransford, *Human Cognition*. This contains many practical findings which teachers will find useful.

As I was correcting the page proofs of this book I was sent a copy of Benny Shanon's *The Representational and the Presentational: An Essay on Cognition and the Study of Mind*. Harvester Wheatsheaf, 1993. I have only had time to browse, but was relieved and delighted to find someone who shares my disquiet about cognitivism and is able to muster a scholarly critique of it.

85. For some revealing light on how journal papers are selected see Standing, L. and McKelvie, S., 'Psychological journals: a case for treatment'. *Bulletin of the British Psychological Society*, **39**, 445–450, 1986. Also Stacey, B. G., 'The uses of psychology journals'. *The Psychologist*, **6**, 12–15, 1993.

4 Perception and Learning

1. For comment on the word 'coded' see Bower, T., *The Perceptual World of the Child*. Fontana, 1977, p. 65.
2. I first came across the concept of 'schemas' in Frederic Bartlett's *Remembering*, Cambridge University Press, 1932. I am much indebted to him. A stronger influence here has been Abercrombie, M. L. J., *The Anatomy of Judgement*. Free Association Books, 1989; first published 1960. For a more recent discussion on 'schema' see Neisser, U., *Cognition and Reality*. W. H. Freeman, 1976. For a recent application (very reminiscent of Abercrombie) see Rumelhart, D. E., *Understanding Understanding*. Centre for Human Information Processing, University of California, 1981.
3. I refer again to Oakley, D. A., 'Cognition and imagery in animals'. In Oakley, D. A. (ed.) *Brain and Mind*. Methuen, 1985.
4. This illustration is taken from Dallenbach, K. M., 'A puzzle picture with a new principle of concealment'. *American Journal of Psychology*, **64**, 431–433, 1951. Reproduced with permission.
5. Gregory, R. L., *Eye and Brain*. Weidenfeld & Nicolson, 1979.
6. Tom Bower shows how a child deprived of visual stimulus in the early months of life may never learn how to see even when it has optimal conditions to do so later in life. See his *The Perceptual World of the Child*. Readers may wonder what happens when a person has intact eyes but sustains an injury in the part of the brain responsible for seeing. For an account with fascinating implications see Weiskrantz, L., *Blindsight*. Oxford University Press, 1986.
7. For important differences between seeing, and hearing language, see the contribution by Turvey in Weimer, W. B. and Palermo, D. S. (eds) *Cognition and the Symbolic Process*. Lawrence Erlbaum, 1982.
8. Boas is quoted to the effect that, when anthropologists first encountered so-called primitive people, and attempted to write those people's language with the letters of their own language, they often jotted down sounds which were irrelevant, and left out sounds which were important. What their jottings most clearly revealed was what their own native language happened to be (e.g. English, French, German). See Proffit, D. R. and Halwes, T., 'Categorical perception: a contractual approach'. In Weimer and Palermo, *Cognition and the Symbolic Process*, Vol. 2.

9. See Buckhout, R., 'Eyewitness testimony', and Neisser, U., 'John Dean's memory: a case study'. In Neisser, U. (ed.) *Memory Observed*. W. H. Freeman, 1982.
10. This is a large topic, highly relevant to this book, and I must summarize my position as best I can:

   (a) References to 'relativism' often include a direct or oblique mention of Einstein. As is well known, his special theory of relativity holds that natural phenomena will look different depending on the position of an observer; or, more in his terms, every physical description of something, like a body moving in space, will be relative to the things around it. Hence, if everything in the universe, including light, were moving at the same speed, it would be impossible to measure that speed. In short, it is how things *appear* from a particular point which is relative, not that 'everything is relative'. Einstein also noted that his work in physics has no implications for life in general. He wrote: 'The present fashion of applying the axioms of physical science to human life is not only entirely mistaken, but also has something reprehensible in it.' For some penetrating comments on this matter see Wilber's Introduction in Wilber, K. (ed.) *Quantum Questions*. Shambhala, 1984. See also Heisenberg, W., *Physics and Philosophy*. Penguin, 1989. I find it remarkable that the social and philosophical inferences made by those who are not physicists themselves, on the basis of what some eminent physicists have written, are often far removed from those which those same physicists have themselves made.

   (b) The belief in 'the social construction of reality' has so permeated thinking in the second half of this century that it has almost achieved the status of a self-evident truth, to question which risks placing oneself among the reactionary, blind, dogmatic, insecure and illiberal. In spite of such risks I note my belief that this position is logically untenable, and pernicious to serious inquiry. I believe it is also destructive of human relationships. For example, in a relativist frame of reference I am unable to distinguish between truth and falsehood, fake and genuine, sincere and insincere, love and hate, or fantasy and reality. In other words, I would never be able to discover, for example, whether I am, or am not, *'really'* 'selfish', or whether that was someone's 'construction' of me.

   (c) The 'relativistic' position is ultimately irrational because, as it is in principle impossible to measure the general validity of a statement couched in its terms, all questioning and discussion must eventually come to an end. (For example, if all beliefs are relative, then that belief must be relative, too, and hence no more valid than any other belief, including its opposite.) This makes its position ultimately impenetrable, making relativism more like an ideology or a faith than a part of rational discourse. For a lucid discussion of what is involved in being rational see Bartley, W. W., Jr., *The Retreat to Commitment*. Open Court, 1984. See also Hollis, M. and Lukes, S. (eds) *Rationality and Relativism*. Blackwell, 1982.

   (d) A striking feature of work written from the relativist/postmodernist position is the absence of concrete pointers in it as to how one might *do* anything, particularly in the work which stresses the importance of practical action. Most of the contributions in Kvale, S. (ed.) *Psychology and Postmodernism* (Sage, 1992) sound like polemics, with the exception of the contribution by Seth Chaiklin, which is like fresh water in an arid desert; even its English suddenly sounds 'real'. Not only are we never told by the other contributors how we might concretely do anything, the only tool they give us, to help us to decide whether what we are doing is stupid or sound, is to see whether it 'works'. That is like using a hammer to open a tin of beans: it works, but there are better ways.

   (e) You can't say that a given film, say, conveys an 'unreal' picture of reality, hence there ceases to be a distinction between reality and fantasy – indeed, these words become meaningless – indeed, the very concept of 'meaning' becomes meaningless.

   (f) It seems to me that the notion of 'the social construction of reality' is more a product of Western alienation than an explanation of it, and much of the postmodernism literature which has come my way reads more like 'intellectualization', and a defence against (or 'denial' of) depression, than a comment on life. How else explain its negation of reality?

   (g) The question raised is ultimately about whether the human mind is inside or outside nature. For a comment on this see note 17 below.
11. For comment on the dramatic decline in American educational attainments see National

Commission on Excellence in Education, *A Nation at Risk*. In Ryan, K. and Cooper, J. M. (eds) *Kaleidoscope: Readings in Education*, 5th ed. Houghton Mifflin, 1988. This book contains many useful articles.

12. Plato, *Protagoras & Meno*. Penguin, 1964.

13. Two and a half thousand years later, here is Spencer Brown (in *Laws of Form*. Allen & Unwin, 1969) saying something similar when discussing the process of discovery in mathematics: 'Even the analogy of seeking something cannot, in this context, be quite right. For what we find, eventually, is something we have known, and may well have been consciously aware of, all along. Thus we are not, in this sense, seeking something that has ever been hidden. The idea of performing a search can be unhelpful, or even positively obstructive, since searches are in general organised to find something which has been previously hidden, and is thus not open to view. In discovering a proof, we must do something more subtle than search. We must come to see the relevance, in respect of whatever statement it is we wish to justify, of some fact in full view, and of which, therefore, we are constantly aware.'

14. Blakemore, C., *Mechanics of the Mind*. Cambridge University Press, 1977. For a review of research in this area see Mayes, A., 'The physiology of memory'. In Underwood, G. *et al.* (eds) *Aspects of Consciousness*, Vol. 2. Academic Press, 1981.

15. See W. B. Weimer's 'Psycholinguistics and Plato's paradoxes of the *Meno*'. *American Psychologist*, **28**, 15–33, 1973. I had not seen this paper mentioned till I read Baars's book, *The Cognitive Revolution in Psychology*. Guilford Press, 1986. I thought it one of the most interesting contributions to the study of learning I had come across. It raised a host of questions, but by then I had almost completed this manuscript. I found it strange to think I had in part been trying to retrace a route Plato had traversed so long ago.

16. Sinnott, E. W., *Matter, Mind and Man*. Allen & Unwin, 1937, p. 43.

17. Schrödinger, E., *What Is Life?* and *Mind and Matter*. Cambridge University Press, 1967. Readers may see how far removed this position is from the one which postulates that the human mind 'constructs' reality. The point is important because those who favour the constructivist position often refer to the work of modern physicists to buttress their position. Schrödinger makes it clear that he considers us and the world one. In writing this book, I repeatedly found myself having to refer to the literature on the relationship between mind and body. It seems to me that this is inescapable in any serious study of learning. I found the following works (in addition to the ones cited) helpful: Sherrington, A., *Man on His Nature*. Cambridge University Press, 1940, often reprinted; Sperry, R. W., 'A modified concept of consciousness'. *Psychological Review*, **76**, 532–536, 1969; and Popper, K., 'Three worlds'. In McMurrin, S. M. (ed.) *The Tanner Lectures on Human Values*, Vol. 1. University of Utah Press, 1980.

18. Gibson, J., *The Senses Considered as Perceptual Systems*. Houghton Mifflin, 1966, p. 267. Gibson also writes: 'If what things afford is specified in the light, sound, and odour around them, and does not consist of the subjective memories of what they have afforded in the past, then the learning of new meanings is an education in attention rather than an accrual of associations.'

19. See Weimer, 'Psycholinguistics'. See also Piattelli-Palmarini, M. (ed.) *Language and Learning*. Routledge, 1980, especially the contributions by Chomsky and Fodor. This book contains many insights into what is sometimes called the 'innate' versus 'constructivist' debate. I regret it came into my hands after I had almost completed the manuscript.

5 Real Learning

1. Reynolds, B., 'Reductionism in literary theory'. In Peacocke, A. (ed.) *Reductionism in Academic Disciplines*. SRHE and NFER-Nelson, 1985, p. 79.

2. I realize I cannot hope for more. For that reason this book is not written as a textbook. If it lacks things such as numbered summaries, that is not due to oversight, but to a certain view of learning.

3. I intend the word 'aberration' to be taken literally. My reason is indicated by the following

comment, often made by psychotherapists on the basis of their clinical practice: 'It is further to be noted that intellectual pursuits as such, whether literary, artistic, scientific or otherwise, appear to exercise a special attraction for individuals possessing schizoid characteristics to one degree or another. Where scientific pursuits are concerned, the attraction would appear to depend upon the schizoid individual's attitude of detachment, no less than upon his over-valuation of the thought-processes; for these are both characteristics which readily lend themselves to capitalisation within the field of science.' Fairbairn, W. R. D., *Psychoanalytic Studies of the Personality*. Routledge, 1972, p. 6.

4. R. D. Laing describes such feelings vividly. See his *The Divided Self*. Penguin, 1965.

5. Weckowicz, T. E., 'Depersonalisation–derealisation syndrome and perception: a contribution of psychopathology to epistemology'. In Royce, J. R. *et al.* (eds) *The Psychology of Knowing*. Gordon & Breach, 1972.

6. For help with this insight I am indebted to Gustavo Delgado-Aparicio in a personal communication.

7. See Zajonc, R. B., 'Feeling and thinking'. *American Psychologist*, 35(2), 151–175, 1980. I came across this interesting paper when I had almost completed this manuscript. See also the early and fascinating paper by Morton Prince, 'Can emotion be regarded as energy?' In Reymert, M. L. (ed.) *Feelings and Emotions: The Wittenberg Symposium*. Clark University Press, 1928.

8. See Claxton, G., 'The light's on but there's nobody home'. This is a clear argument in support of the belief that our ego is a fiction. In Claxton, G. (ed.) *Beyond Therapy*. Wisdom Publications, 1986.

9. I am indebted to Benjamin Lee Whorf here. I take this opportunity to note my debt to my late friend George Stern for drawing my attention to his work. It is interesting to see how Whorf and Vygotsky complement each other so well. See Whorf's *Language, Thought and Reality*, ed. Carroll, J. B. MIT Press, 1973. First published 1956. For some glimpses of what this state 'behind' language may involve see Luria, A. R., *The Mind of a Mnemonist*. Harvard University Press, 1968. Also helpful is Brewer, W. F., 'The problem of meaning and the interrelations of the higher mental processes'. In Weimer, W. B. and Palermo, D. S. (eds) *Cognition and the Symbolic Process*. Lawrence Erlbaum, 1982. For more recent comments see Weiskrantz, L. (ed.) *Thought without Language* (especially the contributions by Premack, Schacter, Horn, Kertesz and Bisiach), Oxford University Press, 1988.

10. For an introduction to the thinking of the deaf see Furth, H. G., *Thinking without Language*. Free Press, 1966. Also Meyers, R., 'Relation of thinking and language'. *Archives of Neurology and Psychiatry*, 60, 119–139, 1948. Slobin also has helpful things to say: see Slobin, D. I. *Psycholinguistics*, 2nd edn. Scott, Foresman, 1979.

11. For this example and several others I am indebted to E. T. Gendlin. See his 'A theory of personality change'. In Worchel, P. *et al.* (eds) *Personality Change*. Wiley, 1964. Also the same writer's 'Focusing'. *Psychotherapy*, 6(1), 4–15, 1961. For other comment on this matter see Wickens, D. D., 'Encoding categories of words: an empirical approach to meaning'. *Psychological Review*, 77, 1–15, 1970. A letter from Einstein is also pertinent here. It is reproduced in Hadamard, J., *The Psychology of Invention in the Mathematical Field*. Dover, 1954.

12. Quoted in Brown, R. and McNeill, D., 'The tip of the tongue phenomenon'. *Journal of Verbal Learning and Verbal Behavior*, 5, 325–337, 1966. These writers note that 'the whole word is represented in *abstract form recall*' (emphasis in original).

13. In Bartlett, F., *Remembering*. Cambridge University Press, 1932, p. 206.

14. Weiskrantz, L., 'Neuropsychology and the nature of consciousness'. In Blakemore, C. *et al.* (eds) *Mindwaves*. Blackwell, 1987. Also Schacter, D. A., *et al.*, 'Access to consciousness'. In Weiskrantz, L. (ed.) *Thought without Language*. Clarendon Press, 1988.

15. In a wish to be clear, I sometimes use the term 'unconscious' when I should perhaps use the term 'preconscious'.

16. I understand that it would be more accurate to say that 'the left hemisphere achieves superiority in the utilization of a multiplicity of descriptive systems which are fully formed in an individual's cognitive repertoire', while the right hemisphere is 'most crucial in the processing of materials to which none of the descriptive systems preexisting in a subject's cognitive repertoire is readily applicable, and in assembling new descriptive systems'. See

Goldberg, E. and Costa, L. D., 'Hemispheric differences in the acquisition and use of descriptive systems'. *Brain and Language*, **14**, 144–173, 1981.

17. See Oakley, D. A. and Eames, L. C., 'The plurality of consciousness'. In Oakley, D. (ed.) *Brain and Mind*. Methuen, 1985.

18. Goldstein, K., *Human Nature in the Light of Psychopathology*. Schocken Books, 1963; first published 1939. Geschwind notes that Goldstein had reported such findings as early as 1908. See Geschwind, N., 'The perverseness of the right hemisphere'. *Behavioral and Brain Sciences*, **4**, 106–107, 1981. Freud noted the same phenomenon but explained it via the concept of 'repression', and it seems to me that it is not difficult to reconcile their positions. See Freud's 'The unconscious', reprinted in *On Metapsychology. The Theory of Psychoanalysis*, Vol. II. Penguin Freud Library, 1984, p. 199. See also Schachtel, E. G., 'On memory and childhood amnesia'. In Neisser, U. (ed.) *Memory Observed*. W. H. Freeman, 1982. I thought this a fascinating paper, among other things because it points to the limitations of language. For a review of experimental work on repression see Holmes, D. S., 'Investigations of repression'. *Psychological Bulletin*, **81**, 632–653, 1974. Holmes suggests that the experimental evidence does not support Freud but I doubt whether the phenomenon can be replicated in a laboratory. For an interesting comment on the way psychoanalytic and sociobiological ideas are beginning to converge see Badcock, C. R., *The Problem of Altruism*. Blackwell, 1986. This is also of interest in view of the strictures by philosophers of science like Popper and Lakatos on the standing of Freud's theories.

19. LeDoux, J. E., 'Brain, mind and language'. In Oakley, *Brain and Mind*, p. 206. I am particularly indebted to LeDoux. See also Volpe, B. T. *et al.*, 'Information processing of visual stimuli in an "extinguished" field'. *Nature*, **282**, 722–724, 1979. Also Gazzaniga, M. S., 'Right hemisphere language following brain bisection: a 20-year perspective'. *American Psychologist*, **38**, 525–537, 1983. In an earlier publication Gazzaniga and R. W. Sperry ('Language after section of the cerebral commissures'. *Brain*, **90**, 131–148, 1967) state that the right hemisphere is conscious. The discussion seems to turn on a definition of the term 'conscious'. In using it I have in mind Bartlett's notion of the organism's 'capacity to turn around upon its own schemata and to construct them afresh'. In another publication we find 'while nonhumans may be found to be aware and even self-aware, they are nevertheless not aware in the unique ways and to the extent made possible by the human verbal system'. LeDoux, J. E. *et al.*, 'Beyond commissurotomy: clues to consciousness'. In Gazzaniga, M. S. (ed.) *Handbook of Behavioural Neurobiology*: Vol. 2, *Neuropsychology*. Plenum, 1979. See also Marin, O. S. M. *et al.*, 'Origins and distribution of language', in the same publication. For comment on how the left hemisphere tends to interfere with the right hemisphere's attempts to deal with verbal stimuli see Levy, J. *et al.*, 'Expressive language in the surgically separated minor hemisphere'. *Cortex*, **7**, 49–58, 1971. Also Levy, J., 'Possible basis for the evolution of lateral specialisation of the human brain'. *Nature*, **224**, 614–615, 1969. For a review of research see Galin, D., 'Implications for psychiatry of left and right cerebral specialisation'. *Archives of General Psychiatry*, **31**, 572–583, 1974. For a general review of the topic of hemisphere differences see Springer, S. P. *et al.*, *Left Brain, Right Brain*, 3rd edn. W. H. Freeman, 1989. For a brief and clear review see Nebes, R. D., 'Hemispheric specialization in commissurotomized man'. *Psychological Bulletin*, **81**(1), 1–14, 1974. For a masterly review of language and the brain see N. Geschwind's paper in *Science*, **170**, 940–944, 1970. For a clinical case report describing the loss of the right hemisphere in a man with a right hemisphere speech centre see Smith, A., 'Speech and other functions after left (dominant) hemispherectomy'. *Journal of Neurology, Neurosurgery and Psychiatry*, **29**, 467–471, 1966.

20. See Ley, R. G. *et al.*, 'Consciousness, emotion, and the right hemisphere'. In Underwood, G. *et al.* (eds) *Aspects of Consciousness*, Vol. 2. Academic Press, 1981. Also Schwartz, G. E. *et al.*, 'Right hemisphere lateralisation for emotion in the human brain: interaction with cognition'. *Science*, **190**, 280–288, 1975 and Jackeim, H. A. *et al.* 'Emotions are expressed more intensely on the left side of the face'. *Science*, **202**, 434–436, 1978.

21. The best single source of evidence I know for this assertion is to be found in the correspondence on 'The Cyril Burt Affair' published in various issues of the *Bulletin of the British Psychological Society* from January 1977.

22. See Freud's *The Ego and the Id*.

23. Spinetta, J. J. and Rigler, D., 'The child-abusing parent'. *Psychological Bulletin*, **77**(4), 296–304, 1972. I thought this a most valuable paper.

24. The most striking review of experimental findings on this topic I know is by Nisbett, R. E. and Wilson, T. D., 'Telling more than we can know: verbal reports on mental processes'. *Psychological Review*, **84**, 231–259, 1977. But see Smith, E. R. and Miller, F. D., 'Limits on perception of cognitive processes'. *Psychological Review*, **85**(4), 355–362, 1978. For further comment see Natsoulas, T., 'Conscious perception and the paradox of blindsight'. In Underwood *et al.*, *Aspects of Consciousness*, Vol. 3. For a discussion and review of the literature see Dixon, N. F., *Subliminal Perception: The Nature of a Controversy*. McGraw-Hill, 1971. For an empirical test of the psychoanalytic contribution see Silverman, L. H., 'Psychoanalytic theory: the reports of my death are greatly exaggerated'. *American Psychologist*, **31**, 621–637, 1976. Any claim made for computer simulations of humans would have to be able to model all of the findings cited by these researchers.

25. For an introduction to this topic and helpful references see Wilkinson, A., *The Foundations of Language*. Oxford University Press, 1971. For comments which show that the kind of grammar taught in school is seldom the kind of grammar used to produce language see Slobin, *Psycholinguistics*. Perhaps I should note here my belief that it is most important for learners to know how to spell and punctuate accurately, and that this can only be 'really' learnt in the context of creative work. For a most interesting work which shows that learning is powerfully a matter of suitable exposure rather than teaching, see Pronko, N. H., 'On learning how to play the violin at the age of four without tears'. *Psychology Today*, **2**, 52–57, 1969.

26. See Frith, C. D., 'Consciousness, information processing and schizophrenia'. *British Journal of Psychiatry*, **134**, 225–235, 1979.

27. Vygotsky, L. S., *Mind in Society*, ed. Cole, M. *et al.*, Harvard University Press, 1978, again explains this well.

28. Although I find his writing opaque, I am indebted to F. M. Alexander here. See his *The Use of the Self*. Gollancz, 1985; first published 1932. For comment on the work of Alexander see Jones, F. P., *Body Awareness in Action*. Schocken Books, 1976.

29. Readers may like to compare this formulation with the interesting one suggested by Newcomb, T. M., 'Persistence and regression of changed attitudes: long-range studies'. *Journal of Social Issues*, **19**, 3–14, 1963.

30. See Simon, H. A., 'The shape of automation', first published in 1960 and reprinted in Pylyshyn, Z. W. (ed.) *Perspectives on the Computer Revolution*. Prentice-Hall, 1970. For an introduction to artificial intelligence see Boden, M. A., *Artificial Intelligence and Natural Man*. Harvester Press, 1977. I began reading this work with interest and admired Margaret Boden's clear writing and sympathetic intelligence. However, as I continued, I became increasingly uneasy. I kept thinking of a character named Bledyard in Iris Murdoch's novel *The Sandcastle* (1954) and the way a female character describes him (in the Penguin edition, p. 81). She says: 'He argues insistently and coherently and with the appearance of logic – but somehow it's just all wrong, there's some colossal distortion.' I must quote another character's reply: 'One has to ask oneself now and then whether it isn't one's own vision that is distorted.' I sense the same 'colossal distortion' in other accounts of artificial intelligence I have read, and readers must make up their own minds. In this respect I have been much helped by Joseph Weizenbaum's highly readable *Computer Power and Human Reason*. Penguin, 1984.

31. It was E. Fromm who first drew my attention to these steps, but I am unfortunately unable to recall where.

32. For a clear introduction to marital problems see Dominian, J., *Marital Breakdown*. Penguin, 1969. For a more detailed treatment see Dicks, H. V., *Marital Tensions*. Routledge, 1967. Both cite much data which links divorce with early experiences.

33. See van den Berg, J. H. *The Changing Nature of Man*. Norton, 1961. I would add that few of the sociological accounts I have read explain why an individual should be affected by social norms in the first place.

34. All this was of course clear to Freud. See his *The Ego and the Id*, reprinted in *Collected Works*, Vol. 11. In this we see Freud attempting to grope his way towards an under-

standing of mental functioning, but still hamstrung by the materialistic conceptions of his time. He was clearly wrong about many things, but then, only mediocrities are always right. For my own part, I am increasingly inclined to believe that Freud's clinical observations were often acute, but the explanations he offered for them often wrong. Thus I am often impatient with what is called his 'metapsychology' (for which he is most famous), and admire his clinical papers such as *Studies on Hysteria*, and Vol. 12 in the *Collected Works*. I also note that the common practice of teaching the topic of psychoanalysis via the works of Freud seems to me like teaching the topic of astronomy via the works of Kepler.

35. John Bowlby shows how and why people sometimes come to deny deeply painful feelings. See his brief and illuminating 'On knowing what you are not supposed to know and feeling what you are not supposed to feel'. *Canadian Journal of Psychiatry*, **24**(5), 403–408, 1979. It seems to me that this writer's *Attachment and Loss* (Vols 1, 2 and 3, Penguin, 1971–81) is the single most important contribution to the topics which Freud addressed published in the last thirty years. For a good introduction to Bowlby's work I would warmly recommend his *The Making and Breaking of Affectional Bonds*. Tavistock, 1979. All the criticisms made of Bowlby's work which I have seen strike me as either missing the essential point, or merely polemics.

36. A vivid description of a person who does not know what she is feeling can be found in Chekhov's short story, 'The Princess', in *The Oxford Chekhov*, Vol. 5. Oxford University Press, 1970.

37. For a most interesting comment on the idea that one must 'own' one's feelings see Eagle, M., 'Psychoanalysis and the personal', in Clark, P. *et al.* (eds) *Mind, Psychoanalysis and Science*. Blackwell, 1988. It is unfortunately true that in much of the psychoanalytical literature fidelity to Freud replaces the generation of testable hypotheses, but I do not think that this explains the vindictiveness with which Freud is attacked by some of the contributors to this volume. For an excellent discussion of these matters see Eagle, M. N., *Recent Developments in Psychoanalysis*. McGraw-Hill, 1984.

38. Examples can be found in Boden, *Artificial Intelligence*.

39. Sacks, O., *The Man Who Mistook His Wife for a Hat*. Pan Books, 1986, p. 12. Not only Sacks's patient speaks like this. Compare his words with Boden's, taken from her 'Does artificial intelligence need artificial brains?' (in Rose, S. *et al.* (eds) *Science and Beyond*. Blackwell, 1986). She is noting how a computer, simulating human intelligence, might pose a question, and uses these words: 'I don't know just what that thing is – but it's about a foot long, with an undulating spotted surface slanting away from the ground.' Because so much of Boden's reasoning is by analogy, the really interesting questions are lost. For example, how could one program a computer to have a sense of 'I'? For a lucid criticism of the notion of artificial intelligence see Wall, P. D. and Safran, J. N., 'Artefactual intelligence'. In Rose *et al. Science and Beyond*. For helpful comment on the way much current discussion on these matters is befuddled by reasoning based on false analogies see Hacker, P., 'Languages, minds and brains', in Blakemore *et al. Mindwaves*. One might here ask how one could model on a computer the reactions of a patient with Parkinson's when given L-Dopa. Sacks's account ties in with much of Freud's work; it even helps to clarify Georg Groddeck's *The Book of the It*. Vintage Books, 1961.

40. The best illustrations I know are provided by Gendlin, in the papers cited earlier. See also Rangell, L., 'Psychoanalysis, affects, and the human core'. *Psychoanalytic Quarterly*, **36**, 172–202, 1962. Also Welwood, J., 'Unfolding of experience: psychotherapy and beyond'. *Journal of Humanistic Psychology*, **22**, 91–104, 1982; and the same writer's collection *Awakening the Heart*. Shambhala, 1983. See also the works of Carl Rogers, Frederick Perls, and especially Arthur Janov's *The Primal Scream*. Abacus, 1973. I believe Janov makes mistakes, but also that he has a central insight of great importance. Another work of interest is Porter, R. (ed.) *The Role of Learning in Psychotherapy* (J. & A. Churchill, 1968), especially the contributions by Sackett and Kubie.

41. Forster, E. M., *Aspects of the Novel*. Penguin, 1970; often reprinted.

42. See Strupp, H. H. *et al.*, 'Psychotherapy experience in retrospect'. *Psychological Monographs: General and Applied*, **78**(11), whole no. 588, 1964; Whitehorn, J. C. and Betz, B. J.,

'A study of psychotherapeutic relationship between physicians and schizophrenic patients'. *American Journal of Psychiatry*, 321–331, 1954; and Gelso, C. J. and Carter, J. A., 'The relationship in counselling and psychotherapy'. *Counselling Psychologist*, **13**(2), 155–243, 1985. For a review of research and a most helpful discussion see Frank, J. D., *Persuasion and Healing*. Schocken Books, 1963.

43.   Dinnage, R., *One to One: Experiences of Psychotherapy*. Penguin, 1989, p. 50. This is a collection of interviews with people who have undergone therapy, and one catches one's breath at the sheer *personal* ineptitude of some of the therapists, and the damage this does to their clients. This closely parallels my own experience as a client and practitioner. Few situations have raised my hair as much as hearing a wacky therapist presenting the case of one of his patients. No amount of mere training overcomes this problem. For a brief introduction to psychotherapy see Storr, A., *The Integrity of the Personality*. Penguin, 1972; Basch, M. F., *Doing Psychotherapy*. Basic Books, 1980 and Malan, D. H., *Individual Psychotherapy and the Science of Psychodynamics*. Butterworth, 1978. I found the latter an especially helpful work in my training, but believe that the effect adduced to 'interpretations' may be as much a matter of the way in which they act as vehicles for something else. A writer whose work I find particularly congenial, and who has affected my own practice, is Peterfreund, E., *The Process of Psychoanalytic Therapy*. Analytic Press, 1983. (I thank Emmy Gut for first drawing my attention to the above.) A writer to whom I am especially indebted here is Ian Suttie. His *The Origins of Love and Hate* (most recent edn, Free Association Books, 1988) is not as well written as it might be, but it is essential reading. Also essential is Ellenberger, H. F., *The Discovery of the Unconscious*. Basic Books, 1970. I should perhaps note my belief that one reason we have therapists is because they respond to a need which society increasingly neglects.

44.   In his *The Theory and Practice of Group Psychotherapy*, Basic Books, 1985, Irving Yalom notes that, when clients are asked to evaluate their experience of therapy, they tend to say they learnt the most from interactions in the group, not the interpretations of the therapist; and when they do mention the therapist, it is more in terms of who she is, rather than what she has said. (This questions the emphasis he places on the cognitive element in therapy and hence his indirect criticism of Janov.) Interestingly enough, other research suggests that successful therapists strongly believe in their favoured orientation.

45.   See the works of Carl Rogers and Eugene Gendlin: Rogers, *On Becoming a Person*. Constable, 1967; Gendlin, 'A theory of personality change'. In Worchel, P. *et al.* (eds) *Personality Change*. Wiley, 1964; 'Focusing'. *Psychotherapy*, **6**(1), 4–15, 1961.

46.   Oliver, W. A., 'Teachers' educational beliefs versus their classroom practice'. *Journal of Educational Research*, **47**, 47–55, 1953.

47.   Combs, A. W. and Soper, D. W., 'The helping relationship as described by "good" and "poor" teachers'. *Journal of Teacher Education*, **14**, 64–67, 1963.

48.   Gonnella, J. S. *et al.*, 'Evaluation of patient care: an approach'. *Journal of the American Medical Association*, **214**(11), 2040–2043, 1970.

49.   Shakespeare, W., *Hamlet*. I, iii. *c.* 1601.

50.   Shakespeare, W., *The Merchant of Venice*. I, ii (Portia). *c.* 1597.

51.   I refer again to Vygotsky's *Thought and Language*. MIT Press, 1962. Long after Vygotsky had died, his colleague Luria wrote: 'It is no exaggeration to say that Vygotsky was a genius. Through more than five decades of science I never again met a person who even approached his clearness of mind, his ability to lay bare the essential structure of complex problems, his breadth of knowledge in many fields, and his ability to foresee the future development of his science.' In Luria, A. R., *The Making of Mind*. Harvard University Press, 1979, p. 38.

52.   I am again indebted to Whorf. See the marvellous last four chapters in his *Language, Thought and Reality*. Whorf's basic thesis is that there must be an agent 'behind' language. See also Fromm, E., *Beyond the Chains of Illusion*. Simon and Schuster, 1962.

53.   Bartlett, F., *Remembering*. Cambridge University Press, 1932, p. 207.

54.   Quoted by Luria in *The Making of Mind*. Luria also draws attention to the fact that, in his work with brain-damaged patients, Kurt Goldstein had noted years ago that the most basic forms of speech are not individual words, but the formulation of ideas as whole proposi-

tions. Goldstein noted that these are always bound up with the motives of people and the conditions in which they find themselves.

55. I believe it is impossible to write sensible psychology unless it incorporates an awareness of material of the kind to be found in works like Lynch, J. J., *The Broken Heart*. Harper & Row, 1977; and Totman, R., *The Social Causes of Illness*. Pantheon Books, 1979. The political and economic context is obviously also very important.

56. See the Summary at the end of Holt's *How Children Fail*. Penguin, 1969; revised edn, 1987. Jerome Bruner also has a good chapter on this matter entitled 'On coping and defending', in his *Toward a Theory of Instruction*. Norton, 1968.

57. This is a paraphrase from Krishnamurti.

58. Consider these comments by Louis de Broglie (who won the Nobel prize for physics in 1929): 'in order that humanity should have been able to adapt itself to live in the world which surrounds us, it would undoubtedly be necessary that there should be already between this world and our mind some analogy in structure; if that had not been so, perhaps humanity would not have been able to survive. Well, it would have disappeared, that is all!' In Wilber, K. (ed.) *Quantum Questions*. Shambhala, 1984, p. 118.

59. For comments on this mystery see Eiseley, L., *The Immense Journey*. Vintage, 1946; Dobzhansky, T., *The Biology of Ultimate Concern*. Fontana, 1971; Dubos, R., *The Torch of Life*. Simon & Schuster, 1962; Hardy, A., *The Living Stream*. Collins, 1965; and Jones, R. S., *Physics as Metaphor*. Sphere Books, 1983.

PART II TEACHING

6 The Transmission Method and an Alternative Approach

1. Wertheimer, M., *Productive Thinking*. Greenwood Press, 1978. For perceptive comments on the quality of teaching in colleges see Klapper, P., 'The professional preparation of the college teacher'. *Journal of General Education*, 3, 228–244, 1959.

2. A helpful guide is Katona, G., *Organising and Memorising*. Hafner, 1967. See also Hohn, F. E., 'Teaching creativity in mathematics'. *Arithmetic Teacher*, 8, 102–106, 1961; and Good, T. L. and Grouws, D. A., 'Teaching effectiveness in fourth grade mathematics classrooms'. In Borich, G. D. *et al.* (eds) *The Appraisal of Teaching: Concepts and Process*. Addison-Wesley, 1977.

3. Rogers, C. R., 'Personal thoughts on teaching and learning'. In Rogers, *On Becoming a Person*. Constable, 1967.

4. In Wragg, E. C., *Classroom Teaching Skills*. Croom Helm, 1984.

5. Miller, A., 'Depression and grandiosity as related forms of narcissistic disturbances'. *International Review of Psycho-Analysis*, 6, 61–76, 1979.

6. Abercrombie, M. L. J., *The Anatomy of Judgement*. Free Association Books, 1989; first published 1960.

7. There is a great deal of research which compares 'the lecture' with 'the discussion' method. None that I have seen would answer the question I have posed; and nearly all of it seems highly unsatisfactory. For a review see Costin, F., 'Lecturing versus other methods of teaching: a review of research'. *British Journal of Educational Technology*, 1(3), 4–31, 1972.

8. See Smith's Introduction, in Smith, B. O. (ed.) *Research in Teacher Education: A Symposium*. Prentice-Hall, 1971. See also Saadeh, I. Q., 'Teacher effectiveness or classroom efficiency: a new direction in the evaluation of teaching'. *Journal of Teacher Education*, 21, 73–91, 1970. Saadeh shows why so much research into teaching has yielded so little, but his conclusions strike me as opaque. See also Mitzel, H. E., 'Teacher effectiveness'. In Harris, C. W. (ed.) *Encyclopedia of Educational Research*, pp. 1481–1486, 1960. For a more recent account of teacher training, mostly based on the 'skills' or 'experience' approach, see Ashton, P. M. E. *et al.* (eds) *Teacher Education in the Classroom: Initial and In-service*. Croom Helm, 1983. For work which shows how even carefully conducted classroom research can yield little see Medley, D. M. and Mitzel, H. E., 'Some behavioural correlates

of teacher effectiveness'. *Journal of Educational Psychology*, **50**(6), 239–246, 1959. The only thing these researchers were able to establish with some certainty is that there is little relationship between how well a teacher teaches, and how effective that teacher's superiors believe he or she is. Few practising teachers will be surprised! For a detailed review of research into teaching see Dunkin, M. J. and Biddle, B. J., *The Study of Teaching*. Holt, Rinehart & Winston, 1974. I was only able to browse through this large book. As with so much 'empirical' work, it contains a mass of data without, as far as I can see, a theory to give the reader a sense of direction.

9. For a brief account of classroom research see Hopkins, D., *A Teacher's Guide to Classroom Research*. Open University Press, 1985. For a succinct comment on the difficulty of doing classroom research see Travers, R. M., 'Criteria of good teaching'. In Millman, J. (ed.) *Handook of Teacher Evaluation*. Sage, 1981. A work that has influenced me is Hamilton, D. and Delamont, S., 'Classroom research: a cautionary tale'. In Hamilton, D. (ed.) *Beyond the Numbers Game*. Macmillan, 1977. But see Hammersley, M. (ed.) *Controversies in Classroom Research*. Open University Press, 1986; and Hammersley, M. (ed.) *Case Studies in Classroom Research*. Open University Press, 1986. Also helpful are Erickson, F., 'Qualitative methods in research on teaching', and especially Biddle, B. J. and Anderson, D. S., 'Theory, methods, knowledge, and research on teaching'. Both in Wittrock, M. C. (ed.) *Handbook of Research on Teaching*. Macmillan, 1986. Though hard to apply to education, I have a hankering for the approach expressed by Platt, J. R., 'Strong inference'. *Science*, **146**, 347–353, 1964.

10. Rosenshine, B. V. and Furst, J., *Teacher Behaviour and Student Progress*. Slough: NFER, 1971. For another review of research, which largely supports the position taken in this book, see Soar, R. S., 'Teacher behaviour related to pupil growth'. *International Review of Education*, **18**, 508–528, 1922. See also Rosenshine's paper in Smith (ed.) *Research in Teacher Education: A Symposium*. See the same writer's review of research, 'Content, time & direct instruction'. In Peterson, P. L. *et al.* (eds) *Research on Teaching*. McCutchan, 1979. For a response, see Peterson's chapter in the same publication: 'Direct instruction reconsidered'. A more recent review of research on teaching by Rosenshine (Rosenshine, B. and Stevens, R., 'Teaching function'. In Wittrock, *Handbook of Research on Teaching*) suggests a more directive teacher, as does Good, T. L., 'Classroom research: a decade of progress'. *Educational Psychologist*, **18**(3), 127–144, 1983. I am unsure whether this reflects better research or a change in educational fashions, for although learners may gain more knowledge when directed closely, they are likely to achieve less real understanding that way.

7 The Teaching Process

1. See Sarason, I. G., 'The effects of anxiety and threat on the solution of a difficult task'. *Journal of Abnormal and Social Psychology*, **62**, 165–168, 1961. Also Thelen, H. T., 'Experimental research towards a theory of instruction'. *Journal of Educational Research*, **45**, 89–136, 1951.

2. A work with many helpful suggestions on how to teach English in a non-didactic way is Elbow, P., *Writing without Teachers*. Oxford University Press, 1973. See also Klippel, F., *Keep Talking*. Cambridge University Press, 1984; and Rinvolucri, M., *Grammar Games*. Cambridge University Press, 1986. I wish I had had the help of such works when I began teaching English!

3. Bransford, J. D., *Human Cognition*. Wadsworth, 1979, p. 119, notes interesting work by Pollchik on the value of giving examples.

4. Some of these comments are based on Fowler, H. W. and Fowler, F. G., *The King's English*. Oxford University Press, 1973, p. 11.

5. Leavitt, H. J. and Mueller, R. A. H., 'Some effects of feedback on communication'. *Human Relations*, **4**, 401–410, 1951.

6. Stuart, S., *Say*. Nelson, 1969. This is a lively account by a teacher of English of his discomfort with the transmission method of teaching and how he moved away from it.

7. Winnicott, D. W., *The Child, the Family, and the Outside World*. Penguin, 1964. Also Greenson, R. R., 'On enthusiasm'. *Journal of the American Psychoanalytic Association*, **10**, 3–21, 1962.
8. Kounin, J. S., *Discipline and Group Management in Classrooms*. R. E. Krieger, 1977. For a more readable account see Kounin's 'An analysis of teachers' managerial techniques'. In Morrison, A. *et al.* (eds) *The Social Psychology of Teaching*. Penguin, 1972. For a comment on Kounin's work see Brophy, J. E. and Evertson, C. M., 'Teacher behaviour and student learning in second and third grades'. In Borich, G. D. *et al.* (eds) *The Appraisal of Teaching: Concepts and Process*. Addison-Wesley, 1977. For tips on classroom management in schools see Marland, M., *The Craft of the Classroom*. Heinemann, 1975; also Wragg, E. C., *Classroom Teaching Skills*. Croom Helm, 1984.
9. For a comment on the concept of 'habituation' see Bower, *The Perceptual World of the Child*, p. 25. Also Humphrey, N. K. and Keeble, G. R., 'How monkeys acquire a new way of seeing'. *Perception*, **5**, 51–56, 1976.
10. See Montgomery, E. C., 'Exploratory behaviour as a function of similarity of stimulus situations'. *Journal of Comparative Physiological Psychology*, **46**, 129–133, 1953; and Berlyne, D. E. and Slater, J., 'Perceptual curiosity, exploratory behaviour, and maze learning'. *Journal of Comparative Physiological Psychology*, **50**, 228–232, 1957; Maddi, S. R., 'Affective tone during environmental regularity and change'. *Journal of Abnormal and Social Psychology*, **62**, 338–345, 1961.
11. The use of the term 'village idiot' is highly questionable. This story is based on a tale I heard many years ago when such a term was considered less offensive than it rightly is now. The term implies feeble-mindedness, and a certain attitude toward it, and for this I cannot think of a modern substitute.
12. For some answers see Brown, N. O., *Life against Death*. Wesleyan University Press, 1959, often reprinted. Also warmly recommended is Becker, E., *The Denial of Death*. Free Press, 1973.
13. For comments on the nature of analogies and their place in learning see Gick, M. L. and Holyoak, K. J., 'Schema induction and analogical transfer'. *Cognitive Psychology*, **15**, 1–38, 1983.
14. For comment on the place of imagination in teaching see Egan, K. *et al.* (eds) *Education and Imagination*. Open University Press, 1988.
15. Egan, K., *Teaching as Storytelling*. Routledge, 1988. Among other things the author questions the assumption that young children are unable to think in an abstract way.
16. Bower, G. H. and Clark, M. C., 'Narrative stories as mediators for serial learning'. *Psychonomic Science*, **14**(4), 181–182, 1969.
17. See Inagaki, K. and Hatano, G., 'Amplification of cognitive motivation and its effects on epistemic observation'. *American Educational Research Journal*, **14**(4), 485–491, 1977. Also Nisbet, J. and Shucksmith, J., *Learning Strategies*. Routledge, 1986; and Entwistle, N., 'Learning from the experience of studying'. In Francis, H. (ed.) *Learning to Teach: Psychology in Teacher Training*. Falmer Press, 1985.
18. A particularly good illustration of learning material, and an evaluation of its use compared with didactic teaching, is Brewer, I. M., *Learning More and Teaching Less*. SRHE and NFER-Nelson, 1985. See also Monk, G. L., 'Student engagement and teacher power in large classes'. In Boulton, C. *et al.* (eds) *Learning in Groups*. Jossey-Bass, 1983.
19. Lifson, T., 'A comparison between lectures and conference methods of teaching physiology'. *Journal of Medical Education*, **31**(6), 376–382, 1956.
20. Anderson, R.C. and Biddle, W. B., 'On asking people questions about what they are reading'. In Bower, G. H. (ed.) *The Psychology of Learning & Motivation*. Academic Press, 1975.
21. West, M. *et al.*, 'Medical students' attitudes toward basic sciences'. *Medical Education*, **16**, 188–191, 1982. See also Neame, R. L. B., 'How to construct a problem-based course'. *Medical Teacher*, **3**(3), 94–99, 1981.
22. Finkel, D. L. and Monk, G. S., 'Teachers and learning groups: dissolution of the Atlas complex'. In Boulton *et al.* *Learning in Groups*. Also Thelen, N. A., 'Some classroom quiddities for people-orientated teachers'. In Silberman, M.L. *et al.* (eds) *The Psychology of Open Teaching and Learning*. Little, Brown, 1972.

23. For an excellent description of good and poor teaching based on worksheets see 'Mixed ability teaching at Beachside Comprehensive'. In Ball, S., *Beachside Comprehensive*. Cambridge University Press, 1981.

24. I once had such a problem. I had replaced all the parts mentioned, one by one, over several weeks, with much sweat and expense, and then discovered that one of the flexible hoses was partly blocked and acting as a non-return valve!

25. For most helpful comments on what goes on in such discussions see Lomov, B. F., 'Psychological processes and communication'. *Soviet Psychology*, 17, 3–22, 1978; Kol'tsova, V. A., 'Experimental study of cognitive activity in communication'. *Soviet Education*, 17, 23–38, 1978; Inagaki, K., 'Facilitation of knowledge integration through classroom discussion'. *Quarterly Newsletter of the Laboratory of Comparative Human Cognition*, 3(2), 26–28, 1981.

26. See Johnson, D. W., 'Student–student interaction: the neglected variable in education'. *Educational Researcher*, 10(1), 5–10, 1981.

27. Yalom, I., *Theory and Practice of Group Psychotherapy*. Basic Books, 1985, p. 157.

8 Classroom Interaction

1. See Rogers, Carl, *On Becoming a Person*. Constable, 1967, and his *Client-Centred Therapy*. Houghton Mifflin, 1951. Another valuable book is Dinnage, R., *One to One: Experiences of Psychotherapy*. Penguin, 1989. She shows how therapists are like plumbers: some do an excellent job, some have no effect, and some cause a great deal of damage.

2. See Christensen, C. M., 'Relationship between pupil achievement, pupil affect-need, teacher warmth, and teacher permissiveness'. *Journal of Educational Psychology*, 51(3), 169–174, 1960. This is a most helpful paper. For a review of research see Ripple, R. W., 'Affective factors influence classroom learning'. *Educational Leadership*, 22, 476–480, 1965.

3. John Holt has some vivid descriptions of this. See his *How Children Fail*. Penguin, 1969; revised edn 1987.

4. I am again greatly indebted to Jane Abercrombie, *The Anatomy of Judgement*. Free Association Books, 1989; first published 1960. For comment on the way classroom topography reflects ideas about learning and teaching see Getzels, J. W., 'Images of the classroom and visions of the learner'. *School Review*, 82, 527–540, 1974.

5. For the importance of learning something well before one goes on to something new, see Rosenshine, B. V., 'Content, time, and direct instruction'. In Peterson, P. L. *et al.* (eds) *Research On Teaching*. McCutchan, 1979.

6. See Collier, K. G., 'Peer-group learning in higher education: the development of higher order skills'. *Studies in Higher Education*, 5(1), 55–62, 1980. For some helpful tips on how to facilitate group work when teaching adult literacy classes see *Teaching Groups: A Basic Education Handbook*. London: Adult Literacy and Basic Skills Unit, 1982.

7. My greatest debt is again to Jane Abercrombie, but two serious omissions in her work should be noted. First, although she discusses the difficulties students experience when they have a teacher who is not didactic, she does not note that teachers also experience difficulties when they attempt to move from a didactic to a less didactic approach. This omission is important because some teachers who find non-didactic teaching difficult often blame their learners for this difficulty. Second, she does not note that even a two-sentence exchange can sometimes serve the same purpose as a 'free group discussion'.

8. In addition to Abercrombie, *Anatomy of Judgement*, the following have helpful suggestions on how to encourage learner participation: Barnes, D., *Language, the Learner and the School*. Penguin, 1969; Bridges, D., 'The silent student in small group discussion'. *Education for Teaching*, 59–66, 1975; Smith, B., 'The noisy tutor in small group discussion'. *Education for Teaching*, 35–38, 1976; Seal, C., 'The discussion group'. *Journal of Further and Higher Education*, 1(1), 22–25, 1977; Seal, C., 'Two views of discussion groups'. *Journal of Further and Higher Education*, 4(1), 51–59, 1980; Beattie, G. W., 'The dynamics of

university tutorial groups'. *Bulletin of the British Psychological Society*, **35**, 147–150, 1982; and Flanders, N. A., *Analysing Teaching Behaviour*. Addison-Wesley, 1970. For suggestions on how to facilitate discussions when teaching a foreign language see Ur, P., *Discussions That Work*. Cambridge University Press, 1981.

9. See Elstein, A. S. *et al.*, *Medical Problem Solving*. Harvard University Press, 1978. Abercrombie, *Anatomy of Judgement*, is again excellent on this.

10. I believe many teachers would agree that one of their most rewarding achievements is when their learners assume a mode of thinking in which it becomes second nature to expect to be given evidence for any position put forward. If so, it is surely something of a paradox that many teachers do not seem to require any evidence for adopting the approach to teaching which they do.

11. I note again the work of Bartley on what it means to be 'rational': Bartley, W. W. Jr., *The Retreat to Commitment*. Open Court, 1984. I am indebted to Walter Weimer for drawing my attention to it.

12. The description of learners given here suggests that some of the currently termed 'core skills', i.e. communications, problem-solving and personal skills, are facilitated by the approach described here. These so-called 'skills' are embedded in the lesson topic, and are a by-product of a certain approach to teaching. There is nothing new in this, of course. What is new is the myth that these abilities can be decontextualized, i.e. that they are discrete 'skills'. This belief is a legacy of positivist philosophy, long since discredited in other disciplines. However, the emphasis currently placed on 'core skills' may do something to counteract the present pernicious drift towards replacing education with training.

13. See Keller, W. D., 'On teaching and learning'. In Burton, T. H. *et al.* (eds) *Excellence in University Teaching*. University of South Carolina Press, 1975.

14. My use of the word 'open' is prompted by the work of Sidney Jourard. See his *The Transparent Self*, revised edn. Van Nostrand Reinhold, 1971.

15. Here I am indebted to Yalom, I., *The Theory and Practice of Group Psychotherapy*. Basic Books, 1985, p. 386.

16. Wispé, L. G., 'Evaluation of section teaching methods in the introductory course'. *Journal of Educational Research*, **45**, 161–185, 1951. Wispé's research was done some time ago, so although the percentages she reports would probably be somewhat different today, my experience has been that the tendencies still hold. This is one of the better papers on this topic I know; however, I believe it suffers from a fundamental flaw. Although Wispé distinguishes between experienced teachers, and graduate students acting as instructors, none of the teachers involved had any systematic training in teaching. But then, nearly everyone who does this kind of research seems to take it as self-evident that teaching does not require systematic study.

17. A good introduction to this large topic is McLeish, J., *The Lecture Method*. Cambridge Monographs on Teaching Methods, no. 1. Cambridge Institute of Education, 1968. Another good introduction is Frenkel-Brunswick, Else, 'Personality Theory and Perception'. In Blake, R. R. *et al.* (eds) *Perception: An Approach to Personality*. Ronald Press, 1951. The most illuminating work on this topic I know is Adorno, T. W. *et al.* (eds) *The Authoritarian Personality*. Norton, 1969.

18. I still haven't quite got over my surprise at finding that this is so. My education began with Young, M. F. D. (ed.) *Knowledge and Control*. Collier-Macmillan, 1971. I am much indebted to these writers.

19. For a work which sheds much light on this topic and is deservedly a classic see Erikson, E. H., *Childhood and Society*. Hogarth Press, 1965, many times reprinted.

20. The most notable I know are the books by John Holt: *How Children Fail*; and *How Children Learn*. Penguin, 1970. See also Kohl, H. R., *On Teaching*. Methuen, 1977.

21. Salzberger-Wittenberg, I., *The Emotional Experience of Learning and Teaching*. Routledge, 1983. I found this a most valuable work.

22. For some glimpses of adult learners see Marsh, J., 'The boredom of study: a study of boredom'. *Management Education and Development*, **14**(2), 120–135, 1983. The picture presented is totally unlike that which is fashionable today in much current writing on adult education. See also the first half of Otty, N., *Learner Teacher*. Penguin, 1972.

23. Abercrombie, *Anatomy of Judgement*, is again most helpful.
24. Haste, H., 'Beyond the barriers'. *The Psychologist*, 3(5), 212–214, 1990.
25. The following is surprisingly relevant here: Cooper, E. and Jahoda, M., 'The evasion of propaganda: how prejudiced people respond to anti-prejudice propaganda'. *Journal of Psychology*, 23, 15–25, 1947.
26. Lindsay, J., *Cézanne: His Life and Art*. Evelyn, Adams & Mackay, 1969, pp. 163, 160.
27. I mention 'therapy' because most current notions about 'student-centred learning' are based on the work of Carl Rogers, whose educational beliefs derived from his work with self-referred patients. I am much indebted to Rogers, but I believe it can be misleading to extrapolate directly from therapy to teaching. Unfortunately, many people in education who advocate being 'student-centred' do not seem to have actually read Rogers. Some of the 'skills'-orientated ones even seem proud of this fact.
28. Dinnage, *One to One*, p. 82.
29. Freud, S., *Group Psychology and the Analysis of the Ego*. In Freud, *Civilisation, Society and Religion*. Pelican Freud Library, Vol. 12, 1985.
30. Bion, W. R., *Experience in Groups*. Tavistock, 1961. I often find Bion's writing opaque and busy teachers will find the material most relevant to them on pp. 29–75. A good introduction to the work of Bion is Rioch, M. J., 'The work of Wilfred Bion on groups'. *Psychiatry*, 33, 56–66, 1970. A helpful book which applies the work of Bion to classroom interaction is Mann, R. D., *The College Classroom*. Wiley, 1970. For cogent criticism of Bion's work as well as much psychoanalytic writing see Sherwood, M., 'Bion's experiences in groups: a critical review'. *Human Relations*, 15, 113–130, 1964. For the idea of 'forming, storming, norming, & performing' see Tuckman, B. W., 'Developmental sequence in small groups'. *Psychological Bulletin*, 63(6), 384–399, 1965. For a review of experimental research on groups, written from the perspective of social psychology, see Brown, R., *Group Processes*. Blackwell, 1988. Alas, I seldom find this view helpful.
31. For helpful comments on such matters see Horwitz, L., 'Projective identification in dyads and groups'. *International Journal of Group Psychotherapy*, 33(3), 259–279, 1983.
32. I am much indebted here to Yalom, *Theory and Practice of Group Psychotherapy*. Although it is important to distinguish between therapy and teaching, teachers should find Yalom's work very useful. His approach is eclectic, and integrates clinical and laboratory findings into a coherent theoretical scheme.
33. The single worst example I have experienced suggests to me that a certain combination of students can produce the most vicious attack. Roughly, in one instance there were two police officers of different age and rank (who struck me as rivals and incipient bullies), a highly intelligent, attractive and destructive young woman, several weak students, one of whom derided the approach taken in this book, one of outstanding integrity who distanced herself from the rest, half a dozen pleasant ones who took the usual uncommitted stance, and a new manager over-keen to establish her authority. At one point I made a remark which, I think, was innocent enough, but it was construed as challenging, and the result was a kind of verbal lynching; and as is common in lynchings, the motives were far from clear to me. At the time I found the experience deeply distressing, but now it is the irrationalism of the occasion which strikes me.
34. For examples of such writing see Cosin, B. R. *et al.* (eds) *School and Society*. Open University and Routledge, 1971. For a better collection see Hammersley, M. and Woods, P. (eds) *The Process of Schooling*. Open University Press, 1976.
35. One of the things that has often struck me about many of the explicitly sociological works on teaching I have read is the extent to which their writers deny people much causal agency. I believe social forces have a far more powerful effect on our lives than is easily appreciated, but many of these works convey the impression that we are all passive victims. In that respect C. R. Badcock (*The Problem of Altruism*. Blackwell, 1986, p. 13) writes, 'it seems that sociology as a so-called "science" contains little or nothing in the way of genuine scientific insight but in reality functions as a vast, defensive elaboration'.
36. The following contain helpful comments on asking questions: Hammersley, M., 'The organisation of pupil participation'. *Sociological Review*, 22, 355–368, 1974; and the same writer's *Case Studies in Classroom Research*. Open University Press, 1986.

37. In a review of research on questioning it has been found that using 'higher cognitive questions has a positive effect on student achievement'. See Redfield, D. L. and Rousseau, E. W., 'A meta-analysis of experimental research on teacher questioning behaviour'. *Review of Educational Research*, **51**(2), 237–245, 1981. For further research and a sustained discussion see Marton, F. and Saljo, R., 'On qualitative differences in learning: 1 – outcome and process; and symposium: learning process and strategies; 2 – outcome as a function of the learner's conception of the task'. *British Journal of Educational Psychology*, **46**, 4–11, and 115–127, 1976. See also Watkins, D., 'Depth of processing and the quality of learning outcomes'. *Instructional Science*, **12**, 49–58, 1983. For some recent findings see Entwistle, A. and Entwistle, N., 'Experiences of understanding in revising for degree examinations'. *Learning and Instruction*, **2**, 1–22, 1992.

38. For some of these examples I am much indebted to Klapper, P. 'The professional preparation of the college teacher'. *Journal of General Education*, **3**, 228–224, 1959.

39. Department of Education and Science, *New Teacher in School: A Report by Her Majesty's Inspectors*. HMI Series: Matters for Discussion 15. London: HMSO, 1982.

40. Rowe, M. B., 'Wait-time and rewards as instructional variables, their influence on language, logic, and fate control: Part One – Wait-time'. *Journal of Research in Science Teaching*, **11**(2), 81–94, 1974. I thought this a valuable paper written in an unfortunate style, which is true of many papers cited in these notes.

41. See Wright, C. R. and Nuthall, G., 'The relationships between teacher behaviours and pupil achievement in three experimental elementary science lessons'. In Morrison, A. *et al.* (eds) *The Social Psychology of Teaching*, Penguin, 1972. I have not made any reference to whether a teacher turns to a male or a female learner when asking a question. There is research which suggests that this may be an important variable, and it draws attention to the question of gender in education, an issue with far-reaching implications. It would be foolish to try to deal with it in the space available here, but I would like to express a regret that, in their understandable reaction to masculine excesses, some feminists appear to have adopted the 'masculine' values so characteristic of the West, instead of trying to foster the more 'feminine' ones which we – especially our children – so sorely need. Having once been a member of the kibbutz movement, I have had a frequent sense of *déjà vu* when these matters are discussed in the UK today.

42. Tizard, B. and Hughes, M., *Young Children Learning*. Fontana, 1984, p. 200.

43. See Beloff, J., *The Existence of Mind*. MacGibbon & Kee, 1962. Although Beloff makes the important point that computers are unable to ask intelligent questions, and although he has other interesting things to say, his work suffers from a basic fault common in the criticisms of artificial intelligence written by philosophers, namely, that their approach tends to be within the context of thought. No matter how critical they are of artificial intelligence, they tend to collude with its basic premiss.

44. In discussing the change in people's thinking during the period commonly called the Renaissance, Wayland Young notes: 'The mystery does not lie in the fact that they found answers; it lies in the fact that they asked the questions which had not been asked for thousands of years. And this is a matter of feeling, not knowledge. The difference between asking a question and not asking it is quite a different kind of difference from that between finding the answer and not finding it. Whether you can answer it is a matter of intelligence and perseverance. But whether you ask it in the first place is a matter of emotion. What emotion? I would say the feeling of being authorized to ask it, the feeling that one is allowed to inquire, and that things and people will not bite if you look closely at them.' Young, W., *Eros Denied*. Corgi Books, 1967, p. 78. There are many other valuable comments in this book.

45. For an illuminating analysis of the personal experiences I have recounted here see Saljo, R., 'Learning in the learner's perspective I & II', Institute of Education, University of Göteborg, 1979.

46. See Solomon, G. and McDonald, F. J., 'Pre-test and post-test reactions to self-viewing one's teaching performance on video tape'. *Journal of Educational Psychology*, **4**, 280–286, 1970. For further references see Wragg, E. C., *A Review of Research in Teacher Education*. NFER-Nelson, 1982.

47.   Alexander, F. M., *The Use of the Self*. Gollancz, 1985, p. 33. Long after I had completed the manuscript, I came across Leon Festinger's paper 'Behavioural support for opinion change' (*Public Opinion Quarterly*, **28**, 404–417, 1964), in which he notes: 'All in all, we can detect no effect on behaviour, of a clear and persistent change in opinion brought about by a persuasive communication.' The same finding was reported by Corey in an even earlier paper. See Corey, S. M., 'Professed attitudes and actual behaviour.' *Journal of Educational Psychology*, **28**, 271–280, 1931.

48.   If the argument in this chapter, and the evidence cited in its support, is reasonably sound, it must have important implications for teacher training. Among other things, the argument implies that having suitable information, finding it relevant, having experiences and reflecting on them are insufficient to bring about appropriate practice. I have also frequently noticed that even a genuine commitment to, or ability to discuss, 'TVEI philosophy' or 'student centredness' is no indicator whatsoever that one is able to teach in a manner consonant with those views. Nor are one-day workshops of much use in furthering such approaches unless the participants are already well advanced in those directions.

49.   I have found that reading John Holt's *How Children Fail* does more to change the attitude of student-teachers toward teaching adults than any book on teaching adults. Abercrombie and Rogers have as big an impact. This is especially the case with many non-graduate student-teachers whose minds blossom with the wider implications of these writers' work after years of fatuous skill-based learning. For some evidence see Patricia Wilson's *Antenatal Teaching*. Faber & Faber, 1990. I mention this in part because an inspector once reported that the reading I recommend 'does not reflect current practices in adult and continuing education and the concentration on early childhood and child psychology is of little relevance' (DES, Report T216/51/0270, 299/88). Perhaps I should add that none of these books is a 'how to teach' manual. One has to read them, work out how to apply what is there to one's own teaching, practise, and then reflect on that practice.

9 Overview

1.   For suggestions in a school setting see Kirk, R., *Learning in Action*. Blackwell, 1987. For suggestions in a college setting see the contributions by P. J. Runkel, and S. Cytrynbaum and R. D. Mann, in Runkel, P. J. *et al.* (eds) *The Changing College Classroom*. Jossey-Bass, 1969. For applications to a Peace Corps training programme see Harrison, R. and Hopkins, R. L., 'The design of cross-cultural training: an alternative to the university model'. *Journal of Applied Behavioural Science*, **3**, 431–460, 1967.

2.   As some readers may have missed a reference to what is commonly called 'non-verbal communication' or 'body language', I should perhaps admit that I have not found the material I have read on this topic very helpful in teaching.

3.   Haramati, S., *Three Who Preceded Ben-Yehuda*. Jerusalem: Yad Izhak Ben-Zvi Publications, 1978. See the section on Baruch Mitrani.

4.   For an introduction see van Ments, M., *The Effective Use of Role-Play*. Kogan Page, 1984. See also Mann, R. D., *The College Classroom*. Wiley, 1970. For a collection of educational games for all ages see Brandes, D. and Phillips, H., *Gamesters' Handbook*. Hutchinson, 1977, often reprinted.

Afterword

1.   If I had read Fodor before I wrote this paragraph, I would have written that I have tried to put forward a 'theory of fixation of belief' rather than a 'theory of learning'. See *Language and Learning*, cited earlier, p. 144.

2.   For a survey of various approaches to theory-building, of exceptional value to teachers, see Phillips, D. C., *Philosophy, Science, and Social Inquiry*. Pergamon Press, 1987.

3.   It may be noticed that, though I noted the characteristics of a good theory on p. 109,

this tells us nothing about how a discovery or a theory is arrived at. That is another story!

4. In one of his books Arthur Koestler writes that he used to go skiing as a young man. When he and his companions reached a mountain, they sometimes had the choice of using a ski-lift, or climbing up. He notes that both ways got you to the top, but that those who used the lift got a view, while those who climbed got a vision.

5. I should be very pleased to hear from anyone who has any comments.

Index

(Only topics and names noted in the main text are cited here.)